Dark Lore

Daily Grail Publishing

Darklore Volume 10
Copyright © 2019 by Greg Taylor (Editor)

Contributing authors retain ownership and all rights to their individual pieces.

All rights reserved. No part of this book may be reproduced, stored, or transmitted in any form without permission in writing from the publisher, except by a reviewer who may quote brief passages for review purposes.

ISBN: 978-0-9946176-5-1

Daily Grail Publishing
Brisbane, Australia
userhelp@dailygrail.com
www.dailygrail.com

Contents

Introduction — 7

The Lost Children of Hamelin • *Maria J. Pérez Cuervo* — 9

Uncovering the Lost Tomb of Osiris • *Ray Grasse* — 23

The Apkallu Initiative • *Kelvin F. Long* — 57

Diabolus in Musica • *John Reppion* — 81

The Great Work of Immortality • *Eric Wargo* — 101

Making the Unbelievable Believable • *Blair MacKenzie Blake* — 127

God is my Rock • *Greg Taylor* — 149

James Tilly Matthews and the Air Loom • *Mike Jay* — 173

Some Faerie Metaphysics • *Neil Rushton* — 191

The Carved Stone Balls of Scotland • *Jeff Nisbet* — 213

The Rogue Egyptologist • *Robert M. Schoch* — 225

Endnotes and Sources — 251

"When you have eliminated all which is impossible, then whatever remains, however improbable, must be the truth."

- Sherlock Holmes

If you would like to be notified of future releases of *Darklore*, please send an email to darklore@dailygrail.com. Please be assured your contact details will not be used for any other purpose.

Editor's Introduction

It has (sadly) been two and a half years since the last *Darklore* release, and in that time the world seems to have gone down a rabbit-hole of sorts. And, apparently, part of this weird new world we live in is the concept of 'fake news!' – a two-word descriptor that now invalidates every revelation from any news source simply by the invocation of those magic words.

Word to the woke: you're not doing anything new. We've understood media sources can be dubious, and the necessity of exercising skepticism and critical thinking when considering information from them, all along. And by 'we', I mean those who do their best to avoid belief systems (or B.S., as Robert Anton Wilson referred to it), and are interested in looking at theories and experiences that lie outside consensus reality, and engaging in speculation about possibilities beyond 'first appearances'.

But the truly 'woke' also understand the necessity of applying that same skepticism and critical thinking to ideas and experiences that are outside the box. As the maxim goes, it's great to keep an open mind, just as long as it's not so open that your brain falls out. Otherwise it's easy to get lost in a world of outlandish theories, and open yourself up to exploitation by con-men and propagandists. Don't 'pick a side', dismissing all information from those you see as your opponents, only accepting evidence that confirms your pre-existing views. Examine each piece of information anew, without bias, as best you can.

And that applies to each new release of *Darklore*. We cover a wide range of rather outré and controversial topics, often presenting outside-the-paradigm ideas. I would hope, therefore, that all readers approach each essay with fresh, but critical, eyes, understanding fully that we not claiming any truths...but equally, that we shouldn't be dismissed as 'fake news'. I hope you enjoy *Darklore X!*

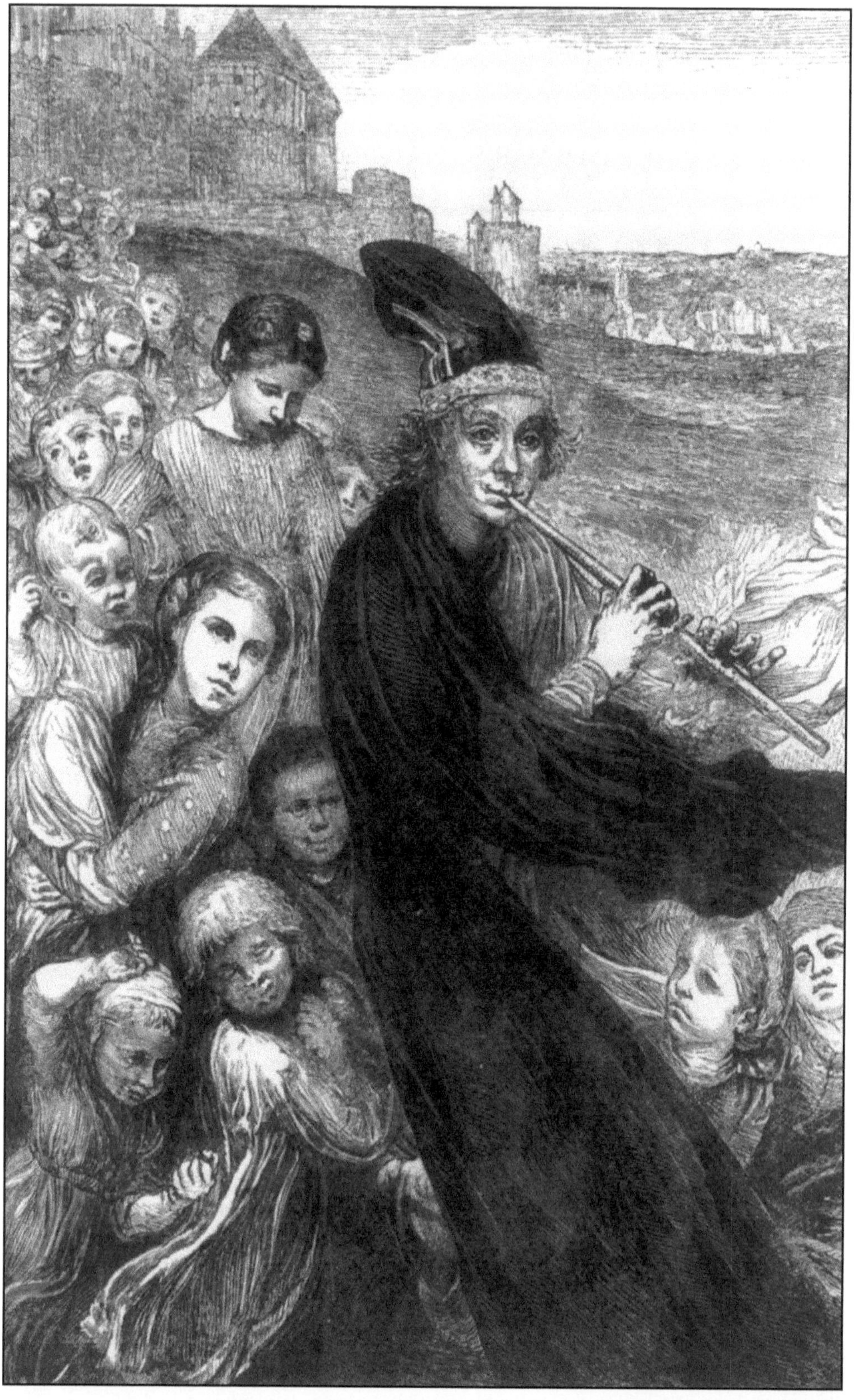

THE LOST CHILDREN OF HAMELIN

Looking for the truth behind the story of the
Pied Piper of Hamelin

by *Maria J. Pérez Cuervo*

Every June, the town of Hamelin in Germany celebrates the anniversary of a macabre event still familiar through children's fairytales more than seven centuries later. But beyond the musical *Rats* and the colourful souvenirs and tourist attractions, the town of the Pied Piper is full of references to a real tragedy – one recorded on the walls of the so-called *Rattenfängerhaus*, or House of the Piper: "In the year of 1284, on the day of Saints John and Paul, the 26th of June, 130 children born in Hamelin were seduced by a piper, dressed in all kinds of colours, and lost at the calvary near the *koppen*."

The town of Hamelin hasn't forgotten this loss. The street where, supposedly, the children were last seen is called *Bungelosenstrasse*:

"street without drums". Even so many years after the event, no one is allowed to play music or dance there. Oral tradition preserved and enriched the story until the Brothers Grimm included it in their compilation of German legends, *Deutsche Sagen* (1816–18). In the Grimms' version, mediæval Hamelin is hit by a plague of rats. A seemingly hero-like figure appears, in the shape of a mysterious stranger dressed in red and yellow clothes. He promises to rid the town of the vermin, and the townsmen promise him money in exchange. The rat-catcher has a strange, almost supernatural gift: he plays a tune on his pipe that lures the rats into the river Weser, where they all drown. But, blinded by their greed, the townsmen refuse to honour their promise and pay the Piper his fee. The Piper leaves the town, plotting his revenge. When he returns to Hamelin, he wears the attire of a hunter. He plays a melody that hypnotises the children, who follow him to the mountains, never to be seen again.

The cruelty of the *denouément* strikes us doubly, because it surpasses our expectations. What initially looks like a classic "Overcoming the Monster" plot turns into a nightmarish tale of disproportionate revenge. The Piper's retribution oversteps the boundaries, suggesting society's ultimate taboo: child murder. This twist is so shocking that many versions have been tempered, with the Piper orchestrating the disappearance of the children only to get the money he is owed; the children go back to Hamelin and the townsfolk learn their lesson. Far from simplifying the story, this presents the Piper as a more interesting hero, a complex, modern one – someone who has to challenge the establishment in order to survive in difficult times. And yet the tale's elements of greed, revenge and infanticide send us back to the Middle Ages, a violent period of deep contrasts. The legend contains enough material to have inspired the popular and the poetic imagination for centuries – but what really happened on that fateful day in 1284, and who was the mysterious Pied Piper?

Traces of the Tragedy

The main difficulty when trying to trace the roots of the legend is the lack of primary sources. The earliest surviving reference to the tragedy of Hamelin is a note in a manuscript copy of the *Catena Aurea* of Heinrich von Herford (c.1370), generally referred to as the Lüneburg Manuscript. According to both this manuscript and the inscription found in the *Rattenfängerhaus*, the events took place on 26 June 1284. There are, however, reports of scholars who accessed earlier documents that are now lost. Dutch physician and demonologist Johann Weyer mentioned in the fourth edition of his *Delusions of the Devil* (1577) some of the historical sources that contained multiple references to the tragedy of Hamelin: "These facts are thus written in the annals of Hammel and are religiously guarded in the archives. They are to be read also in the sacred books of the Church, and to be seen in the painted panes of the same; of which fact I am an eyewitness. Besides, as confirmation of the story, the older magistracy was accustomed to write together on its public documents: 'in the year of Christ and in that of the going out of the children', etc."[1] Weyer was probably referring to the book of statutes

of Hamelin, *Der Donat*, (c.1351), or to a collection of local historical documents called the *Brade*.

The Market Church in Hamelin exhibited another piece of the puzzle, a glass window dating from the 1300s depicting the stranger dressed in multicoloured clothes taking away a crowd of children dressed in white. The window was destroyed in 1660, but it inspired a 1592 watercolour by Augustin Von Moersperg that preserves its essence and represents the main geographical elements of the legend – the town, the river Weser, and the mountain, with a dark entrance to a cave.

The Black Death

Although neither the Lüneburg Manuscript nor the glass window suggest that rats played an important part in the Hamelin events, folklore has assimilated the figure of the Pied Piper with that of a rat-catcher. The first surviving reference to rodents appears in the 16th-century *Zimmern Chronicle* (c.1559–65), followed by Weyer's aforementioned *Delusions of the Devil,* both written almost three centuries after the tragedy. If the rats were most likely a later addition rather than an original element of the Hamelin episode, they gave depth to the tale and resonated in the popular imagination thanks to a play of macabre symbolic associations. The image of a rat-infested mediæval town instantly brings to mind thoughts of the plague. Plagues and epidemics have had a continuous impact on the collective imagination, taking us back to the Ten Plagues of Egypt in Exodus: biblical plagues were a punishment from God. The Piper, able to defy the curse with the power of his music, is thus invested with supernatural abilities.

In mediæval representations, Death presented himself as a skeleton wearing a colourful pied attire, a jester who always laughs last (perhaps the reportedly widespread fear of clowns might even derive from this image). The Pied Piper thus becomes the lord of the rats, the Black Death (known at the time as the Great Death or simply the Pestilence) personified, and the one responsible for taking the lives of the 130 children of Hamelin.

Associations of the Piper with the Black Death aren't limited to the subtext of the tale. The plague has also been used to contextualise the story; Jacques Demy's 1972 film, featuring singer/songwriter Donovan as the Piper, is a good example. However, the peak of Black Death in Europe was between 1348 and 1350, that is, more than 64 years after the date of the children's disappearance if we follow the Lüneburg Manuscript's chronology. The possibilities of an outbreak of bubonic plague in the Hamelin of 1284 are certainly limited. In addition, the plague would have swept away the lives of many people – not just of one town, and not just of its children. Perhaps oral tradition gave the Piper the identity of a rat-catcher after the plague had struck and Von Zimmern preserved this new variation in his 1559 *Chronicle*. Ever since then, the Pied Piper has become the most iconic of rat-catchers. Throughout the mediæval period, it was a well-respected and well-paid occupation, an essential service for towns infested with vermin. But it was a risky business – rat catchers' proximity to rodents made them prone to deadly diseases – and perhaps one that deserved a hero: Rat Catchers' Day is still celebrated on 26 June to commemorate the events in Hamelin.

City of Lost Children

In the earliest accounts of the Hamelin events, we are told that the children were "lost", but not necessarily dead. The Brothers Grimm, at the end of their version, add that "some say that the children were led into a cave, and that they came out again in Transylvania," a conclusion retained by Robert Browning in his 1842 poem *The Pied Piper of Hamelin*. The terms from the Lüneburg Manuscript used to describe the place of the children's disappearance (Calvary, Koppen), have been interpreted in different ways. Historian Hans Dobbertin assimilated the word Calvary, place of the skull, to the word Koppen, meaning head. In the Bible, Calvary or Golgotha was the place of the execution of Jesus – a mountain or a hill. This might suggest that the children of Hamelin were executed, or perhaps the word Calvary is merely used to describe the skull-like shape of a hill, like the biblical Golgotha.

Scholars such as Heinrich Spanuth, Jürgen Udolph and Dobbertin have suggested that the Piper could have been an emissary sent by the ruling nobility to promote a campaign for the colonisation of Moravia, East Prussia, Pomerania or the Teutonic Lands to the East. The expression "children of Hamelin" could have been a general term for all the inhabitants of the town who listened to this brightly dressed "recruiting sergeant", and their exodus a response to politico-economical factors.

In this light, the story of the Pied Piper might be seen to bear certain similarities to that of the Children's Crusade, an extraordinary series of events that purportedly took place in 1212. In both episodes, the border between history and myth is a porous one. The Children's Crusade appears in mediæval sources, but

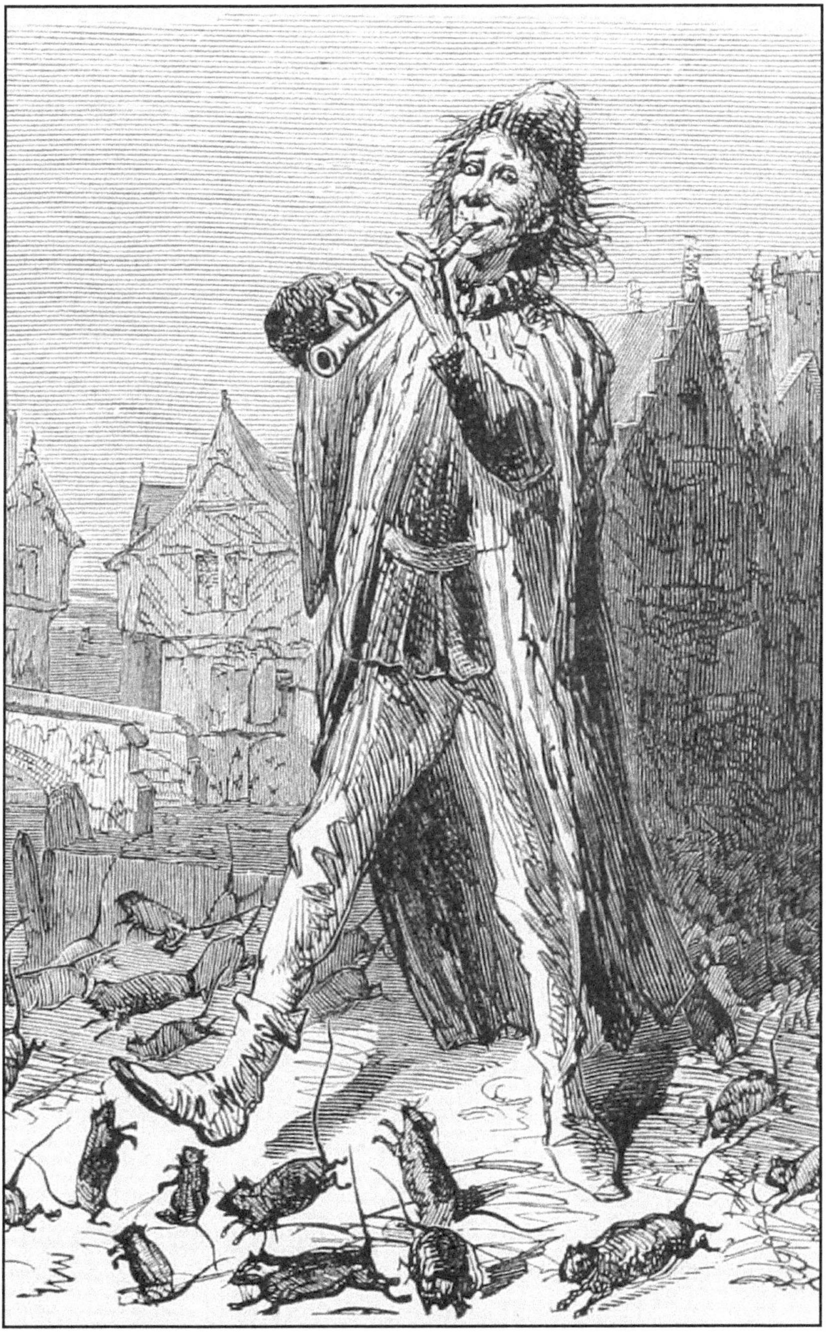

historians now question its authenticity. The crusade was said to have been led by a child shepherd named Nicholas, from Cologne, Germany, who preached that the purity of children would allow them to conquer the Holy Land; the legend says that they starved and died along the way.

Dead can Dance

Another episode that shares features with the Pied Piper events took place in 1237 in the town of Erfurt, 271km south-east of Hamelin. A group of children marched in a dancing procession towards Arnstadt, 15km to the south, where they were said to have collapsed with exhaustion. Unlike the children of Hamelin, the Erfurt youngsters were rescued by their parents, who took them back to their homes. Still, some of them were said either to have died or remained afflicted with a permanent tremor. The events at Erfurt are considered to be one of the first manifestations of the mediæval phenomenon known as the Dancing Mania, usually interpreted as a form of mass hysteria related to religious fervour. Dancing Mania was reportedly spread by "the sight of sufferers, like a demoniacal epidemic, over the whole of Germany and the neighbouring countries to the northwest".[2] Those affected were described as unable to control their movements, or to stop their endless dance, and many were said to have died of exhaustion. As with Hamelin, we have an image of a crowd of children led away by music, perhaps to their deaths.

The Dancing Mania is also known as the Dance of St John, whose festival is celebrated on 24 June, or the Dance of St Vitus, whose day is celebrated on 15 or 28 June, depending on the calendar. It is no coincidence that these three dates are set around Midsummer and the Pagan celebration of the Summer Solstice. Early descriptions of Dancing Mania strongly suggest that its origin was related to

Midsummer celebrations, a vestigial hangover from Paganism, and, as such, condemned by Christians: "No Christian on the feast of St John [the Baptist] or the solemnity of any other saints performs *solestitia* [solstice rites] or dancing or leaping or diabolical chants."[3] Indeed, those affected by the Dancing Mania were thought to be possessed and therefore consigned to mass exorcisms. Traditionally, Midsummer was also considered to be a time of initiation for youngsters. It's possible that the children of Hamelin, like their predecessors from Erfurt, could have been participating in a Pagan ritual, marching off to the mountains while dancing to the music of a colourfully attired piper jester. But, unlike the children of Erfurt, they never returned home.

The Piper as a Trickster

The scarce and enigmatic reports of the loss of an entire generation in Hamelin reverberated down the centuries. Literal interpretations of the story present the Piper as a kidnapper or a psychopathic pederast. This vision has endured in popular culture (even the 2010 remake of *Nightmare on Elm Street* suggests that there are some similarities between the characters of Freddy Krueger and the Piper), but its underlying idea was first expressed five centuries ago, in the work of German physicist and Humanist Jobus Fincelius (*De miraculis sui Temporis,* 1556), who believed that the Piper was the Devil in disguise:

> Of the Devil's power and wickedness will I here tell a true history. About 180 years ago, on S. Mary Magdalene's Day, it came to pass at Hammel on the Weser in Saxony, that the Devil went about the streets visibly in human form, piped and allured many children, boys and girls, and led them through the town-gate towards a mountain.[4]

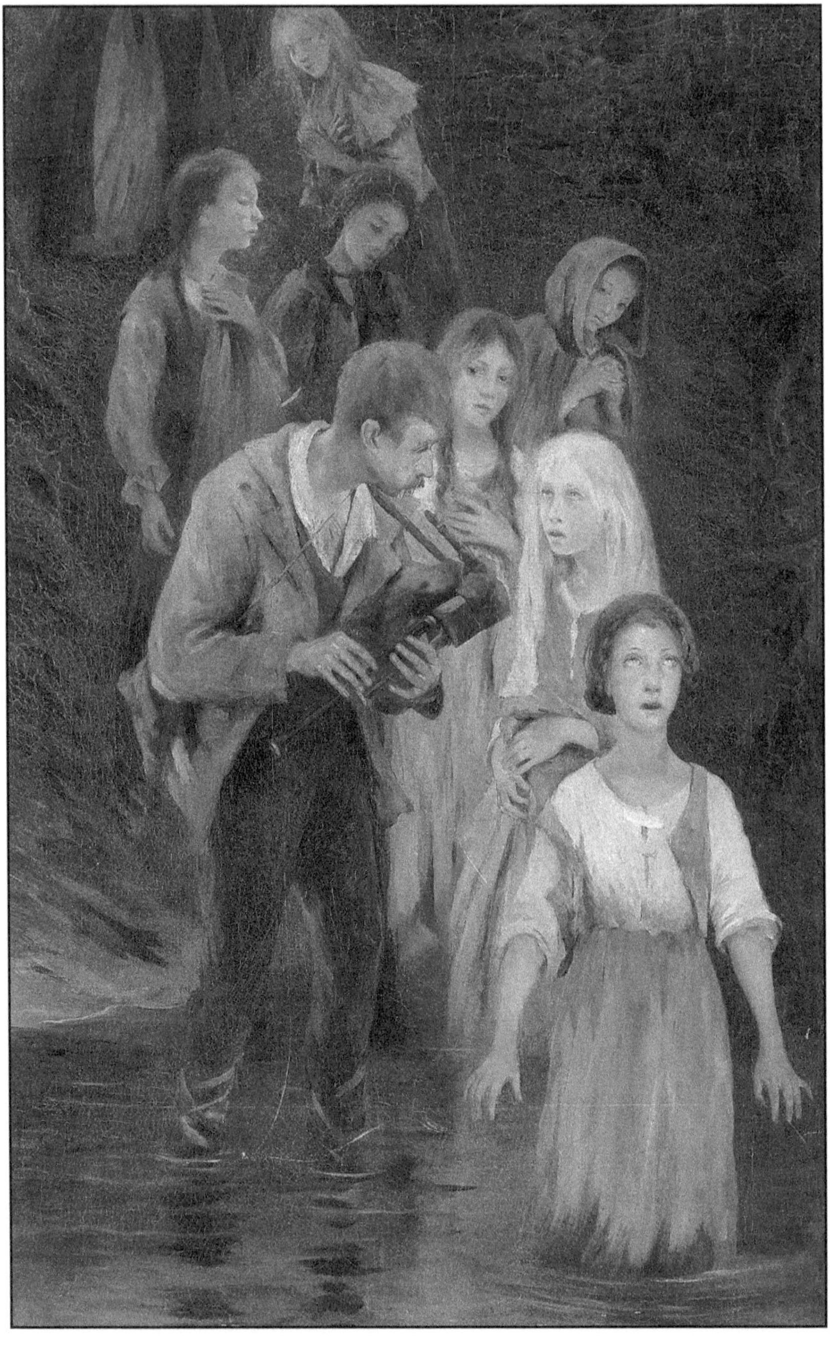

This idea is repeated in Robert Burton's *The Anatomy of Melancholy* (1621), where the Piper turns up as an example in episode two, "A Digression of the nature of Spirits, bad Angels, or Devils, and how they cause Melancholy".

This characterisation of the Piper as a demoniacal archetype always represents him as possessing malevolent intentions and, crucially, supernatural abilities: he is able to lure animals and children with the music of his pipe. Such musical skills recall the Greek god Pan, whose melodies were said to inspire panic and other uncontrollable reactions, both positive and negative. We should remember that with the spread of Christianity, the horned and goat-legged Pagan god lent his attributes to Satan, replacing the fallen angel of the Bible with the image of the Devil.

The 19th century romanticised the figure of the Pied Piper, just as it did with other outsiders – the pirate, the gypsy, the bandit. Goethe's 1802 poem *Der Rattenfänger,* clearly inspired by the Hamelin legend, presents the rat-catcher of the title as…

> the bard known far and wide,
> The travell'd rat-catcher beside;
> A man most needful to this town.

Along similar lines, the most popular retelling of all is Robert Browning's 1849 poem, where the children of Hamelin are happy to leave a town governed by greedy, dishonourable adults. The Piper, the "travell'd rat catcher" of Goethe's lines, arrives in Hamelin offering a fresh start for a new generation.

Appropriately setting the figure of the Piper to music, Goethe's poem would, in turn, be adapted by Romantic composer Schubert and, later, Hugo Wolf. The Romantic take on the Piper contains an idea that has proved unsurprisingly appealing to musicians: the transformation of youth by a mysterious outsider who has inherited the musical skills of Orpheus or Pan – a theme that's been revisited by the likes of Led Zeppelin, Jethro Tull, Megadeth and even ABBA.

Over more than 700 years, the Pied-Piper of Hamelin has become an archetypal Trickster figure. The Trickster is known for challenging the establishment, breaking the rules and spreading anarchy. In his dual nature, he can be seen as malignant or mischievous, but he is also a messenger of the gods and an agent and symbol of transformation. The Pied Piper, like the Trickster, is a shape-shifter who wears a number of different masks – the psychopath, the hero, the rebel… even Death himself. Like Shakespeare's Puck or Barrie's Peter Pan, he spreads a net of enchantment, leading our children to the Otherworld. Whether this Otherworld was a new land to colonise, an altered state of consciousness or the realm of the dead remains a mystery.

Maria J. Pérez Cuervo is a UK-based writer who specialises in history, archaeology, art, myth, and mystery. Her writing appears regularly in *Fortean Times* and *Mental Floss*, and she was one of the contributors to Daily Grail Publishing's *Spirits of Place*. She can be found on Twitter as @mjpcuervo.

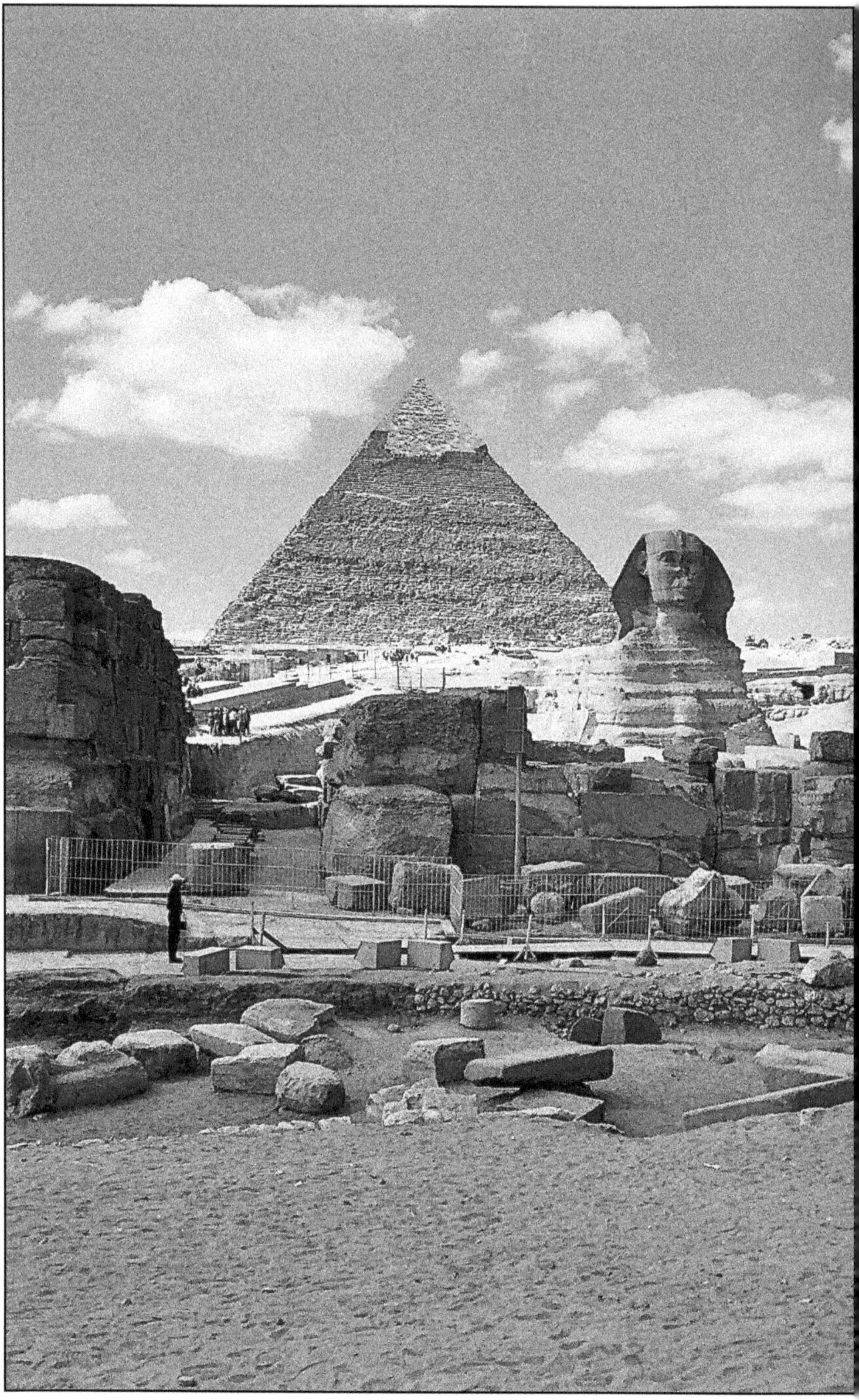

UNCOVERING THE Lost Tomb of Osiris

PERSONAL REFLECTIONS ON AN ARCHAEOLOGICAL MYSTERY

by *Ray Grasse*

I was just 12 years old when I grabbed a shovel from my father's tool collection and began digging a hole in the family backyard. That wasn't just because the thought of digging a hole appealed to me, although that was true, too. It was because I was inspired by the fantasy of a long-distant past, and secret hopes of uncovering lost artifacts from the Native American tribes that once roamed my neighborhood, or perhaps even fossils from the dinosaur era. When my mother strolled out hours later and found me at the bottom of a seven-foot hole, she was horrified and ordered me out immediately, fearful that I might suffocate if those damp walls were to collapse on me. Well, she did have a point.

I've often wondered if our childhood obsessions didn't harbor the seeds of our later interests and ambitions during adulthood. That fascination with the past and "digging deeper" certainly seemed to portend my own, and among other things led to an amateur interest in any and all things related to paleontology, archaeology, and most of all, Egypt. That curiosity lingered well into my adult years and led to a series of unusual experiences I'd eventually have in that extraordinary land. What I'd like to do here is describe one such event that took place in 1997 involving a little-known chamber deep underground on the Giza Plateau that's since been the source of considerable speculation, but also considerable misinformation.

John Anthony West and Friends

But to do that I first need to set the stage by mentioning that throughout the 1990s I worked on the editorial staff of the Theosophical Society in America, located in Wheaton, Illinois. During that time I came to know an independent researcher and lecturer by the name of John Anthony West, who had published a provocative book titled *Serpent in the Sky: The High Wisdom of Ancient Egypt*. I first read his book in the mid-1980s, and was captivated by its theories, which explored the "symbolist" theory of Egypt first articulated by the writer Schwaller de Lubicz (1887-1961). In a series of books and essays, de Lubicz suggested that ancient Egypt possessed a far greater degree of wisdom than generally acknowledged by modern-day academics, and that was subtly encoded in the symbolism of its monuments, architecture, and hidden geometries. One of my duties working for the Society was that of acquisitions editor, so when I discovered that John's book had gone out of print I asked him about acquiring the rights for a reprint, and thus it was Quest Books released a new and updated version of his book.

It was through John that I came to know a Boston geologist by the name of Robert Schoch, as well as an old friend of John's, Boris Said. During this general period the three of them joined forces

John Anthony West (Photo © Ray Grasse)

(along with director Bill Cote) to produce a TV special for NBC called *Mystery of the Sphinx*. First broadcast in 1993, it was hosted by actor Charlton Heston and argued that the Great Sphinx of Egypt might be thousands of years older than commonly dated, as suggested by the unique weathering patterns along its body and the surrounding enclosure.

The special also explained how ground penetrating radar technology they employed on the Giza Plateau indicated there may indeed be a hidden chamber underneath one of the Sphinx's paws, just as predicted by the famed "sleeping prophet," Edgar Cayce, decades earlier. In addition to performing well in the ratings, the show went on to win two Emmys, and triggered debates on the pages of academic journals for years to come.

John's star was definitely on the rise.

Though I kept in close touch with West over the coming years, I began communicating with his partner Boris as well. Or perhaps I should say *ex*-partner, since they had a falling out over a dispute concerning their NBC special. As Hemingway-esque a character as any I've met, Boris lived a life of high adventure, including race car driving and two stints in the Olympics as the head of a bobsled team. He had known John since childhood, but now things had taken a very bad turn – and it all seemed to be over money. Not being privy to the intimate details of that dispute, I can't pass judgment on it one way or another, and leave it for others to make up their own minds about who did what, when, and how.

It was during one phone conversation with Boris in 1996 that I first learned about an intriguing development taking shape in Egypt that he clearly seemed excited about. He described an expedition to Cairo that was being organized along with members of the Edgar Cayce foundation, the A.R.E. (Association for Research and Enlightenment), as well as a mystically-inclined scientist named Dr. James ("J.J.") Hurtak. I knew of Hurtak and his work before, chiefly in connection with a book he'd written in 1973 titled *Forbidden Knowledge: Keys of Enoch*. It was a mysterious but hefty

Boris Said (left) and J.J. Hurtak (right) (Photo © Ray Grasse)

volume that somehow managed to sell over 100,000 copies without any advertising at all, which is no small feat. The purpose of this upcoming expedition would be to explore and film a mysterious chamber roughly 100 feet underground on the Giza Plateau, located several hundred yards behind the Sphinx. It had never been fully investigated before due to the high water levels inside, but now those levels were receding, thus making it more accessible to researchers.

Said had known about this spot on the Plateau for several years already, but at the urging of Hurtak, Boris grew increasingly convinced they would find something important in that spot. As a result, Boris enlisted the involvement of the Edgar Cayce group, and the expedition would be largely bankrolled by a wealthy member of that organization, Dr. Joseph Schor. According to Boris, it was set to take place in February of 1997, and he asked if I'd like to come along and observe the proceedings in a journalistic capacity. It was an offer I couldn't refuse.

Passage to Egypt

Upon arriving in Cairo that first night, I made some calls and arranged to meet a few of the other team members near the front entrance of the Mena House, a posh hotel in the grand colonial style just a stone's throw from the pyramids. As night fell across the Plateau, a small van pulled up to the curb with Boris and Hurtak inside, along with their wives. After some cursory introductions, we headed over to the Great Pyramid where we found others from the team already waiting for us. The gathering on this first night was intended to inaugurate the expedition on an auspicious note.

The sense of anticipation amongst all the team members was electric. We made our way in through the pyramid's entrance and up the long "Grand Gallery," and finally into the King's Chamber. Once we all settled into our spots against the outer walls, Hurtak then led the group through a three-hour spoken ceremony, with his voice and language taking on near-Biblical inflections at times. The litany of topics he covered included the seventy-six names of the Pharaohs, the Nile journey as a symbolic voyage of the soul, an invocation of blessings from the disembodied Pharaohs, the significance of the three stars in the belt of Orion, and the unique sonic properties of this room. There was more: he alluded to the Hall of Records, the importance of the missing pyramid capstone, and the Kabbalistic relationship between the four-lettered name of God and the four corners of the pyramid's base. James casts a very wide net, that was obvious.

With that portion of the ceremony finished, each team member took turns lying inside the sarcophagus for a few moments, while Hurtak and I helped them climb into and out of it safely. By the time the formal ceremony was over, most of the team members were exhausted, some of that due simply to jet lag from the long flight over, while a few others seemed deeply moved by Hurtak's ceremony. Glancing at Boris, I saw tears running down his cheeks,

The vicinity of the well-shaft leading to the "Tomb of Osiris" on the Giza Plateau. The entrance to the underground shaft is on the right, directly in front of the three seated figures, the Great Pyramid is in the background. (Photo © Ray Grasse)

and asked what he was feeling. He said Hurtak's ceremony touched a deep chord for him, though he couldn't articulate why. I found it fascinating, too, but was grappling with such intense back pain from the hard surfaces we'd been sitting for three hours on that I looked forward to returning to my motel room and the comfort of a soft bed.

Old and New

Early the next morning, the investigation began in earnest. "Well, here goes nothing," Boris quipped as we set out before dawn toward the Plateau in his van. The early morning skies around the Plateau exude a quality of clarity and peace quite unlike anything I've experienced anywhere else. Our vehicle was waved past the checkpoint leading to the pyramids, as we drove carefully towards the site where we'd establish our base of operations for the day.

Members of the film crew hauled their elaborate equipment down the steep metal ladder in the well-shaft, while the rest of us milled around up on top, trying our best to find shade as the temperature soared to 100°F. The conversations amongst the team members pivoted around the pressing questions of the day. Was the chamber below simply a natural cavity, as some believed? Or was it an ancient ceremonial room that fell into disrepair? Or might this even be an "anteroom" which connected to another, more important chamber – an ancient library, perhaps? More than one team member was hoping for that possibility.

At one point during the afternoon Egyptologist Mark Lehner came by to check out our group. I'd met him once before, at a conference in Chicago put on in 1992 by the AAAS (American Association for the Advancement of Science), where he and Robert Schoch debated the true age of the Sphinx. At the time, Lehner was probably the most prominent critic of West and Schoch's theories

A close-up of the entrance to the "Tomb of Osiris" shaft, which tunnels under the Khephren Causeway. (Photo © Ray Grasse)

about the Sphinx, and he'd obviously gotten word of our group's presence on the Plateau that day.

Nodding towards the entrance of the shaft, he remarked to a couple of us standing around, in a noticeably teasing way, "So…have you found the Hall of Records down there yet?" (This was in reference to the fabled treasure trove of knowledge theorized by Edgar Cayce).

Though I didn't say anything about it at the time, there was no small irony in his comment. That's because just one year earlier I'd been looking through a neighborhood library and came across a thin volume titled *Egyptian Heritage,* which was a sympathetic treatment of Edgar Cayce's writings on Atlantis, Egypt, and the Hall of Records. The author of the book? None other than Mark Lehner himself – the self-professed skeptic of all fringe theories associated with Egypt. He had apparently started out an avid student of Cayce's theories, but during the course of his academic studies underwent a conversion to a more conservative and evidence-based view of ancient Egypt. Or that's how it appeared in public, anyway; who knows what views he still privately entertained.

Because of that past affiliation with the Edgar Cayce foundation, Mark remained friends with Joseph Schor and his colleague Joe Jahoda through the years. After he walked away from our group, I heard Jahoda say that Mark had climbed down to the bottom of the well-shaft as early as the 1970s, and suspected even then it might hold some real importance. Why, I wondered? "Because of its proximity to the pyramids," Jahoda explained. "It implied to Mark it must have been exceedingly important to the ancient Egyptians. But the water table was too high back in the 70s for him or anyone else to do any further investigation of it."

That first day was a long one, extending well past sunset, as Boris and some of the others lumbered back up the ladder beneath the cobalt sky. As I helped him carry some of his gear back to the van parked several yards away, I was taken aback by the startling sight of green laser beams darting across the plateau around us, creating stunning designs across both the ground and the face of the pyramid behind us. I quickly realized that a sound-and-light show was being staged further down the Plateau for tourists who came here for an educational show about the history of the region; we just happened to be in the line of fire. It made for an anachronistic blend of past and future, with ancient history melding with space-age technology. Yet strangely enough, it all seemed perfectly fitting somehow.

The Discovery

It was sometime over the course of February 18th that the expedition's cameraman, Garrett, made the initial find. He was down in the chamber positioning the tripod for his movie camera when he suddenly realized he was standing on a stone slab of some kind. Clearing away the dirt, it became obvious this wasn't any ordinary rock, since it looked too smooth, too polished. Word quickly percolated back up to the crew members on top, and before long rumors began circulating as to what this might be.

Later that day while everyone was away on break, I climbed down the rusty metal ladder bolted into the sides of the narrow shaft to see what was down there for myself. The shaft is staggered into three distinct levels, I saw. The first level opened out into a relatively small space that was littered with debris, and seemed to be of no obvious significance. From there, the shaft presents a sheer vertical drop of about 70 feet, and the old ladder felt precarious at points. But the descent was exhilarating, too, since I felt as though each step down was transporting me back further in time, to an era and culture thousands of years older than my own. For a split second, my mind flashed back to those feelings I had as a child digging that hole in my parent's backyard, looking for remnants of a forgotten past, almost as if something was coming full circle.

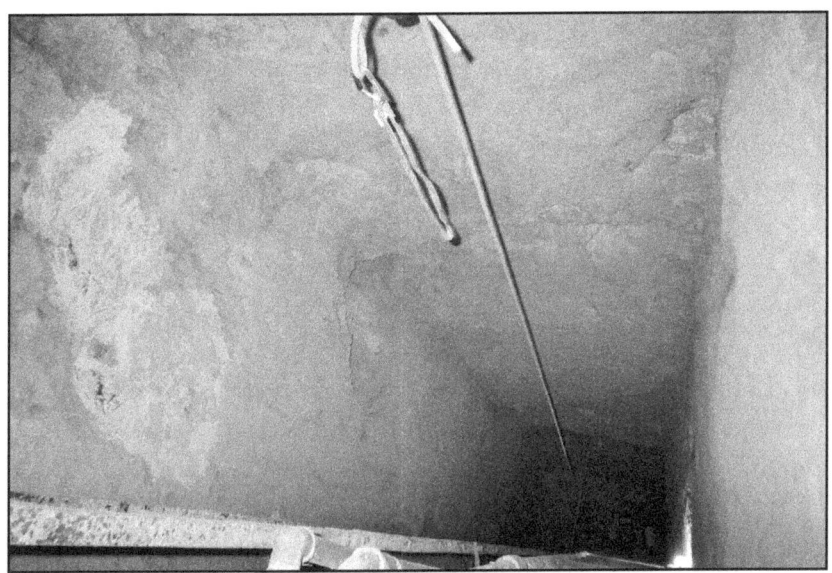

Looking down the shaft, from the first level to the second. (Photo © Ray Grasse)

On the second level of the shaft, with one of two empty sarcophagi visible. The team's cinematographer is on the left, J.J. Hurtak is on the right. (Photo © Ray Grasse)

On the second level is a chamber with seven niches or "cubicles" carved into the rock walls, two of which contained large sarcophagi made of heavy stone. One of those is solid black and surprisingly smooth, almost as if it had been constructed using modern engineering tools. The other one looked rougher and grayish in color. Each of these two sarcophagi is well over 20 tons, I'm told. It boggles the mind trying to imagine how the ancients could have moved these massive objects down into this spot, especially considering there are no signs of damage on the walls of the shaft. Fascinating as all this was, I was anxious to see what was further down the shaft, so I carefully made my way down the ladder to the shaft's bottom, roughly a 30-foot drop.

At first glance, the lowest room almost looked like a rectangular cavern. I was struck by the sense of profound antiquity that permeated it. Some of that was obviously due to the fact that, unlike so many popular tourist sites in this country, it was completely unrestored.

Looking out towards the northwest corner of the lowest chamber in the shaft, with the remains of one of four pillars visible in the middle, and the watery moat along its fringes. (Photo © Ray Grasse)

The air in the chamber was thick and musty, almost suffocating. There was something slightly spooky about it, too, not just because of its ruinous state but the sight of human bones protruding from the muddy water along its edges. That was unsettling in a way, as if I'd intruded onto someone's final resting place. I couldn't help but wonder if there might be something to those legends about curses against trespassers to these ancient sites, so just to play it safe I offered up a few silent protective prayers before venturing in further.

I could see that the chamber was completely flooded along its outer rim on three sides, and that I was standing on a sort of island extending out from the shaft's entrance. At the far end of this quasi-island I noticed the broken remains of two large pillars, both of them square and truncated. To me, the room had more the vague feel of an archaic temple than a conventional crypt.

And there, right before me, amidst the rocks and the mud, I could see the smooth stone surface the others had spoken about, roughly one square foot in size and just a few yards from the entrance into the chamber. It wasn't obvious whether or not this was man-made, but to my untrained eye it seemed too smooth to be natural, as if hinting at something larger underneath.

Theories were abundant amongst the team members up top as to what this might be. Some suspected it was the surface of a sarcophagus, while a few others thought it could indicate a passageway to yet another chamber – perhaps even the legendary Hall of Records itself? Unfortunately the team only had a filming permit, not an archaeological one, so we weren't allowed to disturb anything in the chamber. Just to make sure our curiosity didn't get the better of us, the Egyptians posted an observer to accompany us the entire time, who watched our every move. Considering how much thievery and damage often takes place at many of these sites, I could understand that. But it was frustrating, too, since we knew that removing even a small amount of dirt from around that slab might reveal what it was, or what lay beneath it.

Facing the east end of the 'Tomb of Osiris'. From left: Boris (in back, next to the ladder); Desiree Hurtak, Carol Pate, and an unidentified film crew member. The location of the partially submerged slab was found beneath the large tripod slightly left of center here.
(Photo © Ray Grasse)

This was all about to change, however.

The next day while I was down in the chamber with Boris, Hurtak, and a couple members of the film crew, the Egyptian assigned to watch us unexpectedly climbed back up the ladder to take a bathroom break. Those of us still in the chamber all looked at each other as if reading one another's minds – then piled onto the ground to quickly (and carefully) use our fingers to scrape away as much dirt from around the stone slab as possible. We knew full well this was outside the bounds of official protocol, but we also realized this was a once-in-a-lifetime opportunity, and were determined not to damage anything in the process. Over those next few minutes it quickly became apparent this stone slab must have been carved by human hands, and wasn't simply a natural feature. We were excited, but also mystified. What were we looking at, exactly?

The mysterious slab on the floor of the chamber after several of the team members and myself used our fingers to remove several inches of dirt and mud. (Photo © Ray Grasse)

Word about the exposed slab spread quickly amongst the team members above, and the next day Thomas Dobecki (the team's technical expert) and his two helpers hauled their ground-penetrating radar equipment down into the chamber for a closer look. Scanning the dirt floor of the chamber with his equipment, he detected what appeared to be a hollow space just beneath the slab. He said the stone itself seemed to be about thirty inches thick, and beneath that appeared to be a possible tunnel descending in an easterly direction towards the Sphinx. That ignited everyone's imagination further, since it might indicate a passageway, a hidden chamber, or at the very least, a previously unknown sarcophagus. Boris in particular was banking on the possibility of a secret passageway extending down and out from this room. Was it a tunnel? Or simply an empty space indicating a submerged sarcophagus? Whatever it was, anticipation was growing amongst the team members as to what be in store for us.

The Tide Turns

When Egyptian officials caught wind of what we'd uncovered down below, the whole mood of the expedition changed dramatically. I now saw local officials whispering to one another off to the sides, obviously trying to figure out what to do about this unexpected turn of events. Boris and Joseph Schor tried to play down what had been found while talking with Plateau officials, and began negotiating just how much more research or filming would be allowed from that point on. Boris in particular was anxious to obtain permission for exploring the underground chamber further – especially beneath the mysterious stone slab. But Boris and Joseph now seem blocked at every turn, as the rest of the group began growing restless. It was clear the officials in charge suspected this could turn out to be something important, and did not want to lose control of the situation.

It was a couple of mornings after the initial discovery that I arrived on site to find the film crew busy setting up for an interview with Zahi Hawass, which was planned to take place directly in front of the Sphinx. Several minutes later Hawass himself arrived on the scene. Next to the president of Egypt, he was probably the most well-known figure in Egypt. But he could be a world-class ham, too. For years if you turned on any TV show about Egypt you invariably saw Zahi's face front and center. I always had the feeling Zahi could sniff a camera from a mile away, maybe even 1000 miles. It was well-known that his ambitious streak made him more than a few enemies over the years, both inside and out of Egypt. Boris himself seemed to drift into that category over the years, wavering between warm friendship and ice-cold animosity towards the man.

Yet every time I began to feel like Zahi might be too self-serving for his own good, I'd hear some story which portrayed him in a more favorable light. Like the anecdote my friend Rosemary Clark told about the first time she traveled to Egypt and approached Zahi about spending a night inside the Great Pyramid – this, before it became the fashionable thing to do among New Age seekers. Impressed by her sincerity, he immediately arranged for her to spend the night there alone, undisturbed by guards or other visitors. And when she offered to pay him for his help, he steadfastly refused. As anyone familiar with Egypt knows, finding an official in this country who refused money is a rare thing indeed, and suggests to me there may be a spiritual sensibility lurking beneath all that bluster and bombast.

My own fleeting interactions with Zahi were pleasant enough, but I was curious to know more about the man. Like Mark Lehner, Zahi was a vocal critic of all "fringe" theories about the Giza Plateau; his famously derisive term for proponents of such theories was pyramidiots. Yet interestingly, like Lehner, he allegedly started out as an avid student of Edgar Cayce's writings! So when I saw Joe Jahoda standing off to the side waiting for their interview to start,

Preparing to film an interview with Zahi Hawass in front of the Sphinx. Zahi is in the center, Joseph Schor is to the right of him (in white cowboy hat), Joe Jahoda is to the left, without hat. (Photo © Ray Grasse)

I asked him for his honest opinion of the man, since they'd been friends for decades by that point. Joe proceeded to tell me how he and his colleagues at the A.R.E. helped put Zahi through college back at the University of Pennsylvania years earlier. He spoke with obvious affection for Zahi, citing the difficulties he faced in America as a foreign student on his arrival. "People don't realize how tough it was for him when he came to America. He barely spoke any English at all, yet he managed to make his way through school."

Beneath the Pyramid

Over the next few days negotiations with the local officials dragged on, so Boris decided to use his extra time to finish up some other projects. One of those involved taking the film crew over to shoot some extraneous scenes in the King's Chamber inside the Great Pyramid. But as commonly happens with film projects, this one proceeded at a snail's pace, so I took the opportunity to explore other parts of the pyramid on my own.

This massive structure is an engineering marvel, but also a great mystery on a number of fronts. Aside from the lingering question as to how it was built or how long that really took, there is the problem of its true antiquity. In the 1980s a researcher from the University of Washington, Robert Wenke, carbon-dated samples of mortar obtained from the pyramid which contained wood, charcoal and reed, and yielded the surprising result that it was several hundred years older than previously believed. Later testing conducted by Robert Temple, using a different method, corroborated those results (we'll come back to that later). Findings like those are especially perplexing since they seem to place the construction of the Great Pyramid near the very dawn of Egyptian civilization, long before it's generally believed they had either the knowledge or social organization to accomplish such a feat.

After carefully examining the so-called "Grand Gallery" which cuts at an angle up through the pyramid, I decided to search out the subterranean pit beneath its foundation, which is accessible via a narrow slanted passageway that extends down into the ground several hundred feet. Carved out of the Giza Plateau's limestone bedrock, its narrow size forces visitors to make their way in a crouched-down position for the length of those two-hundred feet. This monument is no playground for claustrophobics, rest assured. The passageway raises questions of its own regarding the building of the Great Pyramid, and how long it actually took to create. As independent researcher Gordon White summed it up,

> Constraint analysis is an engineering technique to determine where the bottlenecks lie in a building project. That is, which steps in a construction cannot be made to go faster and/or also hold up the rest of the project... With specific reference to the Great Pyramid, the descending passage...is only 42 inches square, meaning that only one worker at any one time could be carving it out. This provides a neat and measurable example of constraint analysis: it would have taken almost twice Khufu's reign for a single

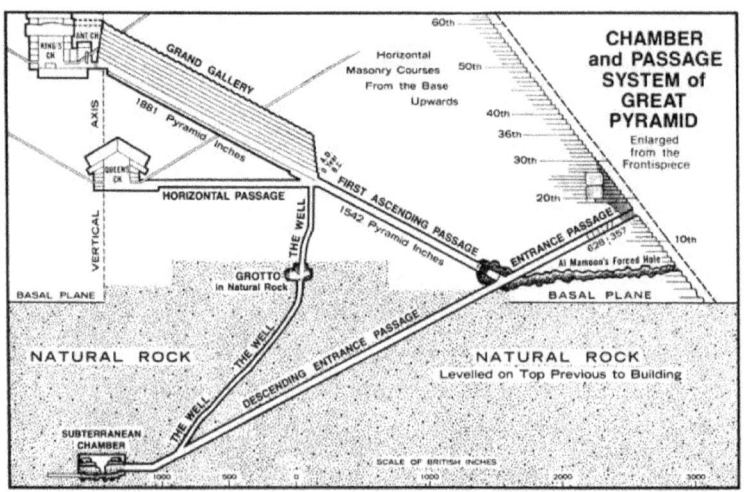

person to carve out this passageway using a dolerite pounder, and that is working twenty four hours a day. Not only is the pyramid too old to be a tomb, its construction cannot fit into the twenty-something year reign of Khufu."[1]

I finally emerged into the pit at the shaft's bottom, which appeared much more roughly-hewn than the rest of the Pyramid. Its original function still isn't fully understood by Egyptologists; while some believe it's an abandoned burial chamber, others suggest it may have served ceremonial or shamanic purposes. The simple fact of the matter is, we don't know.

Standing in the silence of the underground chamber, something about its muffled acoustics caught my attention, so on a hunch I decided to stomp down on the dirt floor as hard as I could. To my surprise, the resonance from that sound seemed to reverberate all the way up through the Pyramid, as if the entire monument had become a gigantic gong. That was remarkable, and reminded me of another experience I had in the Pyramid back during an earlier trip with John Anthony West in 1994. While lying in the sarcophagus and chanting a few obligatory "Oms" with the tour group that day – practically a rite of passage for many of those visiting the Great Pyramid – at one point I hit a certain note that caused the sarcophagus around me to resonate in an uncanny way, and my entire body to vibrate.

Between that sound up in the King's Chamber and this one down inside the pit, it was easy to believe sonic effects like these were intentionally designed to be part of this structure's true function. The more time I spend inside the Great Pyramid, the more I can't help believe this extraordinary structure might represent an advanced magical technology the likes of which we can't fully comprehend now, possibly involving a complex network of intentions, correspondences, and God-knows-what subtle energies, all of which combine to influence – what? The consciousness of humans inside of

Down in the pit beneath the Great Pyramid. (Photo © Ray Grasse)

it? The broader life and destiny of Egypt? Or perhaps even the entire world? I don't claim to know, but I have no doubt there's more to this monument than meets the eye.

After climbing back up from the pit through the passageway, I walked back outside the pyramid and found a ledge slightly higher up on one of its sides, where I sat beneath the stars and watched the lights of Cairo sparkling across the horizon.

Aftermath

The next day I called back home to the States to discover there was a family crisis that needed tending to, so I'd have to head home sooner than expected. But since negotiations with Zahi and company had reached a standstill anyway, it didn't really matter whether I departed sooner or later. As it turned out, the expedition drew to a close without any firm conclusions. Sadly, no treasures or evidence of lost civilizations would be uncovered this time around.

It was roughly one month later that I began noticing rumors on the Internet about the expedition and its supposed discoveries. The speculations were all sensationalistic, ranging from talk about the Hall of Records to alien spaceships uncovered beneath the Plateau. The fact that no hard information about the expedition had been released to the public only fanned the flames of speculation further. Around this time Boris went on the air to talk with popular radio show host Art Bell about the expedition, and thus before an audience of millions spilled the beans about what had taken place that February – in the process invoking the ire of some A.R.E. members who had expected him to keep the team's findings confidential for the time being.

Exactly one year later, on February 16th of 1998, I opened the newspaper to find this story, published by the Reuters news service, with the headline: "Egyptians Find Tomb of Ancient God Osiris." It read: "Sinking water levels have revealed a granite sarcophagus of the ancient Egyptian god Osiris in a 30-metre (98 feet) deep tomb at the Giza pyramids, Egyptian archeologist Zahi Hawass said on Wednesday." Apparently, during the twelve months since our team left Cairo, Zahi and his crew had been busy clearing out the chamber, and discovered that the slab we uncovered was indeed the lid to a stone sarcophagus, or royal coffin. It turned out to be empty, and was partially underwater.

Zahi seemed to feel the chamber and its contents weren't really that old, by Egyptian standards, perhaps dating from the period around 600 BCE, give or take 50 to 75 years. He also suggested the archaic chamber could be the mythical "Tomb of Osiris," described in tradition as a stone sarcophagus on an island surrounded by water, deep underground, where Osiris rose from the dead. Could the chamber we explored be that very spot? According to the press releases, Zahi certainly thought so. He went on to declare this was the most important archeological discovery of his entire career. "I never excavated this shaft before because it was always full of water,"

Zahi said, "but when the water went down about a year ago, we started the adventure."

The most important discovery of *his* career? That took me by surprise, since he made no mention at all of Hurtak, Boris, or the A.R.E., even though they were the ones ultimately responsible for it. But perhaps I shouldn't have been surprised, since Zahi had something of a reputation as a claim-jumper on discoveries set into motion by others. As someone once explained to me, the politics of Egyptology are as bad if not worse than anything you'll encounter in the halls of Washington, DC.

It was one year later, in March of 1999, that Zahi's work down in the chamber was given worldwide TV exposure in the form of a Fox television special titled *Opening the Lost Tomb, Live!*, hosted by Maury Povich. During the prime-time special, viewers were treated to video footage of the chamber itself, images of the half-submerged sarcophagus and its suspended lid, and of course, Zahi himself presiding proudly over his discovery. It was exciting to see how the chamber looked with much of the mud and debris cleared out, and the sarcophagus revealed more fully now. But it was disappointing too, seeing how Boris, Hurtak, and the A.R.E. team were essentially being erased from the history books.

To his credit, though, Boris never let that theft of credit bother him, since he had other projects to pursue, including a TV special that hoped to finally explore the suspected chamber beneath the Sphinx's paw. Both Boris and Joseph Schor were eager to procure financial backing for the project, but knew it wouldn't be easy. In addition to all the baseline expenses involved, there were the large sums of money needed to "reimburse" all the Egyptian officials involved. However it was budgeted, it wouldn't be a cheap project. At one point Boris and Joseph even arranged a meeting with media mogul Rupert Murdoch in his London offices, since he had shown interest in the project. When I asked Boris why Murdoch of all people would want to get involved in something like this, Boris simply answered, "Well, Murdoch is a Mason."

They eventually had their meeting with Rupert, though nothing ever came of it. Boris had his other projects, including ones in Japan, Africa, and Central America, most of them in collaboration with Hurtak. But he returned to the Giza Plateau several more times to do further research into the unique acoustics of the Great Pyramid. After returning from one of those trips, he claimed that what he'd uncovered there would dwarf any other discoveries in Egypt – including the long-sought-for Hall of Records.

He was hesitant to reveal exactly what they found until all the results were analyzed, except to explain how one of them involved strange, wave-like hollows they detected beneath the floor of the King's Chamber. "That's probably what's responsible for the room's unique acoustics," he suggested. He said that a professor from the University of Washington was currently in the process of converting their mountains of data into computer simulations, and those were a revelation to behold.

Sadly, that's the last I ever heard of those findings. Along with a series of legal problems, Boris's health deteriorated, and when he was finally diagnosed with a cancerous lump on his liver he stubbornly resisted chemotherapy. "If I go," he said, "I want to go riding down the Amazon River taking ayahuasca."

During our next few phone calls he sounded increasingly weary and short of breath. In March of 2002, I called to finish up a conversation we'd begun several days earlier about a project we hoped to do involving research being done by my friend Barbara Keller. Boris's long-time friend Beth Melnick answered the phone, and when I asked to speak with him, there was a long pause. She solemnly informed me that Boris had died just the day before. He hadn't gone out riding down the Amazon ingesting hallucinogenic potions after all; he passed away quietly shortly after watching the latest broadcast of the Academy Awards. Which is just as well, since he always had fun watching the ceremony, so at least he went out doing something he enjoyed.

I knew they hadn't spoken to each other in years, so I decided to call up John Anthony West that afternoon to give him the news. He was as taken aback by it as I had been. It's startling when a figure like Boris passes away, since he seemed larger-than-life, maybe even larger than death. But any sadness John felt about Boris was clearly tempered by the longstanding feud which had torn them apart years earlier. Several days later, he posted these words on the Internet:

> Those who met Boris at any time over the course of his 69 years, even briefly, probably will not have forgotten him; physically powerful, radiating an almost superhuman, high octane intensity, with a quick, coarse humor and an even quicker, coarser temper, infinitely resourceful especially when his back was to the wall — which it usually was, since he found ways to make sure that's where it stayed.

Decoding the Tomb of Osiris: What Does It Mean?

As the years went on I heard little else about the Tomb of Osiris, other than more fantastical speculations circulating on the Internet. Those included suggestions that it's actually an inter-dimensional portal which can only be opened by someone with the appropriate DNA. Well, okay.

But in 2016 my interest was sparked anew by research I came across by independent researcher Robert Temple. Temple first gained attention in the 1970s for a controversial book titled *The Sirius Mystery*, suggesting a possible connection between the Dogon tribe further south in Africa and the ancient Egyptian civilization up north. But in a much more recent book, *Egyptian Dawn*, Temple focused heavily on the Giza Plateau itself, and devoted an entire chapter to the Osiris shaft.[2]

Addressing the different levels of the shaft, he suggested it was likely constructed in stages during different historical periods. While the conventional academic wisdom theorized that it dated back to the so-called "Saitic" period, extending from 664 BC to 525 BC – relatively late in Egyptian history – Temple challenged that view, and claimed that it was considerably older. How did he come to that conclusion? That's where things start to get interesting.

As mentioned earlier, the second level of the Osiris shaft contains two large stone sarcophagi. Temple found that the black one with the smooth surface was made of granite, a commonly-used stone throughout ancient Egypt and relatively obtainable for creating ancient tombs and monuments. However, he discovered that the second, more roughly-hewn sarcophagus on that level was carved from a more obscure stone called dacite.

How obscure? Aside from the fact it apparently wasn't used at any other time in ancient Egypt for creating monuments, statues, or sarcophagi, there doesn't appear to be a vein of dacite anywhere in Africa large enough to produce a sarcophagus like the one on the second level of the Osiris shaft. To the best of anyone's knowledge, the dacite deposits closest to Cairo are hundreds of miles away.

That means the Egyptians would have had to transport this massively heavy object overland across great distances, before lowering it down into this relatively narrow shaft. How they managed to do all that is enough of a mystery, but why they did so is just as much of one, especially when you consider how much easier it would have been to simply use the far more accessible Aswan granite. If nothing else, it points to the enormous importance the ancient Egyptians placed on different types of stone and their symbolic meanings.

But that's not the only mystery. One of Temple's projects involved his attempts to date the monuments and objects of the Giza Plateau using a method invented by nuclear physicist Ioannis Liritzis called 'optical thermoluminescence'. While no instruments can carbon date solid stone, thermoluminescence can roughly determine a stone's last exposure to sunlight, which can indirectly help to zero in on a rough time frame. Using that method, Temple dated the construction of the dacite sarcophagus to roughly 2800 BC, give or take 550 years either way – providing us with a window ranging roughly anywhere from 3350 BC to 2200 BC. That raises the intriguing possibility that the dacite sarcophagus could be several centuries older than the Giza pyramids themselves, as conventionally dated. If so, that would make the dacite sarcophagus one of the oldest objects on the Giza Plateau.

But what about the third level down in the shaft, and the granite sarcophagus in the so-called "Tomb of Osiris" that we explored in 1997? When Temple applied the thermoluminescence method to it, he found it was somewhat younger in age – although still much older than Zahi's estimate. It dated back to about 1700 BC, give or take 400 years. That gave it a comfortable range of having been constructed somewhere between 2370 BC to 1270 BC., roughly during the Middle Kingdom.

While that means there could possibly be some overlap between the second and third levels of the shaft, in terms of their age, it does suggest that the second level is older and firmly located within – or possibly even before – the so-called "Old Kingdom" era. Robert Temple thinks that while the second level was originally created as a tomb for important figures, possibly including an early pharaoh, the third level at the very bottom of the shaft was likely created later for more ritualistic purposes. To say it all a little differently, the second level may be more significant for archaeological reasons (due to its great age), whereas the third level seems to be more important for more symbolic and ritualistic reasons.

And what might those rituals within the "Tomb of Osiris" on that lowest level have consisted of, exactly? Inspired partly by the work of Egyptologist Rosalie David, Temple offers up some educated guesses as to what these may have looked like.

At another site in Egypt called Abydos, there are the remains of a sunken temple commonly referred to as the 'Osireion', which was also believed to commemorate the burial and resurrection of Osiris. By studying the rituals practiced there, as described in inscriptions found both in the Osireion and the adjoining Temple of Osiris, one can plausibly reconstruct some of what may have transpired in that chamber within the Giza well-shaft as well. Like the Osireion, *it's possible that the Tomb of Osiris served as a secret place of initiation and ritual re-enactment of the death by drowning, burial and resurrection of Osiris.*

Temple speculates this could have taken the form of the empty sarcophagus being opened, and the priest or pharaoh lying in the container and having the lid placed over them as part of the ceremony. This may have even included the act of "drowning" in the sarcophagus, with the participant using an air tube or the remaining air supply to breathe. Shortly afterwards, when the theorized ceremony calling Osiris to rise from the dead took place, complete with singing and praying, the lid could have been removed and the "resurrected" figure rise up to be "born again." The ceremony may also have been attended by a priestess representing Isis, presiding over the ritual resurrection. As such, the empty sarcophagus in level three could be seen as a symbolic statement in much the same way that the empty tomb of Jesus was seen by his followers as a statement about his resurrection, and of life everlasting.

While this is all purely speculative, I find it compelling, certainly more so than any other explanation or theory about the chamber I've come across thus far. In the end, Temple sums things up this way:

> In conclusion, I should say that the Osiris Shaft can never now be relegated to the status of a secondary feature of the Giza Plateau on the assumption that it is a Saitic burial shaft dating from the period 664 BC - 525 BC. This is now seen to be definitely not the case. The bottom level of the shaft is probably Middle Kingdom,

and Level Two is probably no later than the Fourth Dynasty. And what is more, [the dacite sarcophagus in level two], being made of a unique stone that occurs nowhere else – to our knowledge – amongst the surviving remains of the ancient Egyptian civilization, and being so unexpectedly ancient in date, must now be seen as one of the oldest and most precious of all carved objects to survive in the whole of Egypt. Also, **the 'Tomb of Osiris' must now be viewed as being of extraordinary importance, whether as a mystical burial site, or more likely as a mystical religious site for initiations or ceremonies connected with the Osirian religion during the second millennium BC.** (Emphasis mine.)[3]

A multitude of questions remain about the site and its contents. For instance, some still wonder whether there is a tunnel or channel leading out of the chamber besides the main shaft we entered it through. While we were down in the chamber, for instance, we clearly saw a small cavity off in the northwest corner of the room which appeared to be hacked out of the wall and seemed to lead out beyond the chamber. As of this writing, the latest reports claim that Zahi's crew sent a remote controlled robot through that opening and found that the small channel extended about 150 feet before an accumulation of mud prevented any further exploration.[4]

Another intriguing clue lies in the fact that the water in the moat around the central 'island' where the sarcophagus lies seems to be fed by a natural source. Unlike more polluted water sources further down the Giza Plateau, this water even seems drinkable, and was supposedly used for years as a source of well water for locals. If so, what is the source of the water? As Temple points out, the rock walls and floor of the chamber seem too solid for there to be random leaks. So does it enter through an artificial channel deliberately constructed by the ancients? Apart from the mind-boggling logistical challenges that would have posed for early engineers, it also raises the possibility there may still be an opening of some sort located underwater in that room. Clearly, there is much work yet to be done to unlock the full significance of the Tomb of Osiris, not to mention the Giza Plateau generally.[5]

Some Final Thoughts

Reflecting back on this distant culture, it can almost feel sometimes as though one is looking at an alien civilization, its customs and rituals are so far removed from our own as to seem incomprehensible. Yet despite those differences, we still detect elements that feel strangely familiar to us in some ways.

Consider those theorized rituals which may have occurred in that chamber deep underground, involving the ceremonial death and resurrection of Osiris. Not long after reading Temple's book and his speculations about the chamber, I was invited to watch a friend perform in an Easter pageant being put on by a mega-church in our area. As I watched the actors on stage recreating the death of Christ and his resurrection, complete with a depiction of the stone being rolled away from the tomb, as well as Christ's radiant ascension into heaven (all portrayed with clever lighting and stage effects), I

Down in the pit beneath the Great Pyramid. (Photo © Ray Grasse)

couldn't help notice similarities to what might have unfolded in that archaic chamber. Despite the differences, it's clear that our present-day civilization is still celebrating the death and resurrection of a divine being in ways that echo those of ancient times.

Or consider the simple but ubiquitous Christian practice of baptism itself, in which a person is lowered into water and symbolically "reborn" into a new spiritual life. Looked upon with fresh eyes, this ritual shares an obvious resonance with those in which an initiate or pharaoh in Egypt may have been immersed in water and "reborn" into a new life. Even without the added element of water, some have suggested that the sarcophagus in the King's Chamber in the Great Pyramid served a kindred function, of facilitating the symbolic deaths and rebirths of initiates, priests, or even pharaohs. It's also worth noting that modern Masonic ceremonies feature their own death/rebirth ritual that initiates must undergo to be admitted into their order.

Whether these various rites of death and resurrection in our own time were handed down through the millennia in some direct line of transmission, or simply reflect a perennial archetype that recurs throughout time in various places, it does suggest that our spiritual impulses may not be quite so different from those of our forebears as we'd like to believe.

Ray Grasse is the author of several books, including *The Waking Dream* (Quest Books, 1996), *Under a Sacred Sky* (Wessex, 2015), and most recently, *An Infinity of Gods* (Inner Eye Publications, 2017). His websites are www.raygrasse.com and www.raygrassephotography.com.

Painting illustrating future man finding the archaeological artefact (credit: K. F. Long)

THE APKALLU INITIATIVE

Designing A Minilithic Artefact for Rebooting Human Civilization in the Event of Global Cataclysm

by *Kelvin F. Long*

"The year is 2050. Earth is a thriving metropolis with a population exceeding 9 billion. Progress has been made in harmonising social-cultural tensions around the world and nation-state war is now an infrequent event. A young child of the future steps out into the bright sunshine of a gorgeous new morning. Her day is still ahead of her as she outstretches her arms and smiles at the mellifluous call of the singing birds. But then looking up, she notices something in the distance, a long streak across the sky that is moving rapidly, and seems to be descending towards the ground. It disappears behind the horizon, and shortly later a blinding flash engulfs the world. The girl looks on stunned, eyes struggling against the light to see the gradual build-up of a mushroom cloud that starts to reach high into the atmosphere. The impact event was hundreds of miles away, yet soon it engulfs the world in global climate change and sends tsunamis sweeping over coastal cities destroying all in their path. In response to oceanic earthquakes, the water becomes so big that it pushes across the flat land masses; unrelenting mega white horses to a trampled poppy field below. One day, this will form into wedge-shaped chevron deposits hundreds of feet high, composed of ocean floor micro-fossils. Within days of the event the girl will learn that billions of people are wiped out as human civilization draws to a rapid stagnation. All infrastructure and governments are gone, and only small pockets of communities around the world survive, numbering thousands at best. She was one of the lucky ones, her small community of one hundred people survived just barely on their high mountain-top position. This is fortunate for a girl named Hope."

Introduction

The future is uncertain. Whilst it is important to emphasise the positive reasons for the exploration of Earth and space, it is also important not to be in denial about the risks that really face us; for they are not insignificant. They are many and varied in type. From the potential for nation state warfare, to disease pandemics, to global climate change, to risks from above such as impact events by asteroids or comets or even the possibility of alien invasion. The sure way to guarantee our survival is to follow the lead of Elon Musk and to make the human race an interplanetary species; and indeed to go further with an interstellar species. But until we have reached this point we are vulnerable. The proposal made in this article is not an alternative to the current plans for the colonization of space and the continued building up of infrastructure, but it is a complimentary pathway to increase the probability of human survival into the coming centuries. In particular, it should be taken on board that the assumptions of this project are that a possible future exists where rocket technology no longer even exists as a worst case survival scenario.

The Apkallu Initiative is a proposed project to help reboot human civilization, on the assumption that some small pockets of human communities survive around the world during a global cataclysm, but all the remnants of our industrialised and developed civilization are destroyed. This includes our cities, our farms, our libraries, our infrastructure, and our transport networks; in essence the human race is thrown back to being a hunter-gatherer species and must begin again. It is named after the Sumerian sages who are said to have helped humankind establish civilization and culture, giving us the gifts of a moral code, mathematics, architecture, agriculture and all ways necessary to teach us how to become civilized. The Sumerian civilization is one of the first to appear in recorded history, which included the invention of its own writing form called cuneiform. Before we discuss what the Apkallu Initiative actually is, it is worth reminding ourselves of some essential context.

Impact Threats and Other Risks to Human Survival

We know that objects have impacted the Earth throughout its history and continue to do so today. Approximately 66 million years ago, it is believed that an impact event resulted in the Cretaceous-Tertiary (K-T) extinction. This led to devastation in the global environment and a prolonged winter which affected the photosynthesis of plants and plankton life. It also resulted in the destruction of a plethora of terrestrial organisms, including mammals, birds, insects and most famously the dinosaurs. The object, an asteroid or comet, was 10-15 km in diameter with a likely impact velocity of around 20 km/s and an associated kinetic energy of impact of around 30,000-1,000,000 Gtons TNT equivalent, depending on the assumptions. It left an impact crater in the Yucatan Peninsula in Mexico, and likely created 300 feet high tsunamis over an impact zone of around 3,000 miles.

Another example is Arizona's Meteor Crater, which was the result of a Nickel-Iron object around 50m in size impacting the Earth 50,000 years ago. With impact velocities ranging from 2.8-20 km/s this would have impacted with an associated kinetic energy of 10.7-26.2 Mtons TNT equivalent. Today, a crater remains of the impact event, 1.2 km in diameter and over 550 feet deep.

In 1908 a comet is believed to have impacted eastern Siberia, causing a flattening of a forest 2,000 square km in size. Since no impact crater was found, it is believed that the object disintegrated at an altitude of 5-10 km above the ground. The estimated energy of the air burst explosion was 10-15 Mtons TNT equivalent; depending on the assumptions one makes.

In July 1994 a comet split into 21 fragments ranging in size up to 2 km, and impacted the upper atmosphere of Jupiter with an impact velocity of around 60 km/s. The total energy of these impacts was around 6,000 Gtons TNT equivalent creating dark red spots with some being 12,000 km in size. Had this comet impacted the Earth, it would have posed a major threat to human existence.

During late 2017 we observed the close flyby pass of an asteroid of interstellar origins named 'Oumuamua. Much of the nature of this object remains uncharacterised, but some sensible estimates of the maximum potential impact energy suggest 4.2-46.9 Gtons TNT equivalent, had it impacted the Earth.

Then, in April 2018, an object named Asteroid 2018 GE3 passed close to Earth and was spotted 119,500 miles away, which is closer than the Moon, which orbits at an average distance of 238,900 miles. The object was first observed by the NASA funded Catalina Sky Survey project based at the University of Arizona Lunar and Planetary Laboratory. It was first observed a mere 21 hours before the closest approach to the Earth. The object was estimated to be at least 150-360 ft in diameter.

How many more are out there waiting for us? No doubt some will argue that the impact risks are statistically small and we should not be concerned about them. We know there are many asteroids in our own Solar System, varying in size from 1m up to 1,000 km. Approximately 16,000 objects have been found near Earth, but this is a small fraction of the estimated total that is out there, which varies between 1-2 million. Statistically, this presents a threat to human existence and life as we know it. Indeed, it is the belief of this author that impact events which can lead to global devastation of the human population may be as frequent as 1/1,000 - 1/10,000 years.

In addition to impact risks there are many other threats to human existence. This may include the implications of magnetic field reversal. Such an event occurred 41,400 years ago during the last ice age, called the Laschamp event. It caused a magnetic field reversal leading to a drop in its strength. This resulted in more cosmic rays reaching the Earth and an increased production of the isotopes Beryllium 10 and Carbon 14.

There is also the risk of enhanced solar activity such as through large scale solar flares, or the possibility of the Sun entering unstable periods in its evolution for which our current models of stellar-structure may not take account of. This could be due to the passage of our Sun through the spiral density arms of the galaxy. There are the risks of nation-state war or even global thermonuclear war that could drive us towards extinction, either through direct destruction or through altering the climate. There are the risks of human disease pandemic, which surely must become more probable in an increasing global population. There are the risks of human destruction of elements of the biosphere, such as pollutions of the oceans, soils, deforestation or polluting of the atmosphere. There are the risks that microbes could be introduced into our biosphere from an alien planet that is infectious to our biodiversity.

Then there is the actual risk of alien invasion, from a species set on conquering other lower species or seeking resource acquisition no matter the costs. It may be assessed that some of these are low probability. However, the fact that there are so many risks to the future survival of humankind should be a concern, and it is vital that we take a proactive approach to adaptability and survival, instead of a reactive one when such events occur.

Assumptions of a Hypothetical Near-Human Extinction

Imagine a situation where human-kind is nearly wiped out by some global cataclysm. This could be an impact event or one of the other risks highlighted earlier. In a worst case scenario, but one where some humans survive, we might make the following assumptions:

1. All infrastructure is destroyed, to include buildings, power utilities, city plumbing, dams, transport networks, agriculture and farming, huge portions of the plant and animal kingdom.
2. All information sources are destroyed, to include all the world libraries, computers and electronic memory. It is possible

that some books will be discovered over time as communities explore the rubble remaining from the metropolis. Books would become precious beyond their current value.
3. The global climate is in turmoil and hostile, but with isolated regions of stability such that with determination survival is possible.
4. The geological, climatic, oceanic activity and effects of the cataclysm event, within weeks, months or years will gradually return towards some level of stable Earth.
5. Small pockets of humans survive around the Earth, perhaps 10s to 100s each but with the total not exceeding thousands.

Given this scenario, we can note that the surviving generation will remember the world as it was before. They will use this knowledge to teach their children. At this point knowledge is based upon direct memory. Those children will then grow up, with their parents dying off, and they will remember what their parents taught them and some of those children may even have some memories of the world before. But for the most part we are dealing here with recent history and part mythology. The grandchildren will also be born and grow up, but they will have no direct memory of the world the way it was before. At this point we are dealing with history and mythology. Within the third or fourth generation there is a risk that all knowledge will be lost, and especially if that knowledge is not captured and written down. All received knowledge then becomes both mythology and fantasy.

There are solutions to this practiced by the Native North Americans for example, which is to communicate stories verbally and also use this to impart wisdom, and those stories are accompanied by rituals. However, one cannot believe that such a method of communication does not contain significant information error propagation with each successive generation, compared to the original version.

The Code of Hammurabi, created 1750 B.C, currently housed at the Louvre, Paris
(image credit: K. F. Long)

The History of Humans on Planet Earth

In the event of a global cataclysm, assuming small pockets of human communities survive, but the majority of human civilization and associated technological infrastructure is destroyed, how can we ensure a chance at rebooting human knowledge? Indeed, is it possible that this has in fact occurred in the recent past and this is a part reason for the many megalithic structures on Earth?

Until recently, Sumer was the earliest known civilization in the historical Mesopotamia, and is located in modern Iraq. It dates back to 3,000 B.C and was likely settled around 4,000-5,500 B.C by proto-Euphrateans or Ubaidians. The people from this era are credited for many great inventions and discoveries which led to the advance of their society, including mathematics, geometry, agriculture, architecture, economics and law to name a few. One of the most famous objects discovered from this period is the Code of Hammurabi, a 2.25m-tall stone wall consisting of 282 laws, such as "an eye for an eye" and is the first legal system from the Old Babylonian period.

It is important to note that in the Babylonian creation mythologies, which were written in cuneiform, there are around a thousand lines of text on seven clay tables. The focus of this text is the creation of humankind for the service of the gods. These texts are called the *Enûma Eliš*, and arguably they have a clear lineage to the Judeo-Christian Bible. The cuneiform script was scribed, using a wedge-shaped marker, onto a wet clay tablet and also cylinder seals. These are small round objects typically an inch in length engraved with information. Once dried the inscription was permanent. The information preserved on tablets and seals was cuneiform text but also contained figurative scenes or descriptions of events or objects. Such objects are breathtaking in their clarity, gorgeous in their artistic nature, and contain a wealth of information about the society, its rituals, values, business, science and technology.

Photographs of Sumerian cylinder seals from the private collection of the author
(image credit: K. F. Long)

The *Holy Bible* records a flood story that engulfed all of planet Earth. This is recorded in Genesis chapters 6 – 9, and the flood seems to last for around one hundred and fifty days. Other cultures have recorded similar stories. For example the Sumerian tale of *Ziusudra* and the *Atra-Hasis* also describes a global flood story that is similar to that told in *Genesis*. In the Sumerian story the flood lasts for seven days. An account is also told in the *Epic of Gilgamesh*, which is more similar to the Biblical story. Also, Hindu mythology tells of a great flood in the *Satapatha Brahmana*. It is very easy to dismiss the possibility of a global flood as pure mythology, but the occurrence of a similar story in so many cultures around the world is at least suggestive that it may be a memory of an actual event which many today are regarding as mythology. Indeed, science may be catching up with the past.

Geologists and climatologists study a period in Earth's history called the Younger Dryas, which occurred 12,900 to 11,700 years ago and saw a return to glacial conditions which temporarily reversed the gradual climatic warming after the last glacial maximum which began receding around 20,000 years ago. It led to many catastrophic effects including the decline of the Clovis culture in North America and the extinction of many megafauna which included the mammoths; the last of which survived into the Holocene around 4,500 years ago in Africa, Europe, Asia and North America.

In recent years, evidence is emerging that the Younger Dryas period may have been caused by a cometary impact event on the North American ice sheet, around 12,900 years ago. The evidence for this includes the discovery of a 10 million ton deposit of impact spherules across four continents, and the discovery of a nano-diamond rich layer. In addition, analysis of underground soils indicates massive wildfire and abrupt ecosystem disruption on California's Northern Channel Islands. Scientists have also discovered very high temperature impact melt products as evidence for an air burst explosion. All of this is dated to around 12,900 years ago, at the onset of the Younger Dryas. If this is proven to

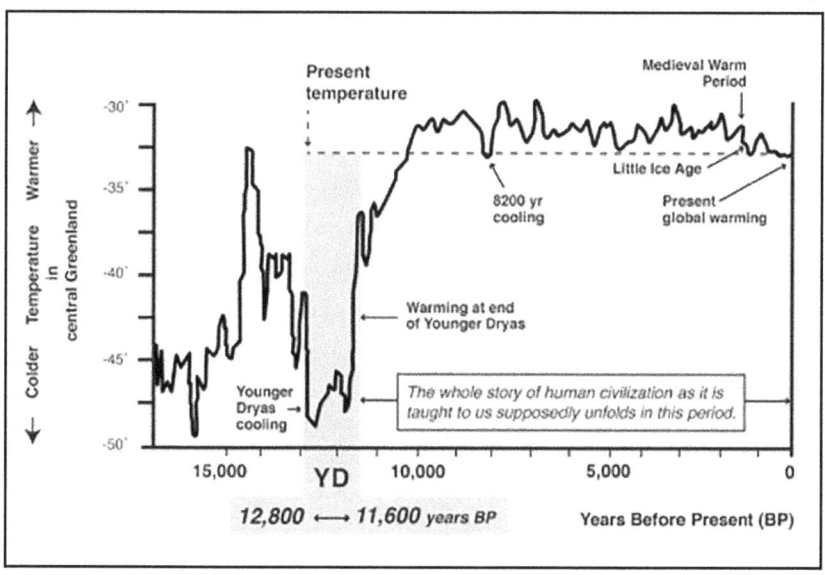

Illustration of the Younger Dryas period

be correct, then a global cataclysm may indeed have occurred in our recent past. Speculating, if any advanced civilizations existed on Earth prior to this date, they may have been wiped out by this cataclysm forcing civilization to start from the beginning again.

At some point in our past we moved from a hunter-gatherer species to an agricultural-farming one, where we embraced the domestication of animals and crops. This is marked by a period called the Neolithic, and occurred around 10,200 years ago. It is considered to be the last period of the stone age and commenced the beginning of the Neolithic revolution. It ended with the emergence of the Copper and Bronze and Iron ages and our new abilities to use metals. It is remarkable that we have apparently exploded technologically and social-culturally over the last 10,000 years or so to the state where we have computers, cars, aeroplanes and communication satellites. What was it that propelled us forward over such a short space of time? Why had we not achieved this level of maturity previously? Was it the formation of a critical population density? Was it global climatic conditions? Was it our tribal nature and inability to get organized? Was it some other existential threat to our existence?

Homo sapiens in our modern form may be several hundred thousand years old. Paleolithic cave art certainly goes back to 40,000 years but may be 60,000 years if we include what is currently being claimed to be art from Neanderthal man. Evidence from the out of Africa hypothesis puts *Homo sapiens* at around 130,000-180,000 years old. But there are alternative versions which claim populations emerging out of Africa as early as 350,000 years ago. Evidence for older findings includes discoveries of anatomically modern human skull fossils at Jebel Irhour in Morocco (315,000 years) and Middle Awash in Ethiopia (160,000 years). The history of human evolution is far from settled and 'thinking man' may be much older than we realised.

Ancient Megaliths

A story from ancient Sumeria is that of an amphibious being called Oannes (also known as Adapa) who apparently taught humankind wisdom. The story was told by Berossus, a Chaldean Priest in Babylon, in 290 B.C. Berossus described Oannes as having the body of a fish but underneath the figure of a man. He is said to dwell in the Persian Gulf, rising out of the waters in day time and furnishing humankind in the instruction of writing, arts and other subjects. Here are the words of Berossus:

> At first they led a somewhat wretched existence and lived without rule after the manner of beasts. But, in the first year appeared an animal endowed with human reason, named Oannes, who rose from out of the Erythian Sea, at the point where it borders Babylonia. He had the whole body of a fish, but above his fish's head he had another head which was that of a man, and human feet emerged from beneath his fish's tail. He had a human voice, and an image of him is preserved unto this day. He passed the day in the midst of men without taking food; he taught them the use of letters, sciences and arts of all kinds. He taught them to construct cities, to found temples, to compile laws, and explained to them the principles of geometrical knowledge. He made them distinguish the seeds of the earth, and showed them how to collect the fruits; in short he instructed them in everything which could tend to soften human manners and humanize their laws. From that time nothing material has been added by way of improvement to his instructions. And when the sun set, this being Oannes, retired again into the sea, for he was amphibious. After this there appeared other animals like Oannes.

Whether this is pure fiction or has any resemblance to historical events does not matter, but it is this story that has given rise to the idea of building what this author is calling a 'minilithic artefact' under the Apkallu Initiative as will be discussed further below. As an aside it is worth noting that in his book *Intelligent Life in the Universe,* written with L. S. Shklovskii (Pan Books, 1977), the astronomer Carl Sagan opened a discussion on the Sumerian civilization with "I came upon a legend which more nearly fulfils some of our criteria for a genuine contact myth".

On planet Earth we know that species rise up and fall and suffer extinction. The fossil record has shown this for many a species. There are also arguments that *Homo sapiens* are not the only occurrence of intelligence on Planet Earth (see for example the recent book *Other Minds* by Peter Godfrey-Smith on the octopus). Why then is it not possible, in the last million years, that an earlier species of man, or other life form on Earth, could have evolved to similar levels of intelligence to that which we possess today, to include a technological level similar in extent? Such a people would predate modern recorded history, and it is at least plausible that some memory of them could be preserved in the creation mythologies of our various ancient cultures.

Many ancient megalithic structures have been found by archaeologists around the world. This includes for example the Great Pyramid and the Great Sphinx in Giza (4,500 years old), Tiwanaku and Pumapunku in West Bolivia (3,500 years old), Stonehenge in England (5,000 years old), Machu Picchu in Peru (550 years old) to name a few. However, recently our linear understanding of human evolution from a hunter-gatherer species to an agricultural-farming one has been placed under scrutiny, by the discovery in 1996 of Göbekli Tepe, a site in the South eastern Anatolia region of Turkey, which may date back to 12,000 years old. The site demonstrates a superior knowledge of construction techniques, geometry and other disciplines and to enable its construction would have required a food surplus to exist – before the arrival of the Neolithic revolution. In addition, it is arguable that to get to a point where you can

Carved pillar at Göbekli Tepe

Gunung Padang (Mohammad Fadli, Creative Commons)

construct something like Göbekli Tepe would take thousands of years of advancement of knowledge in itself. This might suggest that the civilization that built it was 15,000-20,000 years old.

A potentially even older site has also been found in West Java, called Gunung Padang, which was discovered in 1914. It may be the largest megalithic site in South Eastern Asia. Radiocarbon dating puts the site at several different eras spanning 6,500-20,000 years ago, although the dating claims are controversial among archaeologists in Indonesia. A large structure has also been discovered beneath the surface some 15m down and includes large chambers. This discovery, and that of Göbekli Tepe, is telling us that our linear understanding of history is in need of revision.

Interglacial Periods in Earth's History

Given the existence of Göbekli Tepe and Gunung Padang, the idea of an earlier intelligent and advanced civilization existing on Earth is not so implausible. However, were there opportunities in Earth's history for this to occur? An examination of climatic conditions would seem to suggest so.

During the history of Earth there have been five major ice ages, and we are currently in the Quaternary Ice Age at this time, which spans from 2.59 million years ago. Within the ice ages are subperiods known as glacial and interglacial periods.

Recent measurements of the relative oxygen isotope ratio in Antarctica and Greenland show the periods of glacial and interglacial periods throughout history over the last few hundred thousand years. This is a measurement of the ratio of the abundance of oxygen with atomic mass 18 to the abundance of oxygen with atomic mass 16 present in ice core samples, $^{18}O/^{16}O$, where ^{16}O is the most abundant of the naturally occurring isotopes. Ocean water is mostly comprised of $H_2{}^{16}O$, in addition to smaller amounts of $HD^{16}O$ and $H_2{}^{18}O$. The oxygen isotope ratio is a measure of the degree to which precipitation due to water vapour condensation during warm to cold air transition, removes $H_2{}^{18}O$ to leave more $H_2{}^{16}O$ rich water vapour. This distillation process leads to any precipitation having a lower $^{18}O/^{16}O$ ratio during temperature drops. This therefore provides a reliable record of ancient water temperature changes in glacial ice cores, where temperatures much cooler than present corresponds to a period of glaciation and where temperatures much warmer than today represents an interglacial period. The oxygen isotope ratios are therefore used as a proxy for temperature changes by climate scientists.

The Vienna Standard Mean Ocean Water (SSMOW) has a ratio of $^{18}O/^{16}O = 2005.2 \times 10^{-6}$, so any changes in ice core samples will be relative to this number. The quantity that is being measured, $\delta^{18}O$, is a relative ratio calculated as in the units of % parts per thousand or per mil. The change in the oxygen ratio is then attributed to changes in temperature alone, assuming that the effects of salinity and ice volume are negligible. An increase of around 0.22% is then defined to be equivalent to a cooling of 1°C.

There are differences in the value of δ between the different ocean temperatures where any moisture had evaporated at the final place of precipitation. As a result the value has to be calibrated such that there are differences between say Greenland and Antarctica. This does result in some differences in the proxy temperature data based on ice core analysis, and Greenland seems to stand out, such as indicating a more dramatic Younger Dryas period (11,600-12,900 years ago) than other data.

An analysis of this data shows that the climate has varied cyclically throughout its history and is manifest of natural climate change. In particular what emerges out of the data are some interesting lessons about the recent history of planet Earth. Data shows the rapid oscillations of the climate temperature from the average temperature of today, indicative of glacial and interglacial periods. In particular, the data shows that during the Holocene period, beginning approximately 11,700 years before present, the temperature varied between 2-4°C.

It is reasonable to assume that human civilizations under development will do better when the climate is kinder. This means that the warmer it is the better civilisations will do, and the colder it is, the harder the struggles. In particular we can expect that during the conditions of a colder climate that agricultural farming will suffer, and so there will be less food to go around, which will affect both lifespan and population expansion. To support this it is worth noting that the current epoch, the last 10,000 years, has been one of the longest interglacial period for at least the last quarter of a million years and it is reasonable to therefore assume that this is one of the factors which has allowed human development from the emergence of the Neolithic period coming out of the last ice age.

The data also shows that there was a large global warming period known as the Eemian around 115,000-130,000 years ago. The average global temperatures were around 22-24°C, compared to today where the average is around 14°C. Forests grew as far north

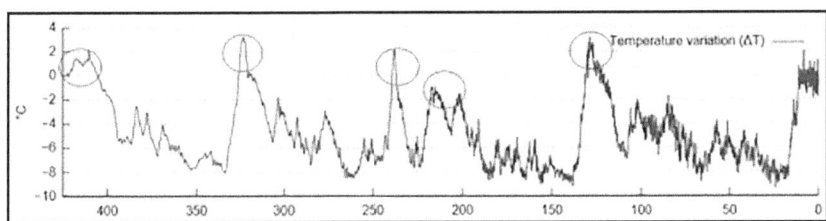

Temperature proxy data showing opportunities for the rise of advanced civilization in recent prehistory

as the Arctic circle at 71° latitude and North Cape in Norway, and Oulu in Finland. For comparison North Cape today is now a tundra, where the physical growth of plants is limited to the low temperatures and small growing seasons. Given that *Homo sapiens* may have been here since around 300,000 years ago, this seems like a major opportunity for the development of human society from a people of hunter gatherers to one of agricultural developers and the development of a civil society.

There have been other interglacial periods that have resulted in global temperatures being either equivalent or above the average today, and the data shows temperature spikes of periods at around 200,000 years, 220,000 years, 240,000 years, 330,000 years and 410,000 years. Each of these interglacial periods will typically last at least 10,000 years.

The Apkallu Initiative

It is fully admitted that much of the above contains speculation, but until we have a firmer grasp of history it would be unwise to rule such possibilities out. We turn our attention then to the future and solving the problem of how to preserve human knowledge in the event of a global cataclysm such that humankind can restart again so that within centuries we mature back to similar levels of today's technological advancement. Ultimately this is a statistical problem, in that by reducing the time of each cycle for maturing to technological capability, one improves the probability of survival. It is sensible to think of this concept as a civilization accelerator.

The Apkallu Initiative is therefore a proposal to construct a minilithic artefact (analogous to megalithic artefacts) that can survive for a time duration exceeding 100,000 years. This duration is chosen for three principal reasons:

1. The recent ice core records suggest that within that time period there may be several opportunities (~4) where the climatic conditions are sufficiently supportive for human existence to facilitate growth beyond basic survival.
2. It approximately corresponds to four processional cycles of the Earth around the equinoxes, which typically last 25,920 years. We note that many of the ancient megaliths seem to have been preoccupied with the measurement of the equinoxes; which may relate to lost memory of previous cataclysms.
3. It is difficult to design for an artefact that can survive longer than this, although desirable.

The artefact would be a form of archaeological-architectural device from the standpoint of future humans who uncover it. The device would be replicated perhaps 1,000 times and distributed around the seven continents of the Earth. Ideally, some could also be placed in space, on the Moon or Mars. The idea is that for any future human surviving a global cataclysm that finds this artefact and studies it sufficiently, it will give them the knowledge they need to rapidly advance human civilization at an accelerated rate.

The artefact would be a form of long distance communication. We have of course attempted message plaques in the past such as the Voyager Golden Record and the Pioneer Plaque. Indeed, the Code of

Hammurabi from the Sumerian civilization is a form of minilithic artefact, but just specific to moral and legal codes. Another example would have been the tablets for the Biblical Ten Commandments.

There is a question of what materials to construct the artefact from. Plastics and metals will likely degrade over thousands of years. Electronic memory is not useful if it is subject to flip switching and also requires a computer interface to read it. It therefore seems sensible to construct the artefact out of stone; perhaps in a similar manner to the Sumerian cuneiform on wet clay tablets. One of the options may be diorite. It would perhaps be useful to depict both logograms, with syllabic and alphabetic elements, as well as phonetics and even determinatives to create appropriate semantic descriptions.

There is a question of what information should the artefact contain. It should contain the foundation knowledge of human civilization. This is a subjective decision. One example we might take lessons from for example was the *trivium* (logic, grammar, rhetoric) and the *quadrivium* (arithmetic, geometry, music, astronomy) of the classical world. Both were considered preparation work before delving into the study of philosophy and theology. In addition to these, the artefact might contain many other disciplines of thought, such as human biology, medicine, architecture, chemistry, physics, law, history, music, language, agriculture, botany, ethics and other subjects. Experts in appropriate disciplines would need to be consulted to derive the say twelve base foundation knowledge or tenets that govern a field from which in principle all else can be derived given time.

The goal of the information content imprinted onto the artefact would be as follows:

1. The continued survival of the human species at peace.
2. The accelerated technological, social-cultural growth of human civilization from an assumed stagnated level.
3. The preservation of moral and ethical philosophy.

There is also a question of what language. One approach would be to take lessons from historical artefacts which contained several languages to ensure future interpretation. This includes the Rosetta Stone (2,200 years old) which contains ancient Egyptian hieroglyphics, demotic and ancient Greek. Another example is the Fuente Magna of the Americas (5,000 years old), found in Bolivia but contains both ancient Pukara and a proto-Sumerian alphabet. Another example is the Behistun inscription (2,500 years old) found in Iran, which contains three different cuneiform script languages, that of Old Persian, Elamite and Babylonian.

There is also the question of the size and shape of the artefact, and although you want it big enough to find, you also want to manage the construction cost of the project. Something around 6 to 12 inches would seem a good optimum size. The exact shape would have multiple surface areas to facilitate different disciplines of knowledge. One idea is a dodecahedron, which has 12 faces.

The proposal of the Apkallu Initiative is to form a team which then designs and leads the construction of such an artefact. This can then be reproduced and distributed to different locations around the world. Some would eventually be displayed in art galleries or museums and some will be lost to the land and sea, but the hope is that in the event of the cataclysmic scenario described above that future humans will stumble across such an artefact, and after studying it, teach their community everything they need to become a civilized and socially-technologically advanced society. Currently no team has been formed, but this article is an initial invitation of interest and anyone interested can contact the web site: https://www.apkalluinitiative.com/

Our ability to become an interstellar capable species depends in the near term on our ability to survive here on Earth or in near-space. The preservation of the deep knowledge and learning of the human experience is critical to this future, if we are to continue to progress, avoid stagnation and decay or even complete extinction or avoid repeating mistakes of the past.

Finally, such a project has the potential to inspire long-term thinking among differing human societies, and so in itself may be a self-perpetuating mechanism toward social-cultural harmonization and increased global awareness of our fragility in the great Cosmos. In addition, because of its interdisciplinary nature, it has the potential to involve all of humanity on its journey, as we jointly work toward a back-up plan to ensure that humanity can survive in the millennia ahead.

> **Kelvin F. Long** was the creator of Project Icarus, the re-design of the Project Daedalus starship of the 1970s, and went on to head the Initiative for Interstellar Studies. An aerospace engineer and physicist, he also served as editor of the *Journal of the British Interplanetary Society* during a critical period in the journal's history. He was the editor of *Beyond the Boundary: Exploring the Science and Culture of Interstellar Spaceflight,* and is the author of *Deep Space Propulsion: A Roadmap to Interstellar Flight* (Springer, 2011).

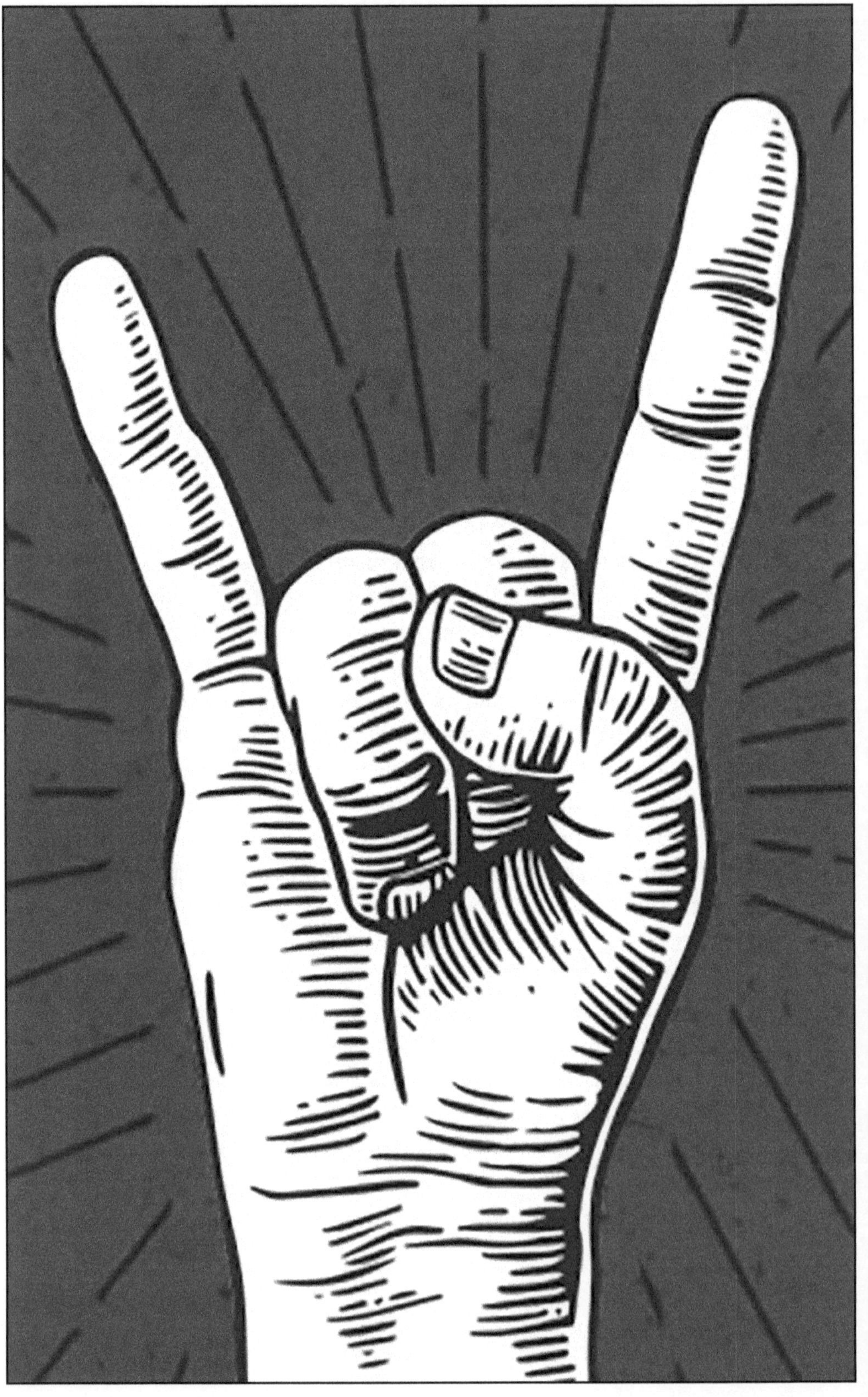

Diabolus in Musica

Rumours of secret pacts with Satan have been rife in the world of music for a long time now, but what are the origins of these supposed record deals with the Devil?

by *John Reppion*

Theophilus the Penitent is a Catholic Saint whose life (and death) was recorded by his sixth century contemporary Eutychianus of Adana. Eutychianus's account tells how, having humbly turned down a job as a Bishop, Theophilus was then ousted from his position as an archdeacon by the man who accepted the Bishophood. Theophilus' solution to this was a novel one to say the least; he sought out a necromancer who put him in touch with Satan to whom he offered his soul in exchange for the Bishop job. The Devil had Theophilus renounce Christ and the Virgin Mary and sign a contract with his own blood used as ink, and the deal was done. In later life Theophilus (quite understandably) felt a bit worried about the pact, and decided to repent, praying to the Virgin Mary for forgiveness. After forty days of fasting, the Virgin appeared to him and verbally chastised him. Theophilus begged forgiveness and Mary promised to intercede with God. He then fasted a further thirty days, after which Mary appeared to him again, and granted him absolution. However, Satan was unwilling to relinquish his hold over Theophilus, and three days later, Theophilus awoke to find the damning contract on his chest. He then took the contract to the legitimate bishop and confessed all that he had done. The bishop burned the document, and Theophilus died out of sheer joy to be free from the burden of his pact.

Theophilus's bargain with the Devil is very much the blueprint for the 16th century German legend of Faust, which has in turn become the archetype for the tale of one who sells their soul to the Devil. "Faustian" is defined thus: *"pertaining to or resembling or befitting Faust or Faustus especially in insatiably striving for worldly knowledge and power even at the price of spiritual values; 'a Faustian pact with the Devil'."*

Theophilus wanted a better job, Faust wanted unlimited knowledge and worldly pleasures, but what about fame and fortune? The trope of a musician selling his her soul to Satan is one so familiar it has become a cliché, but where does it originate from? It's often said that the Devil has all the best tunes, but when exactly did Lucifer's songwriting career begin?

Symphony for the Devil

Born in 1692 in what was then the Republic of Venice, Giuseppe Tartini was the child of aristocratic parents who had it in their minds that their son should grow up to become a Franciscan friar. Tartini studied divinity and law at Padua University where he also received the basic musical training mandatory for all would-be monks. In his late teens Tartini secretly married a favourite protégée of the archbishop of Padua, who was so outraged he ordered the young man's arrest. Disguised as a monk, Tartini fled from Padua and took refuge in a monastery at Assisi. It was while in hiding there that Tartini first began to take an interest in the violin. Though his career did not begin in earnest until his mid twenties, Giuseppe Tartini went on to become a world renowned composer, and a musician of such technical proficiency that it was rumoured he had an extra digit on each hand (he didn't).

Tartini contributed to the science of acoustics by his discovery of the difference tone, or combination tone (also known as the Tartini tone): a psychoacoustic phenomenon where a third note is perceived when two other notes are played. He devised a theory of harmony based on affinities with algebra and geometry, originally set forth in his 1754 work *Trattato di musica* ("Treatise on Music") and later expanded into *Dissertazione dei principi dell'armonia musicale* ("Dissertation on the Principles of Musical Harmony"). Some would doubtless call what Giuseppe Tartini had a God-given talent but, that being the case, his skills certainly didn't escape the notice of The Opposition. Joseph Jérôme Le Français de Lalande recorded in his 1769 book *Voyage d'un François en Italie, fait dans les années 1765 & 1766* ("Journey around France and Italy, in the years 1765 & 1766") a story told to him by Tartini himself:

> One night, in the year 1713 I dreamed I had made a pact with the devil for my soul. Everything went as I wished: my new servant anticipated my every desire. Among other things, I gave him my violin to see if he could play. How great was my astonishment on hearing a sonata so wonderful and so beautiful, played with such great art and intelligence, as I had never even conceived in my boldest flights of fantasy. I felt enraptured, transported, enchanted: my breath failed me, and I awoke.
>
> I immediately grasped my violin in order to retain, in part at least, the impression of my dream. In vain! The music which I at this

time composed is indeed the best that I ever wrote, and I still call it the "Devil's Trill", but the difference between it and that which so moved me is so great that I would have destroyed my instrument and have said farewell to music forever if it had been possible for me to live without the enjoyment it affords me.

Nevertheless Tartini persevered, striving to recapture some echo of that incredible work fiddled out by Old Nick in accordance with their pact. The resulting work, *Il trillo del diavolo* ("The Devil's Trill sonata"), became the musician's best-known composition, although (owing at least in part to its supposed daemonic inspiration), it was not published until Tartini was already thirty years in his grave.[1] It would seem that, when it comes to the contract for such unholy collaborations, the Devil really is in the detail.

The Devil's Violinist

Born in Genoa, Italy in 1782 (twelve years after Giuseppe Tartini's death), Niccolò Paganini grew up to become the most celebrated violin virtuoso of his era, leaving his mark as one of the pillars of modern violin technique. He also, so the story goes, sold his soul to the Devil.

A gifted musician from childhood, it seems that rumours of Paganini's diabolic assistance first began when some claimed that his mother must have made some Devilish pact on his behalf. Like many a child-star since, Paganini found the excesses of fame too much to cope with. In his teens he became an alcoholic, contracted syphilis, and accumulated massive gambling debts. He disappeared from the spotlight for three years but returned in 1804 at the age of twenty-two with a talent so incredibly increased that, again, rumours that a contract with Old Scratch must have been signed were rife. The musician cut an imposing figure; he always dressed in black, was tall, thin, pale, and gaunt (owing partly to the loss of most of his teeth, and the use of mercury in treating his syphilis). He also had unusually long and flexible fingers which some later posited may have been due to a genetic condition, perhaps either Marfan syndrome or Ehlers-Danlos syndrome. He was, in essence, very much a Gothic character, and this was something both his audience and the press of the time seemed to adore about him. In 1831, for example *The Athenaeum* magazine described Paganini as "very Zamiel (Samael being a demon, then recently portrayed in the German opera *Der Freischütz* ("The Marksman") as a man dressed all in black) in appearance, and certainly a very devil in performance".

In May 1832 Henry Cole, first director of the Victoria & Albert Museum in London, saw Paganini in concert at "the Opera House" (King's Theatre) and recorded the event in his diary.

> I never heard any instrumental music which so perfectly realized the idea which his playing was intended to convey. One piece, the witches under the tree of Benevento was so admirably characteristic that you could [imagine] the Vizards & Witches capering before you in all attitudes.

The particular piece Cole alludes to is *Le Streghe* ("The Witches Dance") which had its own legend attached to it. It was said the G string of Paganini's violin was not made of catgut (which even then was never actually made from cat's guts, but usually sheep or goats), but from the intestine of a murdered mistress of his. A portion of *Le Streghe* is played exclusively on the G string, but Paganini went further than this, creating an entire composition, *A Preghiera* (AKA *Moses Fantasy*) for the G string. This piece, based upon a theme from Gioachino Rossini's opera *Mosè in Egitto* ("Moses in Egypt") was supposedly played spontaneously by Paganini after his other three strings snapped one after another during a public performance in Italy. Paganini is reported to have

Contemporary poster for Niccolò Paganini's London debut

paused, announced "And now, Paganini and one string!", and launched into the tune to rapturous applause.

So many of the legends attached to Paganini are not only impossible to verify, but also to source; tales of doppelgängers of the performer being seen in the audience at his performances, of lightning striking his bow on stage as he played, of his glowing "fiery" eyes, and more, are so often repeated and reprinted that their origins are for the most part obscured. What is well documented however, is the musician's tragic demise.

In May 1840 Paganini was ill and near death. The Bishop of Nice (where Paganini was at the time) sent a local parish priest to him to perform the last rites. Paganini refused the sacrament. Some say this was because he believed he would yet recover, others that it was his pact with Satan which prevented him from accepting. He died suddenly a week later. Due to the lack of last rites, and the persistent rumours of his infernal treaty, the Church denied Paganini's body a Catholic burial in Genoa. It took four years and an appeal to the Pope before the Church allowed the body to be transported to Genoa, but Paganini was not actually allowed to be buried until 1876. Paganini got his fame, fortune, and adulation, yet he also suffered decades of terrible ill health, was feared and stigmatised, eventually dying penniless and excommunicated. Once again, the Devil seems to have delivered on his contract, but the cost was a high one for Paganini.

Hell Hound on my Trail

Although he was (and is) best known for his violin playing and composition, Paganini was also an avid guitarist, and perhaps that gave Satan an idea for his next big signing.

Robert Leroy Johnson was born in Hazlehurst, Mississippi, in May 1911. Johnson had an interest in music at an early age, known as a harmonica and jaw-harp player in school, but it wasn't until he picked up a guitar that magic began to happen.

The earliest exponents of acoustic guitar blues that we know of include Charley Patton, Son House and Willie Brown. Patton had been born in southern Mississippi before the turn of the 20th century and was playing around the Southern states by 1914, singing songs such as "Down The Dirt Road Blues" and "Pony Blues". As well as clever rhythmic playing, his guitar style included slapping its body, playing it between his legs and behind his back. Patton teamed up with guitarist Willie Brown in the 1920s and then befriended preacher and blues man Son House. House's own "Preaching The Blues" would have a considerable influence on a young Robert Johnson.

Johnson was fascinated by the music of these men and followed them around, watching them perform. He even showed them a little of his own fledgling guitar playing, but these Bluesmen were – so the story goes, at least – scathing of the young boy's abilities. So Johnson went away and he got better. Lots better. So much so in fact, and so quickly, that there were rumours that he'd had a little help from a certain Man in Black whom he'd had a meeting with at the crossroads near Dockery Plantation one midnight. Playing the Blues was secular; the antithesis of the Church music that "good Christians" were supposed to play. As such, being a Blues musician – singing about earthly pleasures and human failings – was likened to "selling your soul to the Devil" by many, respectable people in Mississippi. When Johnson's sixteen year old wife, Virginia Travis, died in childbirth in 1929, some said it was a punishment for the music Johnson made, and the path which he had chosen. Whatever the reason, Virginia's death (and that of their unborn child) was very much the catalyst for Robert Johnson to begin his life on the road as a touring (wandering, really) Blues guitarist.

Between 1932 and his death in 1938 Johnson travelled the Mississippi Delta, Mississippi, and Arkansas, also venturing as far as

Chicago, Texas, New York, Canada, Kentucky, and Indiana. A quiet though friendly, figure, Johnson would perform under different assumed names, giving little or nothing of his origins or background away. He reportedly had a knack of seducing women with his music, and it was the hospitality of these women which Johnson largely relied upon for his food and lodgings while on his travels. In August 1938, this proved to be the undoing of the twenty-seven-year-old guitarist. The woman whom he chose to woo with his music that fateful evening was married, and her husband poisoned Johnson's whisky. Robert Johnson died three days later in agony. So, Johnson got what he asked for; he learned to play the guitar better than any of his idols and got to tour around just like they did. He even got a fair dose of whisky and women thrown into the bargain, but because the Devil loves his ironies, those proved to be his undoing. But the story of Robert Johnson does not end with his death; it is his legacy which many would argue has become Satan's greatest musical recruitment tool.

Between 1936 and 1937 Robert Johnson recorded twenty-nine songs for the American Record Corporation. These songs were released on eleven 78rpm records through the Vocalion label. Though the records were not hugely successful during Robert's lifetime, countless musicians and historian alike have argued since that they laid the foundations of Rock and Roll: the real "Devil's Music" of the 20th century.

IF 6 WAS 9

In English occultist and ceremonial magician Aleister 'The Great Beast' Crowley's 1912 work *The Book of Lies,* Chapter 69 is headed "THE WAY TO SUCCEED – AND THE WAY TO SUCK EGGS!":

> This is the Holy Hexagram. Plunge from the height, O God, and interlock with Man! Plunge from the height, O Man, and interlock with Beast! The Red Triangle is the descending tongue of grace; the Blue Triangle is the ascending tongue of prayer. This Interchange, the Double Gift of Tongues, the Word of Double Power ABRAHADABRA!-is the sign of the GREAT WORK, for the GREAT WORK is accomplished in Silence. And behold is not that Word equal to Cheth, that is Cancer. This Work also eats up itself, accomplishes its own end, nourishes the worker, leaves no seed, is perfect in itself. Little children, love one another!

The title, and the above quoted paragraph, are (in case you hadn't noticed) none-too-subtle references to the "69" sex position, which facilitates mutual oral sex between two people. Following the publication of *The Book of Lies,* Crowley became involved with the secret religious organisation Ordo Templi Orientis (O.T.O.) which incorporated Sex Magick as part of its rituals and teachings. The writings of Crowley were to have a significant influence upon the Rock and Roll music of the 1960s, as were the recordings of one Robert Johnson.

In 1961 Columbia Records released a two album collection of all of Robert Johnson's recoded material entitled "King of the Delta

Blues Singers". Although the release wasn't a huge hit at the time, it proved to be an influential one.

> Brian Jones had the first album, and that's where I first heard it. I'd just met Brian, and I went around to his apartment-crash pad, actually, all he had in it was a chair, a record player, and a few records. One of which was Robert Johnson. He put it on, and it was just – you know – astounding stuff. When I first heard it, I said to Brian, "Who's that?" [Brian replied] "Robert Johnson". I said, "Yeah, but who's the other guy playing with him?" Because I was hearing two guitars, and it took me a long time to realize he was actually doing it all by himself. […] You know, you think you're getting a handle on playing the blues, and then you hear Robert Johnson – some of the rhythms he's doing and playing and singing at the same time, you think, "This guy must have three brains!"

These are the words of guitarist Keith Richards whose band, The Rolling Stones (just in case you haven't heard of him, or them before), went on to record a version of Johnson's "Love in Vain" for their album *Let it Bleed*. Crowley appeared amongst the many famous and infamous faces on the cover of The Beatles' 1967 LP *Sgt. Pepper's Lonely Hearts Club Band* (it's perhaps worth mentioning that Lennon had asked for Hitler to also be included, but he was removed at the last minute). The Stones' own 1967 album – a foray into psychedelia which many argue is their equivalent of *Sgt. Pepper's,* either by accident or design – also dabbled in occult symbolism; Mick Jagger is dressed in a black wizard's outfit on the cover, and the record was entitled *Their Satanic Majesties Request*. Even so, it was not '67 - nor '68 when their album *Beggars Banquet* featured the controversial "Sympathy for the Devil", a song sung from Lucifer's perspective – but '69 when everything seemed to take a somewhat darker turn.

Brian Jones, founding member of The Rolling Stones, was found dead at the bottom of a swimming pool with his system full of alcohol and drugs. Jones was twenty-seven years old, the same age that Robert Johnson had been when he drank that bottle of poisoned whisky somewhere near Greenwood, Mississippi, and the same age at which so many musicians seem to have died since (the so-called 27 Club, whose members include Jimi Hendrix, Janis Joplin, Jim Morrison, Kurt Cobain and Amy Winehouse). The Beatles played their final gig that year, the same year the Manson Family killed nine people in Los Angeles. The hippie era – free love, flower power, and all that went with it – was coming to an end, and overhead dark clouds began to gather.

The Black Sabbaths

It began in 1969 with "Black Sabbath", and by "it" I mean US psychedelic rock band Coven's debut LP *Witchcraft Destroys Minds & Reaps Souls* – widely regarded as the very first overtly satanic record to be released. This album marked the first appearance in music of the sign of the horns, inverted crosses, and the phrase "Hail Satan". The album's final track, "Satanic Mass" was just that – a thirteen minute Black Mass which, again, was touted as the very first to ever be recorded and released.

During a 1986 interview between MTV VJ Martha Quinn and Black Sabbath's Tony Iommi, the television personality caught the legendary guitarist off-guard.

"Speaking of the early days of Black Sabbath, I found – I swear – the wildest thing," she says.

As Iommi looks on apprehensively, Quinn pulls something out from behind her chair: a copy of Coven's 1969 debut album.

"Have you ever seen this record before? Coven?"

"No."

"This is a Chicago band. You never saw this before? This album came out in 1969..."

Quinn turns the album around to show that a member of the band is credited as Oz Osbourne and its opening track is titled "Black Sabbath". Conveniently cropped out of the frame is the album's gatefold art that featured a naked, skull-adorned woman splayed across a ritualistic altar. Iommi continues to deny knowledge of the band, laughing uncomfortably, "1969? We were there first."

The birth of Coven and that of Black Sabbath does seem to have been a case of Simultaneous Invention, or zeitgeist, or if you prefer; something that was waiting in Ideaspace to be discovered by likeminded musicians at that time. The story of how Birmingham's Black Sabbath became the originators of Doom and what they considered "horror film music" is a fairly well-documented one. Originally a blues band called Earth, bassist Geezer Butler was a big fan of the fiction of Dennis Wheatley (whose books sold in their millions in the '60s, several of which were adapted in to Hammer Horror films) and this led to an apparently brief fascination with demonology and the Black Arts. During this occult phase, Butler had a vision of a black robed figure standing at the foot of his bed. This was enough to scare him out of his dabbling. Soon after Geezer and guitarist Tony Iommi were showing their bandmates some new ideas they'd come up with when the pair unexpectedly launched into the same ominous riff,[2] despite neither having heard the other play it previously. The dark and disturbing melody reminded vocalist Ozzy Osbourne of Butler's weird experience and he quickly penned lyrics inspired by it.

> What is this that stands before me?
> Figure in black which points at me
> Turn around quick, and start to run
> Find out I'm the chosen one Oh no...

Taking its name from a 1963 Boris Karloff horror film, the song was dubbed "Black Sabbath" and soon the band took the name as their own.

"That's when it all started to happen," Tony Iommi told Sabbath biographer Mick Wall in 2014. "The name sounded mysterious, it gave people something to think about, and it gave us a direction to follow".

Yet it wasn't just horror-film-inspired posturing; Catholic-raised Butler felt that the influence of the devil was very strong at the time. "It's a satanic world," he told Rolling Stone in 1971. "The devil's more in control now. People can't come together, there's no equality. It's a sin to put yourself above other people, and yet that's what people do".

With Butler serving as principal lyricist and Iommi as the musical architect, Black Sabbath pursued such themes as war, social chaos, the supernatural, the afterlife, and the timeless conflict between good and evil. The group was a product of the late-Sixties. It was a time when youthful idealism had begun to ebb amid the war in Vietnam, the influx of hard drugs, clashes with authority figures, and the bruising realities of working-class life (low wages, grim labour) that lay ahead for many of them. Yet, unlike Coven, Black Sabbath were never really a satanic band per se.

"We arrived at the height of the Vietnam War and on the other side of the hippie era, so there was a mood of doom and aggression," guitarist Iommi told writer Chris Welch in 2003. Black Sabbath were never devil worshippers or practitioners of witchcraft, as many believed. Quite a different picture of the band is painted in such songs as "After Forever" and Ozzy's frequent flashing of the peace sign during Sabbath concerts.

Jimmy Page of Led Zeppelin, a big fan of Aleister Crowley (so big in fact that he bought The Great Beast's old home and lived in it) was one of the very few musicians rumoured to have made a deal with the devil. Page told Rolling Stone at the time, somewhat obliquely, "I don't really want to go on about my personal beliefs or my involvement in magic. I'm not interested in turning anybody on to anybody that I'm turned on to. If people want to find things, they find them themselves".

Led Zeppelin guitarist Jimmy Page (courtesy Dina Regine, CC-by-SA licence)

In the very nearly half a century since 1969 there have been countless rock and metal bands who have used the image of the Arch Fiend and the trappings and symbolism of Satanism as part of their image: from the Norwegian Black Metal church burnings of the early 1990s to the Scooby-Doo villain-esque costumed antics of Ghost BC. The Devil himself doesn't seem to have taken much of an interest in the genre, however. Could it be that Satan just isn't really a fan of Metal? Or is it that he's far too canny a manager and producer to be dealing in such a niche genre? After all, if you want to reach the widest audience possible, why not go for the most accessible form of music?

Lucifer Goes Pop

Google "musicians who sold their soul" in 2018, and the list reads like a Best of 21st Century Pop Spotify playlist. No longer, it seems, do people bother to ask to be the world's finest violinist, or guitarist in exchange for their immortal soul, rather they ask for the fame itself; to become charismatic, beguiling, to be adored, powerful and rich. Beyoncé, Jay-Z, Rihanna, Katy Perry, and Lady GaGa are just a few of the names which crop up time and time again. However, it is not Satan who these celebrities are supposed to have sold their souls to. At least not directly. The Devil has a very forward-thinking PR team these days, and he's been set up as something of an Atheist icon thanks to The Church of Satan.

The Church of Satan was officially founded in San Francisco, California, on Walpurgisnacht, April 30, 1966, by Anton Szandor LaVey. Although it uses all the occult trappings that musical groups like Coven did, the church presents Satan as a deliberately outrageous antithesis to the Christian God and to Christianity itself, which its adherents see as stifling, corrupt, and unhealthy. "Do as thou wilt shall be the whole of the Law" is one of the mottos of The Church of Satan (that is, "do whatever you want, whatever pleases you, whatever you desire [so long as it harms no-one but yourself]"), a motto borrowed so it happens from the writings of Aleister Crowley. In this context then the worship of Satan becomes a harmless anti-religion, wherein those doing the worshipping don't even really believe in the deity ("the loveliest trick of the Devil is to persuade you that he does not exist" as Charles Pierre Baudelaire wrote in 1864). So, who or what is it that Katy Perry has made her black bargain with, if not Satan? The Illuminati, of course.

The Illuminati are the shadowy secret society which controls… well, pretty much everything… but especially, it seems, the international entertainment industry. According to complex.com:

> According to theorists, the Illuminati have been conspiring to establish a "New World Order" that would set up a single government to control the planet. The Illuminati supposedly has agents who control movies, music, banks, governments, and other powerful institutions, and their influence, combined with strategic decisions, will result in this totalitarian one-world government, or another sinister outcome. Theorists have pointed to other secret societies, like Skull and Bones and the Bilderberg Group, to claim that they're front organizations for the Illuminati.

The Illuminati is essentially that one big company that runs all the smaller companies; it's the Disney or the Time Warner of the secret society world (and presumably runs both of those), but is that as far as it goes? In the early 1900s, Christian fundamentalists claimed that the Illuminati's New World Order would be a sign of the coming of the Antichrist. Aha. So, who owns the Illuminati? Satan does. He liked the whole show so much he bought the company. Every music video, every Superbowl performance, every Coca-Cola commercial, is a secret Satanic ritual beaming corruption not just into the ears, but the eyes, hearts and minds of all those impressionable young folk the world over. The only safe course of action therefore seems like an absolute rejection of 21st century popular culture and a return to the simpler, purer, more Godly entertainment of yesteryear. Shun the Satanic works of Rihanna and Madonna, and crank up the Black Sabbath.

> When you think about death do you lose your breath or do you keep your cool?
> Would you like to see the Pope on the end of a rope do you think he's a fool?
> Well I have seen the truth, yes I've seen the light and I've changed my ways
> And I'll be prepared when you're lonely and scared at the end of our days.
>
> -- from "After Forever" by Black Sabbath, lyrics by Geezer Butler.

John Reppion is an English writer based in Liverpool. A lifelong fascination with folklore, forteana, weird and forgotten history runs through all of his work, from comics (co-authored with his wife, Leah Moore), to Weird Fiction, to his essays and articles. His website is moorereppion.com and he can be found on Twitter @johnreppion.

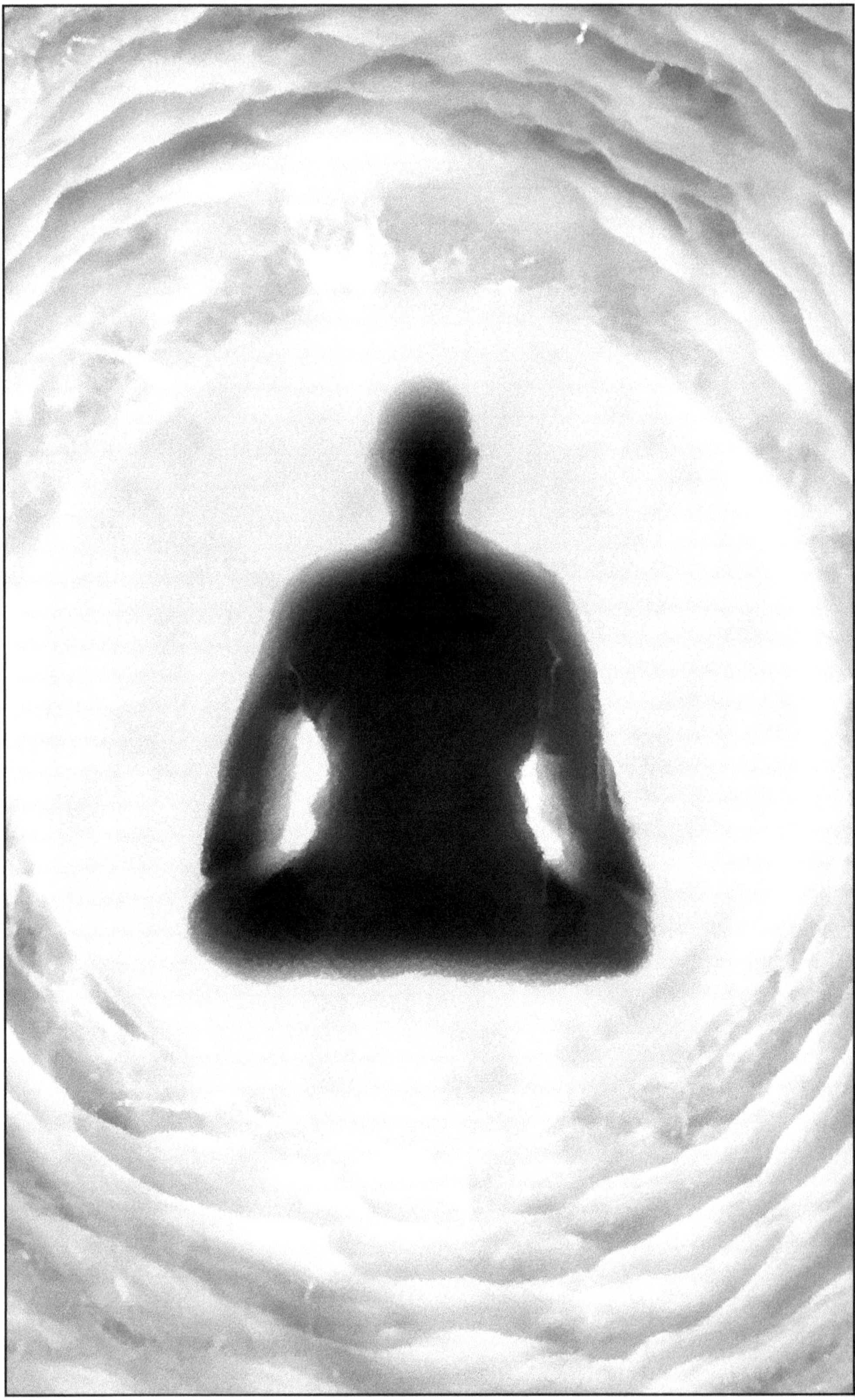

the GREAT WORK of IMMORTALITY

Astral travel, dreams, and alchemy[1]

by *Eric Wargo*

From the growing number of books, websites, and YouTube instructional videos on the topic, having out-of-body experiences (OOBEs) – or attempting to – is an increasingly popular pursuit. OOBEs are a type of dissociative state in which one feels and perceives one's subjective awareness to be dislocated from the physical body, yet distinctly retaining a first-person perspective while interacting with a recognizably real environment such as one's bedroom. In some cases, experiencers confusingly see and interact with their own body from outside.[2] Theosophists and psychical researchers a century ago called it "astral projection," but practices aimed to induce such states have much more ancient roots. Whatever you call it, it is an exercise having obvious intersections with the current revival of interest in psychedelics and shamanism. And there is no altered state more germane to investigating the nature of consciousness and its relation to the brain – the famous "mind-body problem."

Naturally, modern interpretations widely vary as to what is really happening during such experiences. Psychical researchers in the past tended to accept that consciousness does somehow detach from the body (yet remaining connected to it by an umbilicus-like "silver cord" sometimes seen by experiencers). The 1929 book *The Projection of the Astral Body*, a collaboration between an articulate lifetime "projector" Sylvan Muldoon and psychical researcher Hereward Carrington, is an early, comprehensive descriptive and theoretical examination of the phenomenon.[3] In his 1971 classic, *Journeys Out of the Body*, Robert Monroe, a former television executive, described his own method of inducing these states and detailed numerous seemingly discarnate experiences in what he called "Locality I" – recognizably real environments – as well as more exotic settings corresponding to the Theosophists' "astral planes."[4] More recently, an Australian energy worker named Robert Bruce has repackaged the Theosophical theory and its Eastern Tantric equivalents in modern, Western terminology and describes rigorous mental and physical exercises to aid practitioners in inducing these states.[5] These and many other writers have no doubt that consciousness actually leaves the body during OOBEs.

Others with a more scientific bent are naturally skeptical, regarding the seeming realness of OOBEs as a cognitive or memory trick.[6] Psychologist Susan J. Blackmore experienced a vivid OOBE after smoking hash as a young adult and initially thought her experience proved that consciousness could indeed exist beyond the body. However, after investigating the phenomenon as a scientist, she ended up concluding that these experiences have a psychological, not parapsychological, explanation – that they are related to phenomena like sleep paralysis and lucid dreams. Although her position on discarnate states is skeptical, her 1982 book *Beyond the Body* is a comprehensive and sympathetic historical, psychological, and parapsychological assessment of the subject of OOBEs.[7] More recently, in his exploration of Buddhist psychology and neuroscience, *Waking, Dreaming, Being,* Evan Thompson presents a similar narrative of youthful belief in the realness of his OOBEs followed by mature doubt, as he learned more about the neurobiological correlates of first- and third-person perspective-taking.[8] For these writers, OOBEs are not disembodiment but *altered* embodiment occurring in a state of dream lucidity.

It is thus necessary, when addressing OOBEs, to discuss lucid dreams (and related states such as sleep paralysis), since whether or not they are exactly the same, they do seem to lie on a continuum and are induced in the same way. Like OOBEs, lucid dreams were totally disregarded as false memories until just over three decades ago. In the 1980s, a Stanford graduate student in psychology and skilled lucid dreamer, Stephen LaBerge, devised an experiment in which he would make specific eye movements within a lucid dream that could be observed by a colleague at his bedside. The experiment was successful, and it was a milestone in winning long-overdue legitimacy for an experience that Buddhist dream yogis (and lucky laypeople like LaBerge) had been enjoying for millennia.

Setting aside for a moment the question of what OOBEs "really" are – actual journeys beyond the body or just lucid dreams that seem like it – it is increasingly clear that these were crucially important experiences in ancient mystical traditions. For instance, achieving these states may have been the aim of the ancient Greek shamanic practice of *incubation* – sensory deprivation in caves – as has been described in the writings of Peter Kingsley.[9] And thanks to the work of Jeremy Naydler[10] and Algis Uždavinys,[11] it is increasingly clear that descriptions of spirit travel in Egyptian sacred "funerary" texts did not simply refer to the travel of the soul in the afterlife; they reflected a proactive shamanic exercise undertaken during life. Egyptian mystics actively practiced out-of-body travel, in other words, as the ultimate philosophical preparation for death.

OOBEs may have also had more mundane applications in the ancient world. Given the intelligence-gathering role of prophets in ancient Israel and the link between OOBEs and ESP as observed by U.S. government-funded ESP research in the 1970s,[12] it would not be far-fetched to guess that the Egyptian priesthood might have employed OOBEs along with other shamanic techniques in what we would nowadays call "psychic spying" on behalf of the state. One could easily imagine Egyptian priests performing a service to the kingdom much like psychics did to the U.S. and U.S.S.R. during the Cold War.[13]

The Middle Eastern and European traditions of alchemy that evolved out of the Egyptian mystical tradition would have carried on these practices, albeit disguised under layers of increasingly "materialistic" symbolism. Carl Jung famously illuminated the inner aspect of alchemy, arguing that the Great Work consisted of projecting unconscious mental stuff into material transformations, using laboratory processes and procedures as a symbolic control panel in personal journeys of individuation.[14] But given what we now know of the ancient shamanic practices of Egypt that gave rise to alchemy, European alchemy's Eastern analogues in Tantra and Yoga, and the pagan shamanic traditions that persisted on the margins of mainstream Christian culture in Europe, it becomes ever clearer that alchemical explorations would have gone, and indeed must have gone, much beyond active imagination and the projective processes Jung described. The real philosophic gold for some (or many) alchemists may have been fearlessness in the face of death – figurative "immortality" – achieved by self-induced OOBEs.

Spirit and Soul

Crucially, and perhaps counterintuitively, the prerequisite for developing one's astral capacity, in various ancient as well as modern traditions, was to cultivate not simply a Cartesian dualistic conception of *psyche* and *soma*, mind and body, but also to further subdivide the subtle psychic part of our nature into at least two distinct components of its own. Pagan and folk traditions all described a *spirit* with a dim animal-like awareness that was distinct from our more rarified and active, willful, conscious component, equivalent to what in Christian tradition came to be called the *soul*. Spirit and soul were separate entities, not synonyms as they are for most people today.

In general, the feminine, animal-like spirit was roughly equivalent to what the psychoanalytic tradition would later call *the unconscious,* but it was thought capable of leaving the body when we sleep. The Egyptians called it *Ka*. For pagan Europeans, it was our spirit double or feminine spirit guide. Claude Lecouteux, in his study of European pagan/shamanic traditions about spirit doubles, shows that this component not only took nightly trips remembered as dreams but also was responsible for ghost and poltergeist phenomena as well as animal familiars.[15] As an enlivening force, the spirit was closely allied to our breath (whence the name, *spiritus*). Linked to our physical body, it was also connected to our bones in some intimate way. Much later, in the Theosophical tradition, it came to be known as the "etheric double";[16]

modern New Age writers like Bruce write of an "energy body" (Monroe's term is "Second Body") that is more or less equivalent.

This feminine, energetic spiritual component contrasted and actually clashed with the more rarified, conscious, aware component allied to masculine, rational, awake thought. Although this "soul" component was capable of heavenly ascent after death or during ecstatic states, in daily life it was more imprisoned in the body than the spirit component. Indeed, the two parts of the subtle self resisted being in direct contact when not together animating the awake physical body. This soul component was the *Ba* of the Egyptians (capable of ascending and uniting with the transcendent *Akh*) and corresponds to the Theosophists' "astral" (as opposed to etheric) components of the self. It is more or less equivalent to what many writers nowadays call *consciousness*: the center of awake, aware subjectivity, and in many metaphysical traditions, capable of transcending the physical body and surviving bodily death.

Such a tripartite division of our earthly existence into body, soul, and spirit seems remarkably universal across non-Judeo-Christian cultures. Whatever you call these subtle psychic components, shamans throughout the world, including in Medieval and Dark Age Europe, claimed the ability, through meditative practice and sometimes use of drugs, to yoke them together and thereby achieve the feat of leaving their bodies consciously. And, some of the most mysterious texts of 16th and 17th century alchemy show indirect and direct evidence that, whatever else they were up to, alchemical adepts were also attempting precisely these difficult journeys "beyond the body."

Lambspring

The clearest example is *The Book of Lambspring,* an alchemical poem that first circulated as a manuscript in the late 16th century and was later published with a series of beautiful illustrative engravings. It

"The Astral Dream", by Jeroen van Valkenburg (CCSA licence)

asserts that the key to riches, long life, and king-like sovereignty over one's existence is a process of taking the separate subtle components, soul and spirit, consciously uniting them, and leading them out of the body and back again. Among the various symbolic expressions of this are the imagery of a deer and unicorn living in a forest (emphasis is mine):

> The sages say truly
> That two animals are in this forest:
> One glorious, beautiful, and swift,
> A great and strong deer;
> The other a unicorn.
> They are concealed in the forest,
> But happy shall that man be called
> Who shall snare and capture them. …
> If we apply the parable to our Art,
> We shall call the forest the Body.
> That will be rightly and truly said.
> The unicorn will be the Spirit at all times.
> The deer desires no other name
> But that of the Soul; …
> *He that knows how to tame and master them by Art,*
> *To couple them together,*
> *And to lead them in and out of the forest,*
> *May justly be called a Master.*
> For we rightly judge
> That he has attained the golden flesh,
> And may triumph everywhere;
> Nay, he may bear rule over great Augustus.[17]

Lambspring gives us further explicit indication of his belief/assertion that the soul and spirit actually leave the body during the alchemical work in the second half of his book, where he replaces the symbolism of forest, unicorn, and deer with the more humanized symbolism of Father (body), Son (spirit), and an angelic Guide (soul). The Guide leads the Son out of the body of the Father, brings him up to the top of a "mountain in India" and carefully leads him back. This process of separating and reuniting – *separatio* and *coniunctio* – is one of the most central and universal motifs in European alchemy, but it is nowhere more explicitly identified as a process of leading the consciousness and spirit out of the body as it is in this book. The famous alchemical motto *solve et coagula* – "separate and reunite" – can refer on one level to this process.

On its own, Lambspring's book would be pretty unhelpful to a modern person attempting to actually achieve an OOBE, but the author's symbolism resonates strongly with the methods emphasized by contemporary teachers of the subject. The Theosophical tradition, which placed great emphasis on astral projection as a means of accessing cosmic consciousness (the Akashic Records, etc.) and communicating with ascended and alien intelligences, carefully emphasized the crucial role of the lower, denser etheric double – the subtle, energetic envelope or spiritual vehicle that could detach from the physical body on its own (dreaming) or which could, through effort, be yoked to the astral component (conscious awareness or soul) to achieve a conscious astral flight. The key to leaving the body consciously, in other words, was uniting the astral and etheric components, which, as I mentioned, ordinarily don't mix well together. (The resistance of the unconscious and conscious minds to commingle is of course a major theme in Freudian and Jungian psychoanalysis too, and may be seen as a kind of parallel here.)

Robert Bruce, for instance, teaches meditative exercises and a unique method of "tactile imaging" to cultivate a finer-tuned awareness of the physical body and its subtle energetic aspect (equivalent to the energy body with its *nadis, chakras,* etc. described in Asian systems) as a prerequisite to developing proficiency with astral travel.[18] The separation experience at the outset of an OOBE is universally described as a vividly energetic sensation that may also resemble sensations familiar to those who have "raised their kundalini." There is no indication in Bruce's writing that he is familiar with pagan folk traditions about the detachable spirit double, but clearly, despite using a modern computer idiom of "downloading" astral memories etc., his metaphysics are basically the same.

To my mind, the strongest evidence that Lambspring was referring to the refined, dream-like but compellingly real-seeming state we would now call the OOBE comes from the testimony of modern astral travelers like Bruce that the key to decoupling alert awareness from the sleeping physical body is actually to be found, counterintuitively, in the reentry – the *coniunctio* part rather than the *separatio*. Lambspring places special emphasis on this: The Guide says to the son, "I will not let thee go alone; From thy father's bosom I brought thee forth, *I will also take thee back again.*"[19] It signals a special concern with the process of reuniting the soul/spirit with the body as intrinsic to the success of the astral venture.

The purpose of "careful reuniting" is not safety, as one might naturally suppose: Despite instinctive fears of permanent separation, there are no known cases when an astral traveler has failed to awaken safe and sound (although, of course, we might never know it if it did happen). Rather, caution must be exercised because the conscious portion of the self (i.e., soul or astral body) must remain in contact with the spiritual/etheric body, lest all recollection of the experience be lost. *If you can't remember it when you awaken/return, it's like you never went.* Consequently, a crucial part of some modern training in OOBEs focuses on developing the capacity to remember it after the fact, because an unremembered OOBE is no OOBE at all. Bruce suggests that we are astrally projecting all the time but largely lack memory of it.

Thus, Bruce's method focuses on initially keeping flights brief and then celebrating and recording one's small successes. This may be the most valuable and even crucial piece of advice he gives: Developing a habit and a practice of recording dreams in the morning is a crucial preparatory step toward having a remembered astral journey. It is true of any kind of dream-work, in fact. Even if OOBEs are more than "just" lucid dreams, the same induction methods work for both, not to mention the necessity of keeping records afterward.

ATALANTA FUGIENS

Anyone who knows the extraordinary value of attention to dreams (even in a simply psychoanalytic or Jungian vein) knows you will have a hard time remembering a dream or its crucial innocuous-seeming details if you don't write it down right away, or at least jot down a few words to jog the memory when you have time to record it more fully later in the day. My favorite 17th-century alchemical text, *Atalanta Fugiens* by Michael Maier, contains among many other things a coded recommendation about keeping a dream diary, likely as preparation for more advanced Tantric or OOBE exercises.[20]

The title of this lovely collection of engravings and accompanying poems and musical fugues, literally "Atalanta Fleeing," refers to Ovid's story about the race between the beautiful fleet-footed virgin Atalanta and her would-be suitor Hippomenes. The central secrets of alchemical books are often hidden in plain sight right in their title pages, and this is true of *Atalanta Fugiens*. The frontispiece depicts various scenes from the Atalanta legend, whose hermetic themes are indexed obliquely by the 50 emblems and commentaries in the book.

Atalanta was the fastest in the land – so fast she couldn't be caught – and would only marry a suitor who could beat her in a race. Hippomenes wins the race (and her hand in marriage) by availing himself of three gold apples given to him by Venus; during the race, he throws the apples on the ground, one by one, each time catching Atalanta's attention and slowing her down. After winning the race,

Title page from *Atalanta Fugiens*

Hippomenes steals a kiss from his new bride in Aphrodite's temple and the couple (as punishment from that goddess) are turned into lions. The conflict of two lions (and/or dragons) resulting in their ultimate union – again, soul and spirit which do not initially get along but which, with difficulty, can be forced into a productive merger – is a near-universal alchemical motif.

We are meant to ask, what is it that flees and how can you stop it from fleeing? The name Atalanta, meaning "equal in weight or value," does not really give a clue to the nature of the volatile substance. But Hippomenes himself can tell us a lot. The name can be parsed firstly as hippo-menes or "horse mind," which by itself signals that we may apply the wild-etymological method that the great 20th-century adept Fulcanelli called *cabala* (from *caballus*, horse), and re-divide the word however we see fit.[21] The most obvious re-parsing is *hip-pommes,* or "dropped apples," which doesn't tell us anything we didn't already know. But there is a very similar Greek word, *hypomnema*, which meant a reminder, a note jotted down. It happens that Emblem VI depicts this process explicitly: A farmer tosses gold coins onto furrowed ground (a gesture similar to Hippomenes tossing golden apples), accompanied by the motto: "Sow your gold in the white foliate earth." Hippomenes thus seems to be a pun for the very thing indicated by "white foliate earth" with its "sown gold" – that is, *hypomnema*, precious reminders of something fleeting, jotted down (sown) in the white pages (*folia* or leaves) of a notebook.

Keeping records of laboratory procedures and results and the visible changes occurring in the retort would be an obvious interpretation here, not to mention the ultimate creation of a book that will serve to guide others: the alchemical text itself as the Great Work. But are consciously observed chemical reactions, however fleeting, so ephemeral (or volatile) that they are completely forgotten unless fixed in the very moment they occur? I don't know, but it is a very distinctive quality of dreams and related phenomena like hypnagogic/hypnopompic images that they evaporate very quickly and must be seized immediately after they occur or they are really lost forever. Quick note-taking is required to fix this volatile substance.

There is way, way more that could be said about *Atalanta Fugiens*, which contains enough fascinating imagery to reward years of perusal and study. But let me move on to a third alchemical text that most explicitly addresses the link between dream life and OOBEs and also uses its own brilliant symbolism for dream recording.

Mutus Liber (Enlightenment by Means of Dew)

The 1677 alchemical masterpiece *Mutus Liber* (or "Silent Book") is a series of mostly wordless alchemical cartoons by a writer with the pseudonym "Altus," depicting a complicated esoteric process undertaken by a pair of adepts, one male, one female.[22] (Sometimes it is described as a male alchemist and "his" female assistant, wife, Tantric *soror mystica,* or Jungian Anima, but the book gives no cause to privilege the male figure over the female – they both seem to play equally important roles.) This book is another example of an alchemical text that hides its cipher in plain sight, right on its title page.

The frontispiece depicts Jacob's famous dream in Genesis 28, of angels ascending and descending a ladder to heaven. Any reader would know that, in that story, right after he awakens, Jacob anoints the stone he has used for a pillow *beth-el,* "House of the Lord"; until the arrival of Christ himself in the Old Testament's sequel, this stony pillow is perhaps the clearest and most literal expression of the Philosopher's Stone in the Bible. But more crucially for the book we are concerned with here, the Jacob frontispiece includes three backwards chapter/verse numbers in Hebrew, each referring to Biblical passages about heavenly "dew." The centrality of dew in this book is also signaled cleverly by the roses framing the scene: Rose is

Jacob's ladder illustration from *Mutus Liber*

Collecting dew in sheets, illustration from *Mutus Liber*

a pun on the Latin word for dew, *ros* (which should also give you a clue to the real meaning of the rose in other esoteric contexts, such as Rosicrucianism).

In subsequent panels, the alchemists are depicted engaging in various laboratory operations utilizing dew that has been initially collected in an array of sheets during spring mornings, the season being symbolized by a ram and bull, Aries and Taurus, rampant in the background (although the animals could have other connotations[23]). As a means of collecting literal nocturnal moisture, wringing out sheets one has suspended on posts in a field seems that it might be highly impractical. But "dew" is not meant to be taken literally here.

Adam McLean's diagram of the process, provided in his Magnum Opus Hermetic Sourceworks Commentary, is invaluable for keeping track of the operations and the dense symbolism in *Mutus Liber*.[24] For another modern interpreter writing under the name Eli Luminosus Aequalis, these sheets represent the five senses, and his subsequent analysis depicts a noetic, epistemic, and Tantric process.[25] I agree with many of Eli's interpretations, but I think he is wrong about the ingenious symbolism of dew itself and its collection on bedsheets: What else is it that appears in the early morning hours and evaporates quickly with the dawn, and that one might carefully and quickly collect ideally while still lying in bed? The same thing Maier represents by the fleeing Atalanta, and the same thing Jacob is shown in the process of doing right on this book's title page.

Mutus Liber is actually pretty explicit about what we are supposed to do with this figuratively dew-like substance collected over a series of spring mornings. Subsequent panels depict an elaborate process of distilling and then mixing the dew's various components in different combinations. The process begins with what I believe to be isolating repeated dream motifs from other symbolic stuff and what Sigmund Freud (in his *Interpretation of Dreams*) called "day residues"[26] and then using the recurring motifs as mnemonic triggers to wake up inside the dream (lucidity). This is the mnemonic-induced lucid dreaming (MILD) method recommended by LaBerge,[27] and it may be taken as the equivalent of yoking soul and spirit and exiting the sleeping body consciously, as in Lambspring. Eli too argues that this part is about lucid dreaming. I imagine though that, at the time Altus was writing, there would have been no distinction between "mere" lucid dream experiences and what we would now call OOBEs or astral travel.

Developing lucid dreaming capacity is useful for achieving a full-on OOBE, and lucid dreams are the more common experience when the latter fails. Also, it is only in preparing for and interpreting an OOBE as such that one needs to first understand (or, be persuaded) that the spiritual component is distinct from consciousness imprisoned in the body (i.e., the first phase of the *Mutus Liber* process), which then enables one to learn to unite the consciousness with the spirit while leaving the body behind (the second phase), and lastly bring them together, followed by repetition of the process over time such that it becomes easier (lather, rinse, repeat).

So, *Mutus Liber* is essentially a Baroque astral projection manual disguised as chemistry: The stuff of dreams is the *materia prima*, the murky raw material that must be taken, analyzed, worked with, to create true philosophic gold: a special "blended" state in which the soul (alert consciousness) fully joins with the spirit double (or "energy body") on its nightly travels. Successive separations and conjunctions (returns) exalt the self and lead to enlightenment. Over the course of the book, the curtains behind the alchemists progressively open, letting more and more light into their workshop.

Why All the Secrecy?

Beliefs in the separability of consciousness from the body prior to death were antithetical to Christian theology: Humans possessed just a single subtle principle, the soul, which departed the body only in death. Jesus was the singular exception, the only person possessing a divine spirit as well as a soul. As a result, all ordinary human phenomena hinting at spirit – from dreams and visions and mystical and other altered states of consciousness to manifestations of what we would now call the paranormal, like ghosts or psychic phenomena – were at least distrusted and were often relegated wholly to the category of the demonic.[28] You could say, mainstream Christianity successfully robbed religion of spirit, replacing it with faith.

Whether or not we nowadays accept that each person possesses both detachable components, the work of Lecouteux (for Europe), Naydler (for Egypt), and other scholars makes clear that it was firmly a part of pre- and para-Christian folk psychology, supported by infrequent but remarkable experiences like spontaneous OOBEs, lucid dreams, sleep paralysis episodes, near-death experiences, drug experiences, and so on. The continuity of shamanic practices under various alternative labels (black magic, sorcery, witchcraft, etc.) in Christian Europe was certainly genuine, even if their prevalence and power were exaggerated by Church authorities. Alchemical explorers of consciousness would have pursued these techniques, marvelously and densely disguising their efforts under their chemical symbology.

Thus, in their writings alchemists perpetually did a subtle dance around this issue of our subtle self: Is it one thing or two? When they wrote explicitly about soul and spirit as distinct, it was important to emphasize either that they were referring to physical chemistry – in which *spirits* are light volatile distillates (like alcohol) and the "soul" of a substance could stand for its oily and more distinct extracts – or alternatively, to insist that "the two are really one." We see this evasiveness clearly in Lambspring's opening verse. The author says "the sages will tell you" that the body contains a soul and a spirit and that "nevertheless they are one."[29] He then leans in and whispers: "Now I tell you most truly, cook these *three* together … and hold your tongue about it."[30] He seems to be saying that body, soul, and spirit really are three things, but if you are smart, you won't admit to holding such a belief.

The extent to which the Christian duality of the person influenced subsequent rationalist, materialist tradition has been less acknowledged. Enlightenment science and the rationalist tradition carried forward the Christian presumption of a singular mental principle that might somehow be distinct from the body, as in Descartes. The soul and body required no third intermediary, no third term mediating them or yoking them together, other than God Himself. The result has been an almost complete erasure in "official" philosophical and scientific discourses of the ancient and pagan traditions about spirit doubles, as well as lingering confusion about what *spirit* and *soul* mean. Many people now use the terms interchangeably, unaware that there was once a meaningful distinction.

To this day, we have difficulty conceptualizing a consciousness that is not somehow unified, yet we also perpetually have trouble conceiving how these two radically different things, consciousness and the physical body, could be linked together. They seem to need a mediator that our psychologies and metaphysics completely lack. Descartes' famous search for the seat of consciousness in the pineal gland is emblematic of the felt need for some mysterious mediating principle to yoke the soul to the living body.[31] It was of course the genius of Freud and his followers like Jung to renew our sense of the psyche's plurality, resolving it into the conscious and unconscious components as well as parsing psychological functions in various other ways. But even Jung and the analytical psychology he inspired continue to implicitly see the psyche as one thing, even if the individual has delusionally lost sight of this unity through a refusal to "own" certain components of self. In other words, spirit and soul are merely aspects of the same underlying consciousness that would realize its unitary wholeness through individuation.

The Jungian writer James Hillman, for instance, described the soul as the humid enclosed "valleys" where we live surrounded by the familiar local particulars of our lives, and the "spirit" as the

mountain peaks to which we may at times loftily ascend, attaining a clearer, more objective, more far-seeing view.[32] These are *loci*, in other words, places our singular consciousness moves between, not actual separable components of our being. Lambspring's "mountain in India" where the soul and spirit ascend in tandem, would make no sense in Hillman's framework.

Laughing at Death

OOBEs provide many experiencers with enhanced validation of the separability of consciousness from the physical body and, as an inevitable corollary, its possible survival of bodily death – priceless to humans living in the constant terror of mortality. Thus, it is no wonder that, in the centuries before they could potentially be reduced to quirks or malfunctions of the material brain, such experiences constituted an "elixir of immortality" (i.e. as proof of immortality), as well as a talisman of power and health and courage. Once the son and father are reunited in Lambspring's final verse, "they produce untold precious fruit. They perish never more, and laugh at death."[33] Assurance of the independence of consciousness from the body would indeed tend to make one brave in life, and this courage would tend to produce power and success.

The methods for inducing OOBEs are, and have always been, various. Examining the writings of the 16th century alchemist Heinrich Khunrath and his contemporaries, Hereward Tilton concludes that Khunrath's work described (and concealed) processes that resulted in the creation of diethyl ether – a potent anaesthetic.[34] Anesthetics are notable for producing profound dissociative or out-of-body experiences. Ether may have been literally the philosopher's stone for Khunrath, which supports the idea that European alchemists were indeed engaged in a project of exploring and using altered states of consciousness, facilitated by chemicals.

On the other hand, what a user gains in facility of entering an altered state using drugs may be canceled by the difficulty of controlling the experience and, in the modern world at least, easy dismissal of the experience's validity. Thus, while entheogens may provide an important taste of out-of-body or lucid-dream-type experiences, the holy grail seems to be the production of these experiences solely through meditation and other non-chemical techniques. The original alchemical text, the *Tabula Smaragdina* or Emerald Tablet, which describes a heavenly ascent and descent, drawing down the power of "the above" into "the below," tells us that "the wind carried it in its belly," which points directly to meditation as the method to achieve this Great Work. The link between breath (the original meaning of *spirit*) and thought is well-known in many traditions, and so it was surely central to ancient contemplative practices and trance.

As I mentioned at the outset, there are now plenty of guides out there to enable one to learn to have OOBEs and ascertain for yourself whether they are merely a subset of lucid dreams – obviously the only scientifically and socially acceptable materialist interpretation – or something more. I've mentioned a couple of useful ones. Even if its language is somewhat outdated, Muldoon and Carrington's *Projection of the Astral Body* remains the most interesting book on the subject. It discusses some techniques for inducing these experiences and discusses their links to other phenomena like sleep paralysis (what was then called "astral catalepsy") and hypnic jerks ("repercussion"). An earlier series of articles from around 1920 by projector Oliver Fox and later published as *Astral Projection* is less comprehensive but also more personal and more frank about the difficulties and disappointments inherent in the practice, such as the increased difficulty of having such experiences with age.[35] There are also many excellent guides to lucid dreaming available. Most of them repackage Stephen LaBerge's ideas; the best, like B. Alan Wallace's *Dreaming Yourself Awake*, incorporate Tibetan "dream yoga" techniques.[36]

Caveat emptor: Depending on how old you are, having OOBEs may prove much more difficult than enthusiasts like to claim. Despite a few spontaneous OOBEs when I was a young adult and a couple sporadically over the course of my adult life, intentionally bringing one on in my late forties by following instructions in various sources proved extraordinarily difficult – only one deliberate success and a few unexpected, spontaneous ones, as well as many "flight attempts" resulting in lucid dreams or other precursor phenomena like sleep paralysis and strong energy- or Kundalini-like sensations like those described in the manuals. Lucid dreaming is much easier but still, in my experience, difficult to induce on command without the aid of nootropic supplements.[37]

But the efforts are worth it. Lucid dreaming alone is supremely exhilarating and empowering – famously a route to gaining control over one's fears and nightmares, much the way virtual reality is used to desensitize people from phobias or train extraordinary and dangerous skills. Actual OOBEs in "Locality I" (Monroe) or the "Real

Time Zone" (Bruce) – that is, experiences in which the immediate physical environment really seems to be perceived and interacted with – are even more profound and strange. Once you've glimpsed such states, whether spontaneously or in altered states induced by drugs or meditation, they really may become an obsession.

Real-seeming isn't necessarily the same as real, of course. Although LaBerge's experimental proof of lucid dreaming in the 1980s gave a new legitimacy to the paradoxical phenomenology of being awake while the body is asleep, in the same stroke it cast doubt on the *ontology* of (allegedly) discarnate states. It placed a new burden on OOBE experiencers (and by extension, people reporting related phenomena like near-death experiences or NDEs) to prove that what seemed like a real environment traversed by their discarnate consciousness was anything other than a particularly realistic dreamworld. It particularly cast doubt on the reality of the more exotic "astral planes" visited by Theosophists and the higher dimensions of reality described by Monroe and Bruce.

On the other hand, one hallmark of these states that is not so readily dispelled by contemporary neurobiological explanations is the acquisition of veridical (confirmable) information that could not otherwise be obtained by the experiencer. Astral-traveling individuals, as well as people having NDEs, frequently learn news that is only confirmed later. As mentioned previously, facility with OOBEs has long been linked to psychic abilities like clairvoyance, and several of the foremost remote viewers associated with the U.S. Defense Department-funded Star Gate program and the ESP research conducted at Stanford Research Institute in the 1970s linked their psychic abilities directly to OOBE experiences.[38] One possibility is that what may "feel" like consciousness's transit beyond the body in space could instead be a *temporal* displacement of conscious awareness – that is, being "in body" but displaced in time. Does veridical information acquired "out of body" really come from the experiencer's future? I have suggested elsewhere that the next paradigm for theorizing OOBE and related phenomena may focus on their precognitive aspects.

As they say in science journals, "more research is needed."

Yet, unlike most other big questions in science, which require expensive tools and research teams to answer, the mind-body problem (and by extension, perhaps, consciousness's relation to time itself) is one that we can all explore for ourselves, using an exquisite instrument we all possess. All you need is your body, your breath, a notebook handy by your bedside, and a dose of patience to undertake an exploration that has ancient and hallowed esoteric roots. Unlike the ancients, who may have depended on esoteric instruction from a teacher, or the alchemists forced to ponder the obscure symbolism in a few rare texts, abundant instruction is now only a few clicks away. So, traveler, what are you waiting for?

Eric Wargo has a PhD in Anthropology from Emory University and writes about science fiction, consciousness, and the paranormal at his blog The Nightshirt (www.thenightshirt.com). He is the author of the book *Time Loops: Precognition, Retrocausation, and the Unconscious* (2018, Anomalist Books).

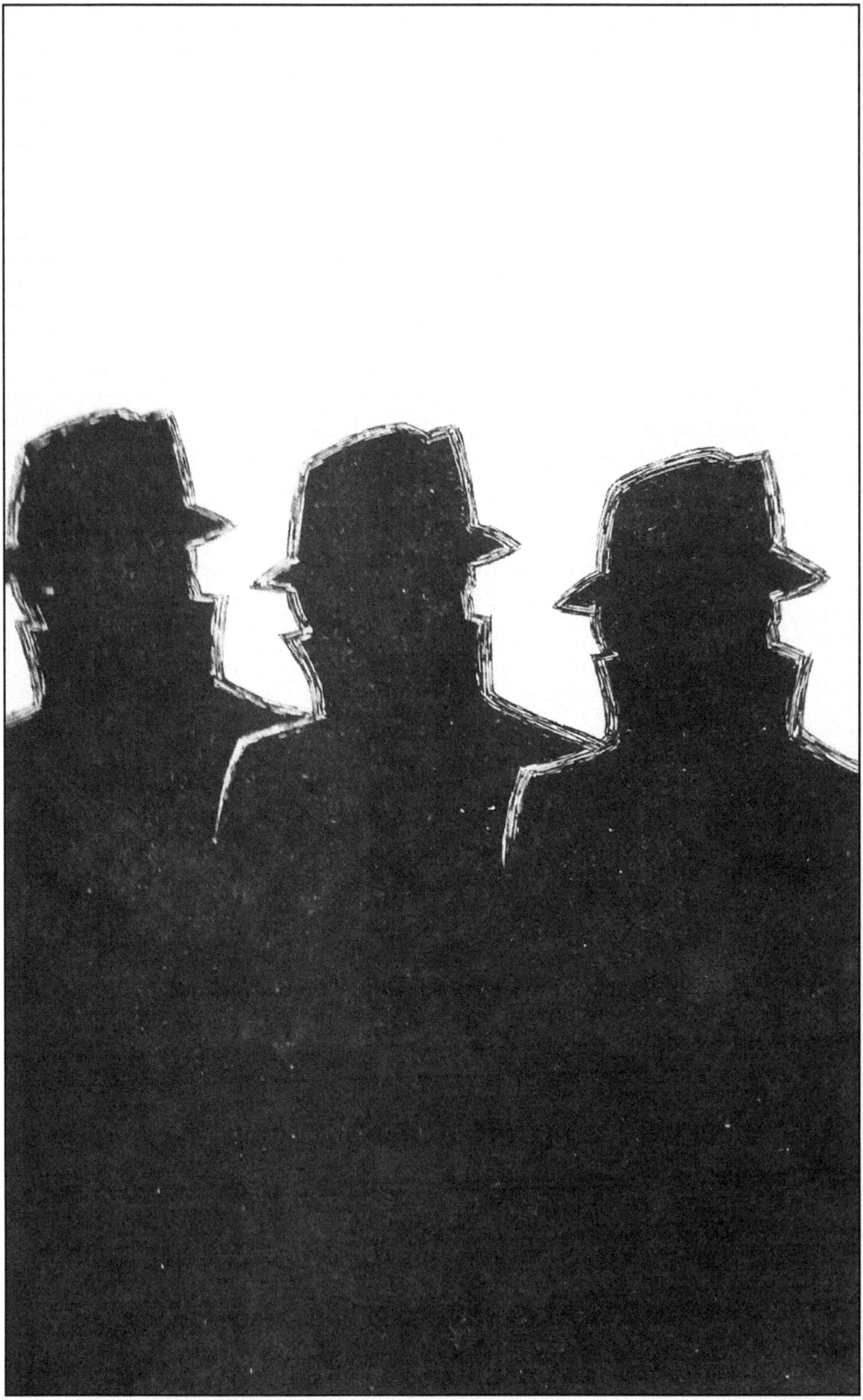

Making the Unbelievable Believable

The M.I.B. of Saucerer Gray Barker

by *Blair MacKenzie Blake*

Gray Roscoe Barker was oddly out of place, and not just because of the ill-fitting black rayon suit that clothed his six-foot-six frame, or that he had aspirations to be in a drama club rather than to butcher hogs or plough fields while attired in overalls. He was the only member of his poverty-stricken family in Braxton County, West Virginia to attend college. After graduating in 1947 he briefly taught English at a high school in Ellicott City, Maryland. Intimidated by the locals, he moved closer to his birthplace in Riffle – a town so small that it didn't appear on maps – landing a job as a drive-in movie projectionist. Ambitious by nature, he was soon operating a theatrical film buying-booking agency in Clarksburg, as well as being a consultant for educational audio-visual equipment. His strong work ethic afforded him luxuries that most of his neighbors in the Mountain State weren't accustomed to. This included a red sports car that he drove on frequent business trips. In those pre-interstate days, the treacherous route wound through the drabness of abandoned coal tipples and decrepit houses where half-naked children licking peach butter on tilted porches gazed back at him with blank expressions. It was local color like this that led to assumptions by outsiders of inbreeding by those who lived in these rundown backwaters. Although stories of physical abnormalities were often exaggerated, Barker took notice of any questionable defects related to the shuffling of the genetic deck and filed them away for reasons that only he knew.

Having grown up with Appalachian folklore, storytelling appealed to him, especially anything that was weird and frightening. He got a kick out of scaring his three nephews with spooky tales of things that went bump in the night. Lacking other means of entertainment, the kids delighted in their uncle's outré antics. But the initiator of this macabre amusement was also frightened by something. He harbored fears of the surveillance state, and with good reason. The terrible secret that he tried to hide would gradually be reshaped into abstractions that would be the inspiration for hit television series and Hollywood blockbusters a half-century later.

Even though he would never capitalize on paranormal concepts that he introduced, he could have earned a great living with his more down-to-earth business endeavors. But the fates had determined otherwise. The great trickster in the sky deflected any opportunities that might come his way in the form of a mysterious event that occurred on a late summer night in 1952.

The Braxton County Monster

While sipping orange juice in a local diner, Barker read a U.P. article about some high strangeness that recently took place in the town of Flatwoods. The first wire reports spoke of things that rivaled those B horror films in the silver canisters that he distributed to the drive-ins.

Since the incident occurred practically in his own backyard, he sent a telegraph to the editor of *Fate* magazine, asking if he had any interest in a write-up. (Note: The founder of *Fate*, Raymond A. Palmer, was also the editor of pulp journals like *Amazing Stories*. Later, many researchers would claim that Palmer and Barker were cut from the same cloth – both publishers being opportunist hucksters hoping to cash in on the flying saucer craze and all things paranormal.) He promptly received the following reply:

> STORY PROBABLY HOAX BUT INVESTIGATE RIGOROUSLY. DON'T SPECULATE SIMPLY STATE FACTS.

A week later Barker visited Flatwoods to set things straight about the creature that terrified seven town folk. The initial sighting by several boys playing sandlot football on the school playground was of an object that looked like "a silver dollar rushing through the air" while covered in flames. Thinking that a flying saucer might have landed on a nearby hilltop, those who were more excited than afraid decided to hike up the rugged terrain to the farmer's property (accompanied by the mother of one of the kids). When they arrived at dusk, a pulsating spherical object in the sloping pasture off in the distance distracted a few of them, while others tentatively approached an eerie haze that engulfed the immediate area. They were shocked to see an enormous figure standing under a large oak tree. As if reacting to the beam of a flashlight shined at it, the monster's eyes shot back a brilliant greenish-orange ray. While gliding towards them with irregular motions that none of the traumatized onlookers could later duplicate, it emitted a nauseating metallic odor that irritated their throats and nasal passages as they beat a hasty retreat to call the local sheriff.

Although the creature was described as having a towering man-like shape that "looked worse than Frankenstein", Barker suspected that this "monster" was most likely a machine. Its reflective sheen might have been the protective covering or spacesuit for the curious occupant of the saucer, or even an escape pod ejected by the distressed craft.

While conducting his investigation, conflicting stories puzzled him. Some of these holes would be filled in many years later by other researchers who concluded that the Flatwoods incident was only part of a more complex sequence of events in which several unusual aeroforms had been intercepted by military fighter jets after being sighted over the east coast. Some of the UFOs might have been damaged by missiles fired by the F-94 Starfires.

These later reports involved government disinformation tactics and visits by enigmatic strangers who removed evidence. This included tar grass-like stains on the woman's beautician uniform and fragments of metal with anomalous properties that were pocketed at the scene by a local photojournalist. Many of the new details uncovered in the Flatwoods investigation contained elements that figured prominently in Barker's early writings about the Men In Black – those notorious silencers of witnesses to UFOs.

After three days of investigating – due to the short deadline that he was given – Barker submitted the eyewitness accounts from tape-recorded interviews. "The Monster and the Saucer" appeared in the January 1953 issue of *Fate*. It was Barker's first published article concerning possible visitations by otherworldly beings. Despite claims of being sensationalistic, it was actually fairly straightforward, as the editor had requested. The court jester of "ufoology" – as Barker's closest friend and saucer hijinks collaborator, James Moseley, later called him on account of his oft-exaggerated reports – had somehow managed to restrain himself...at least for the time being.

What's Doin' with the Saucers?

By September in the same year as his debut article in *Fate*, Barker tested his unique style by self-publishing tales of anomalous objects zipping through the skies. "We may even try to have some harmless fun now and then. But you will know when we are serious and when we are trying for a laugh." This was stated in the first issue of *The Saucerian*, Barker's periodical that chronicled the frenzy of sightings that the public was enmeshed in during the early 1950s.

The mauve-blurred text of the "saucerzine" would set the tone for other amateurish publications that his Ditto machine churned out as part of his new mail order business. As he was busy running down leads on the phone and tapping the keys of the Royal typewriter between gulps of scotch, his subscribers eagerly swallowed his colorful yarns. Squibs from his critics didn't bother him – both the saucer debunkers and the serious researchers. He was enjoying his role as an entertainer. If he continued to stir things up with his deliberate hokum, someday he might obtain the key to unravel the enigma. That's what he really wanted.

The Notorious Three

Albert K. Bender had the key. The mystery of the flying saucers was no longer a mystery. As the director of the "International Flying Saucer Bureau" – a civilian organization based in Bridgeport, Connecticut that conducted and shared UFO research – he promised his members that a startling revelation would be published in the next issue (July, 1953) of his quarterly journal, *Space Review*. But, the scheduled announcement never appeared. Instead, he cryptically advised "those engaged in saucer work to be very cautious." Barker, who was a state representative of the IFSB before he accepted the post as their Chief Investigator, was greatly troubled by the sudden news that Bender was planning to shut down the club and abandon saucer research altogether. What might he have discovered that caused him to drop out just as the organization was attracting new members? It didn't seem likely that his friend had simply lost interest in the saucers. As a factory supervisor for the Acme Shear plant, was he overwhelmed that the IFSB had become so successful? Or had someone or some thing threatened him because he had discovered the truth of the elusive phenomenon?

Bender refused to answer these questions, leaving members of the IFSB and his friends to speculate what had caused him to do a

Albert Bender's cover illustration for *The Saucerian*

complete 180. He might have inadvertently offered a clue when he said that "they wouldn't be happy" about an illustration that he had already done as a favor for one of Barker's 'zines. The cover of the November 1953 issue of *The Saucerian* depicted spacecraft launching platforms that protruded from crater-like openings. Whether this saucer base was on the moon or at some remote location on the Earth was still up for question.

It would be years after the publication of Barker's only successful book, *They Knew Too Much About Flying Saucers* (1956), that Bender, who had become a minor celebrity as a result of being featured in the work, reluctantly provided the answer to the question(s) that had so intrigued its author.

In his own book, *Flying Saucers and the Three Men* (1962), Bender revealed in lurid detail what actually happened to him. Initially Barker expressed having reservations about publishing the book, believing that his friend would be ridiculed and the field of ufology discredited. Some could be forgiven for thinking that he was sincere.

Bender explained that he had wanted to carry out an experiment: March 15, 1953 would be "World Contact Day." He urged all members of the IFSB to participate by simultaneously sending a telepathic message to the occupants of interplanetary craft that were observing the earth. After Bender repeated the message, his bedroom became filled with a yellow mist and he smelled a foul odor. Small blue lights flashed in his mind as he experienced a throbbing headache. He received an inaudible command: "Please be advised to discontinue delving into the mysteries of the universe. We will make an appearance if you disobey." A couple of weeks later three shadowy figures wearing dark clothing and Homburg-style hats materialized in his bedroom and handed him a coin-like object. He was told to squeeze the amulet with the radio on while repeating the word, "Kazik."

When he later followed their instructions, he was somehow transported into a large circular room with unusual glittering surfaces. A person appeared and told him that the aliens were extracting a valuable chemical from our seawater and that their base of operations on the Earth was inside an enormous cavern in Antarctica. Stranger still, when the person showed Bender his normal appearance, this closely resembled the description of the hideous Flatwoods monster that had frightened the country folk in Braxton County.

One might be tempted to think that Bender had let himself become involved with occult forces, and that he had misinterpreted evil spirits for interplanetary visitors. After all, Barker did include photos of Bender's bedroom in his stepfather's house: monster movie motifs and cheesy Halloween decorations covered the walls. In light of this juvenile "Chamber of Horrors", it seems more likely that the dark denizens of his subconscious mind were attempting to hush up the director of the IFSB's arrested development... until Barker got involved.

Moon Potatoes Have More Protein

With the profits from *They Knew Too Much About Flying Saucers*, Barker had started a small publishing venture that he called "The Saucerian Press." The first book to be issued was *From Outer Space To You* (1959) by Howard Menger, a sign painter from New Jersey who had become a frequent guest on a popular late-night radio program hosted by Long John Nebel. In interviews, Menger claimed to have numerous encounters with space people. These were mostly gorgeous women in shimmering outfits that didn't like to be encumbered by brassieres (too bad all of his Polaroids turned out so fuzzy!). Between mystical conversations with the otherworldly visitors, Menger ran errands that included shopping for department store clothing so that the Venusians and Martians wouldn't be too conspicuous amongst Earthlings. For his service, he was given a saucer ride to the moon where he was presented with a souvenir lunar potato that was much higher in protein than spuds grown in Idaho. Far out adventures like this were great for the book, but as soon as it left the press, Menger did a vanishing act. Once again Barker had been deserted by an author, and had no one to promote the book. A year later the contactee resurfaced on Nebel's new television show, only to recant all of his earlier statements. Maybe he had been mistaken about the encounters in the woodlands – it was all in his mind – or, perhaps, he had been duped as part of a military experiment to gauge the public response to possible alien

contact. Barker was left to wonder if Menger, too, had been silenced by some hostile specter. Either way, he made the decision to abandon hardcover bindings in favor of stapled cardstock.

Fair Dinkum Cobber

"Unfortunately, I have to read them before I publish them." This was Barker's reply to Fortean expert John A. Keel after he remarked, "some of the dullest stuff in the literary world appears between covers with brightly colored saucers on them." Keel could have been referring to any number of Barker's Saucerian titles, but perhaps the most hackneyed of all was *UFO Warning* (1967) by New Zealand researcher John Stuart. Was it for this reason that he sent a mailer to his charter subscribers stating that due to the shocking nature of "the most unusual UFO book ever published", those who feared being traumatized by the negative side of saucerdom could select another title? Adding another nice touch, the leaflet contained a warning that if the staples on the enclosure were "molested or broken", the recipient was advised to notify the sender at once.

Stuart was thankful that the fair dinkum (Stuart's nickname for Barker) had accepted his word when other researchers deserted him, although Barker did acknowledge that the book was unpleasant to publish and that it would be unpleasant to read – even for his "specialized audience." For those that opted for a different selection, *UFO Warning* concerns a researcher and his young female co-worker who are hot on the trail of the saucers. Unfortunately, busybodies in the neighborhood take notice of their nightly meetings (complete with snifters of brandy) and all too soon their reputations are blackened. As the 'shocked' reader tries to guess who will seduce who into taking off their clothes, the two manage to deduce that the saucers are based in… Antarctica.

Ignoring the warnings from phantom callers, the female (of course) is attacked by a lecherous furry monster with lime green skin, red veins and webbed feet that leaves scratch marks on her desirable figure.

Fortunately for all involved (except the baddie), this causes the two to discontinue saucer research and puts an end to their late hour rendezvous. Taking some liberties, one could make a case that certain details in the book foreshadowed the hypnosis-induced memories (or confabulation) of clinical procedures recounted by modern experiencers (mental suggestions, scoop marks, etc.), but as Saucerian artist, Gene Deplantier's illustration in the book clearly shows, no 'screen images' were involved.

THE SILVER BRIDGE

In 1970 Barker wrote a book that he was proud of. Unlike the deliberate crackpottery that he hawked to make a quick buck, *The Silver Bridge* was literature – spellbinding prose with murky psychological underpinnings that was said to be a tribute to his idol, the Italian film director, Federico Fellini. The book was based on his firsthand investigation of a manlike creature with fiercely-glowing red eyes that haunted the residents of Point Pleasant, West Virginia in 1966. Described as having a massive wingspan when it ascended like a rocket from its 'home' in an abandoned WWII munitions complex, the flapping spectacle was dubbed the Mothman. Soon, locals connected sightings of the menacing cryptid with a flurry of UFO activity in the area. Later, its conspicuous activity was believed to be an ominous portent associated with the collapse of a suspension bridge that spanned the Ohio River and killed nearly 50 people stuck in rush hour traffic on December 15, 1967.

Reported accounts written from his neutral point of view as "The Recorder" were blended with fictional creations in a structured mosaic. Considering the anecdotal scenarios, much of the work was deeply personal, and the reader must decide whether

Barker's masterpiece is a *Twilight Zone*-like social commentary or launching platform for a more complex interpretation of paranormal phenomena? Barker seemed to be asking if the spaceships and their occupants were temporary constructs that disguised something even stranger, with the purpose being to manipulate human behavior? This broader concept of 'aliens' as inter-dimensional materializations that have managed to co-exist in tandem with humankind was also proposed by researcher Jacques Vallee as part of a new approach to the UFO puzzle, but in 1970 it was quite a departure for Barker, whose mimeographed rags mostly contained fanciful tales involving nuts-and-bolts interplanetary machines.

In one of the chapters we are introduced to a humanoid named Indrid Cold, who claimed to be "a searcher" from "Lanulos in the constellation of Ganymede." The stranger in the shiny outfit emerged from an elongated metallic craft that caused a stereo salesman named Woodrow Derenberger to suddenly stop his Ford Econovan on a rain-slicked stretch of highway.

After interviewing the seemingly level-headed West Virginian, because of certain incongruencies in his descriptions of the interior of the flying contraption (bunk beds, CB radio, etc.), Barker wondered if the 'reality' of other ephemeral beings like Mr. Cold "depends a great deal on the authority of their interpreter?" If such individuals weren't objective entities, then what was the true nature of the robotic silencers that materialized and evaporated in the aftermath of UFO sightings? If not actors of some government agency, were they, too, an environmental aspect of veridical perception?

KOOKIE BOOKS AT GIANT ROCK

As devotees of the benevolent space brothers arrived in droves for the 1970 Interplanetary Spacecraft Convention at Giant Rock Airport in Landers, California, Barker donned a crushed straw hat and filled his assigned stall with what he privately referred to as his "kookie books." The trusty spirit duplicator had been working overtime at his sister Blanche's house in West Virginia and he gambled on a cross-country airline ticket that the attendees would be anxious for more cosmic revelations from Venusians with shoulder-length golden hair. However, as part of his contradictory stance on all things ufological, when he later sought to preserve the festive atmosphere of contactee George Van Tassel's final desert shindig in *Gray Barker at Giant Rock* (1976), rather than publish a retelling of the repetitive platitudes

based on theosophical doctrines or dire warnings from our galactic brethren about the atomic bugaboo, he produced an entertaining account that focused on the quirky personalities at the event. He wanted his readers to vicariously experience the memorable events, and to achieve this he employed a literary technique resembling a frame narrative, or story within a story. As with *The Silver Bridge* (though not nearly as esoteric), the human condition outweighed the alien viewpoint, unless we are to believe that Barker had been muzzled by sinister figures in black suits that shared his nostalgia.

Men in Blue, Blue-Green & Blue-Violet

In *Darklore* Volume III (2009), I wrote about a rare Saucerian publication known as "The Varo Edition" of *The Case for the UFO* (1955) by M.K. Jessup. The Saucerian facsimile reproduced hand-written notes scribbled in a paperback copy of Jessup's book, and the source of these annotations still puzzles UFO researchers.

At the time I hadn't read Barker's further thoughts on the notations in his even scarcer book entitled *After The Philadelphia*

Experiment (1984). Though I often wondered if the highly sought after Varo Edition could possibly have been an elaborate hoax perpetrated by Barker, after obtaining its follow-up, my suspicions grew deeper. Before continuing, a little background is necessary for those not familiar with what was once considered to be the "fantastic key to the flying saucer mystery."

As the story goes, a paperback of Jessup's book was sent anonymously to the Office of Naval Research. The dog-eared copy had been heavily annotated with three distinctive shades of ink that seemed to represent three different annotators. Although the comments were bizarre in the extreme, and appeared to be the product of a deranged mind, certain personnel at the ONR "indicated direct interest in some of the material therein."

So intrigued were they, in fact, they arranged for the Varo Corporation – a defense contractor engaged in classified aerospace projects – to clandestinely duplicate 25 copies of the marked up book, even going to the extra trouble of running offset stencils through the office duplicator so that the marginal notations would be distinguished by a separate color of ink.

Rumors began to circulate in the UFO community that the government had reproduced the mind-boggling 'discussions' of the annotators because they knew too much about military experiments associated with alien technology. Eventually, a few persistent researchers managed to get their hands on one. However, in series of 'bad luck', all of the copies quickly disappeared. Because the grammatical peculiarities had a decidedly alien tone, nefarious activity by the MIB was believed to be responsible. Even Jessup was found dead, having apparently committed suicide by acute carbon monoxide poisoning after driving his station wagon to a sunny park in Florida. When no autopsy was performed, there were allegations of foul play and leading the charge was Barker.

As to how Barker obtained his copy, he said that "the impossible happened" when an unnamed researcher decided to get rid of her

UFO material and transfer the files to him. "Among the voluminous papers was a copy of the Varo Edition!" (Only, in Barker's case, misfortune didn't follow, especially when he charged his subscribers $32.50 for the privilege of owning the Saucerian reprint.)

Sometime later, in an incredible 'coincidence', a shady character named Carlos Miguel Allende showed up unannounced on Barker's doorstep in Clarksburg one day just as he (and Moseley!) were discussing the enigmatic drifter. Allende had previously sent Jessup (and the ONR) several letters about a naval destroyer that had been rendered optically invisible during a military experiment involving Einsteinian physics. The letters had a similar weirdness to the puzzling comments scrawled in the copy of Jessup's book, and, as such, Allende claimed to be the sole annotator. Indeed, Allende has been described as an ingenious prankster and one investigator recently claimed to see other books marked in his idiosyncratic style. Still, it seems rather fortuitous that, besides the original three letters, only a few of the extensive annotations had been published prior to Barker's sneak peek (or tease) in *The Strange Case of M.K. Jessup* (1963).

As another example of possible deception, Barker claimed to have received a letter from someone who noticed that the Varo Edition "displayed a wide knowledge of the theosophical movement founded by Helena P. Blavatsky." Of course, since many of the occult beliefs transmitted to the Russian mystic by the ascended masters would have already been familiar to Barker, the analog becomes just another facet of the ruse. Commenting further on the letter, Barker suggested that the awkward writing style of the Varo notations was reminiscent of the stilted speech of the MIB, and even compared the trans-Tibetan adepts with the swarthy-complexioned silencers.

One has to wonder what motivation the government would have for reproducing the penned ramblings even (particularly) if they contained oblique references to a military experiment involving electromagnetic camouflage? It would seem that the only one with anything to gain was Barker. In over 35 years of diligent searching I have never seen any trace of an original 1950s Varo Edition. I do, however, own a faded Xerox copy that is lacking the Saucerian preface. This might be telling – in a couple of ways. Whether or not Barker hoaxed the annotations we may never know. What we do know is that he had no qualms about presenting fiction as fact.

Ufoology 101

In 1966 Barker presented "The Lost Creek Saucer" on the lecture circuit. Although this appeared to show a classic Adamski-type bell-shaped UFO bobbing around in scratchy 16 mm color frames, it was actually a toy-sized ceramic model dangling from a fishing pole that Barker shot from a Chevy pick-up with his Bolex camera. Diehards (and the really gullible) still insist the 'fake of a fake' is the real McCoy, despite Moseley fessing up in Ralph Coon's 1995 documentary, *Whispers From Space.*

While boozing it up, the mischievous duo of Barker and Moseley also forged the famous "Straith Letter." Using blank U.S. State Department stationary, they typed a letter to contactee, George Adamski, claiming the department had confirmatory evidence of his (outlandish) claims and encouraged his work. And then there were the articles by Dr. Richard H. Pratt, who was listed on the *Saucerian* masthead as a scientific consultant. Pratt was a pseudonym of a young writer named John C. Sherwood, who had submitted a sci-fi story to Barker about the UFOs being time machines from a future earth civilization. Barker convinced Sherwood that the story would be better suited if presented as fact, and offered to publish it as such in one of his newsletters. Sherwood went along with the deception until after Barker's death, writing in the *Skeptical Inquirer* that he was no longer able to stomach the fraud after seeing that it had been rehashed in *Gray Barkers MIB… The Secret Terror Amongst* (1983).

Barker was even said to have edited out ufologist J. Allen Hynek's cameo appearance from the film, *Close Encounters of the Third Kind* when shown in West Virginia theaters. Perhaps this was payback for the former debunker's repeated swamp gas explanations or maybe because of disparaging remarks made by the highbrow professor to Barker's more humorous approach to ufology.

Barker considered such capers as harmless entertainment. It was a way to keep the UFO field going during lulls in activity. Besides, such trickery might actually ferret out valuable information.

Killed Three Times

Although the scare tactics employed by the MIB usually had the opposite effect of shining a spotlight on the matter, in one case a victim was killed three times by the darkly clothed nemeses (only to be resurrected each time by a rejuvenating machine). According to Barker's article in *Flying Saucer Magazine* (1959), this happened to Prince Neosom of the Planet Tythian when the bushy-haired specimen of intergalactic royalty was incarnated on the Earth as Lee Childers.

The story was recounted in *Those Sexy Saucer People* (1967) – a virtually unobtainable paperback that, despite its scandalous cover illustration, is for the most part a typical overview of the UFO phenomenon. Well, at least until the chapter about "The Virgin and the Spacemen." In his pamphlet, *The Last Prom*, Ralph Coon claimed that Barker's enterprising hand was behind the sci-fi sleaze. But even a master leg-puller couldn't expect any sane person to believe that diamonds from Mars were used to finance the abduction of a pretty woman going to a meeting about Theosophy that ends up being violated on a spaceship by twenty-four horny spacemen that look like Greek gods!

In the 1980s Barker began to take an interest in alien abductions that included disturbing medical procedures. Had he wondered if

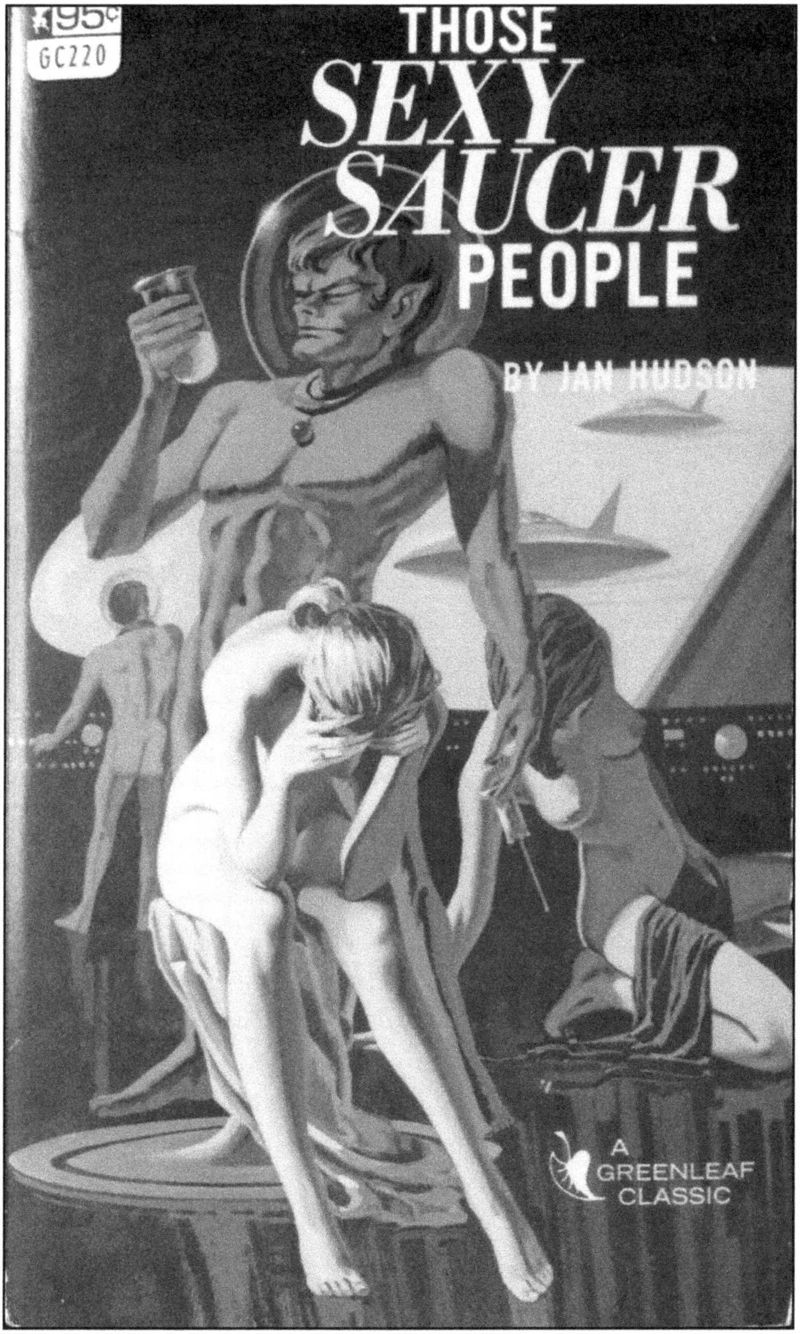
95¢
GC220
THOSE
SEXY
SAUCER
PEOPLE
BY JAN HUDSON
A
GREENLEAF
CLASSIC

some more down-to-earth MIB had been probing into biological theories involving genetic variants that might explain the puzzle of his own sexual orientation? (No, not an exophile.) If so, he might have contributed a chapter to *Those Sexy Saucer People* that involved sterilized coitus performed in an egg-shaped craft in which a nonhuman female lifeform barked like a dog during the act with her male captive. But, other sexual escapades with buxom space nymphs that would surely wear down the batteries of the MIB were most likely written by someone else with tongue planted firmly in their cheek.

The Waldomore

Although doctors told his sister Blanche that Gray died from white lung disease his death in 1984 was very likely the result of AIDs.[1] Sadly, only four people attended the funeral. Today, most people in Clarksburg either don't know who Gray Barker was or remember him as a bankrupt alcoholic that supplied exploitation films to a chain of drive-in movie theaters. Some have claimed that he was blacklisted in the city for being a homosexual. Fortunately, his prolific output has been preserved in an antebellum mansion in West Virginia known as the Waldomore. There, in "The Gray Barker Room", among the embellished accounts of an indefatigable researcher and flying saucer folklorist, you might even find *A UFO Guide to Fate Magazine* (1981) that he painstakingly assembled using his Radio Shack Daisywheel printer.

As for his fixation with the MIB, during the McCarthy era, the unspeakable would be disguised by his hyper-imaginative mind as a menacing presence that suppressed the extraordinary truth. The Brothers of the Shadow had inflicted on him a kind of amnesia, not unlike the mental suggestions induced by the high-tech auralgesiac devices that caused Jessup to take his life. The secret terror amongst him that became so lucrative for Hollywood would become his legacy as he moldered in the grave. Perhaps he finally got his answers – the key to the enduring mystery. For those who can't ignore his ufoological larks, one hopes that the man will at least be appreciated as a true *lekjaz*, or storyteller, to be eulogized by future generations as one of the key figures during the golden age of saucerdom… unsilenced as he was.

Blair MacKenzie Blake is the author of *The Othering* (a novel), *Ijynx*, *The Wickedest Books In the World – Confessions of an Aleister Crowley Bibliophile*, *The Curious Diary Entries of Verity Pennington* (a short story) and one of the writers of *Remember the Future*. He has contributed essays to numerous esoteric-themed magazines, including *The COSM Journal, Sub Rosa, Silkmilk* and *Dagobert's Revenge*. For over 18 years, BMB has been the writer/content manager for www.toolband.com and www.dannycarey.com. He currently resides in Las Vegas, NV.

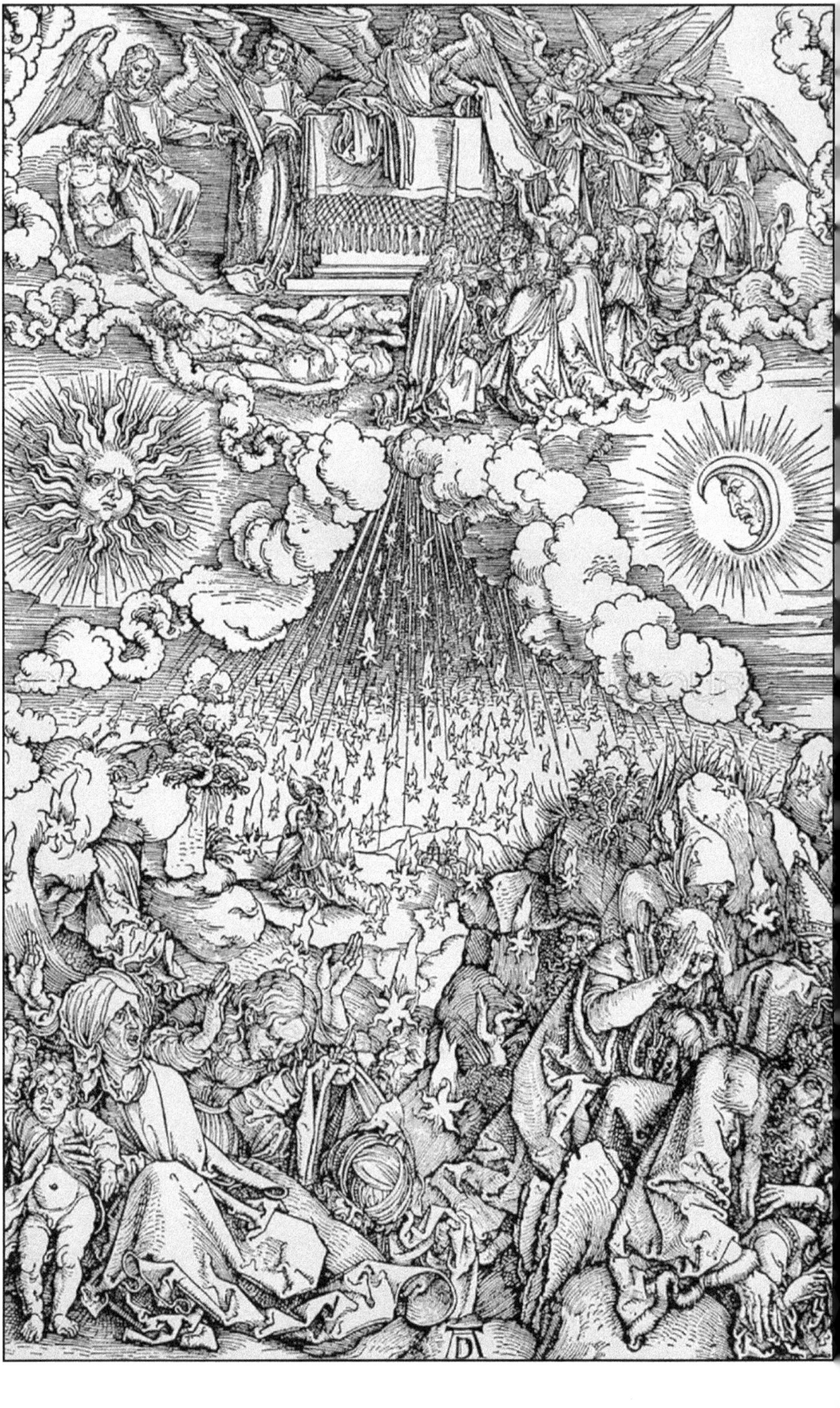

GOD IS MY ROCK

Were meteorites the earliest gods of humanity?

by *Greg Taylor*

In 1938, while the world's focus on Hitler's Nazi regime was firmly on the abhorrent activities they were undertaking in Europe, a division of his infamous SS was involved in an expedition to a far-off land. Led by the eminent zoologist Ernst Schäfer, under the auspices of the *Ahnenerbe* (Bureau for the Study of Ancestral Heritage), the research group traveled to Tibet, at the time regarded by some as the original source of the Aryan race. It is claimed that Schäfer's group returned to Germany with a number of sacred artifacts from the mysterious land, including a robe believed to have been worn by the Dalai Lama himself.[1] But none were more intriguing than a religious statue depicting what appeared to be the Tibetan god of the North, Vaisravana. The reason? Carved across Vaisravana' chest was a swastika symbol – and though the original meaning of this particular symbol was as the Tibetan Bön culture's designation of the sun, it would no doubt have been of great interest to the Nazi expedition.

As World War II broke out, the statue is said to have disappeared into the archives of a private collector for the rest of the century, until only recently re-emerging into public view in 2007. Then, in 2012, it made headlines around the world when an investigation by scientists found that it was likely carved out of an ancient iron meteorite that fell to Earth in Mongolia 15,000 years ago (how could a headline like "Buddhist 'Iron Man' found by Nazis is from Space"[2] not go viral?).

According to the researchers, the fact that hard, iron meteorites are an "inappropriate material for producing sculptures" suggested it was likely that whomever created it was "aware of the outstanding (extraterrestrial) nature of the object".[3] Iron from meteorites has been recognized in ancient cultures around the world as a sacred material, and so it seems only apt that it would be used to create a religious sculpture.

But while there have been some concerns in recent years as to whether the 'Nazi Iron Man from Space' might actually be a modern forgery,[4] it is a known fact that in ancient cultures, meteorites were not just sculpted into gods – but sometimes were believed to be the gods themselves, fallen from the sky.

Rock Gods

Put yourself in the mind of an ancient person, without a modern understanding of what the objects in the sky are. You are minding your own business around your campfire at night, when suddenly one of those mysterious star things – suspected by some to be the gods themselves, watching over humanity from on high – falls from the sky, making thundering sounds and catching fire. It lands nearby, burying itself in the sand – and upon uncovering it, you find a massive chunk of iron. Would you think it might be a god fallen to Earth?

'Nazi Space Buddha'

The evidence from historians throughout the ages suggests that the answer to this question might be 'yes'. Indeed, the 2nd century Christian theologian and historian Clement of Alexandria is said to have concluded, based on numerous historical accounts, that "the worship of such stones [is] the first, and earliest idolatry, in the world".[5]

The following examples of historical references to the worship of stones fallen from the sky are offered by Edward King in his 1796 book *Remarks concerning stones said to have fallen from the clouds, both in these days and in antient times*:

> [T]he learned Greaves leads us to conclude that [the famous image of Diana at Ephesus was] nothing but a conical, or pyramidal stone, that fell from the clouds. For he tells us, on unquestionable authorities, that many others of the images of heathen deities were merely such.

Herodian expressly declares that the Phoenicians had…a certain great stone, circular below, and ending with a sharpness above, in the figure of a cone, of black colour. And they report it to have fallen from heaven, and to be the image of the sun.

So Tacitus says, that at Cyprus, the image of Venus was not of human shape; but a figure rising continually round, from a larger bottom to a small top, in conical fashion. And it is to be remarked, that Maximus Tyrius (who perhaps was a more accurate mathematician,) says, the stone was pyramidal.

And in Corinth, we are told by Pausanias, that the images both of Jupiter Melichius, and of Diana, were made (if made at all by hand) with little or no art. The former being represented by a pyramid, the latter by a column.[6]

A key point in identifying these sacred stones as originally being meteorites is that they are often not simply referred to just as "fallen from heaven", but are also commonly described as being conical or pyramidal in shape. A 1936 paper, "The Image which Fell Down from Jupiter", by C.C. Wylie and J.R. Naiden, discusses the image of Venus at Cyprus noted above ("the image of Aphrodite/Venus in the sanctuary at Paphos was simply a white cone or pyramid") along with a number of other cases of conical/pyramidal stones fallen from heaven and worshipped:

[T]he emblem of Astarte at Byblus was a cone; and the image of Artemis (Diana) at Perga in Pamphylia was also a cone. We are told that the images of the sun god, Heliogabalus, at Emesa in Syria was a cone of black stone with small knobs on it, and that it appears on coins of Emesa. We are told that the sacred stone of Cybele brought from Pessinus to Rome during the second Punic war was a small black rugged stone, but we do not know whether it was of conical shape. We are also told that conical stones, which were apparently considered sacred, have been found at Golgi in Cyprus, in the Phoenician temples at Malta, and in the shrine of the Mistress of Torquoise in Sinai.

Similarly, black, conical stones were said to be venerated in the temple of Heliopolis-Baalbek, while the Nabataean god Dushara was worshipped in the form of an obelisk or "an unhewn four-cornered blackstone".[7]

And while we no longer have physical evidence of these sacred stones – known as *baetyl* stones, and sometimes also as (or related to) the sacred *omphalos* of ancient times – to inspect them first hand, as they have since been lost and destroyed, we don't need to put our trust only in the descriptions of ancient historians to know their shape, as the images of many of them are preserved for us on coins of the time that depicted them sitting within temples.

This recurring pyramidal or conical quality seemed to baffle the renowned anthropologist James Frazer, who stated that "the precise significance of such an emblem remains as obscure as it was in the time of Tacitus". However, it doesn't seem as strange once we consider that this conical/pyramidal shape is common in actual stones fallen from heaven – meteorites – caused by passing through

the atmosphere in a stable orientation, which results in the leading surface being flattened or rounded.

As Wylie and Naiden suggest:

> These images show that the stones were the shape of typical meteorites... It is a well-known fact that the blunt cone is the most common and typical shape for meteorites. In primitive times, as now, an occasional meteorite was seen to actually fall. The fall from the sky was naturally regarded as miraculous, and the stone was often placed in a shrine. The priests told the worshippers that this image was not made with human hands, but that it fell from heaven.[8]

Conical black meteorite

Further Confirmation?

The "certain great stone" fallen from heaven mentioned above that Herodian references was the 'Black Stone of Elagabalus' (or Heliogabalus). Elagabalus was the Phoenician local name for the Sun God at Emesa, where there was an impressive temple dedicated to the god, which contained a statue of the deity that wasn't made by human hands, but instead…

> …was an enormous stone, rounded at the base and coming to a point on the top, conical in shape and black. This stone is worshipped as though it were sent from heaven; on it there are some small projecting pieces and markings that are pointed out, which the people would like to believe are a rough picture of the sun, because this is how they see them.[9]

The Black Stone would later be moved to Rome, after the temple priest Antoninus – at the age of just fifteen – became emperor of the Roman Empire "through the money and intrigues of his grandmother, and the murder of the Emperor Macrinus". However, the reign of Antoninus and his 'rock god' was rather short:

> To the great disgust of the Roman Senate and people, [Antoninus] brought with him from Syria the image of his god, the sacred stone, and himself continued before it his priestly service with all its fantastic forms and gesticulations… He built another temple in the suburbs of Rome, to which the Emesa stone was carried in procession every year, while the populace were entertained with games, and shows, and feastings and carousings.

> Herodian thus describes this performance: 'The god was brought from the city to this place in a chariot glittering with gold and precious stones, and drawn by six large white horses without the least spot,

superbly harnessed with gold, and other curious trappings, reflecting a variety of colours. Antoninus himself held the reins – nor was any mortal permitted to be in the chariot; but all kept attendant around him as charioteer to the deity, while he ran backward, leading the horses, with his face to the chariot, that he might have a constant view of his god.... The people attended the solemnity, running on each side of the way with tapers and flambeaux, and throwing down garlands and flowers as they passed."

The reign of a foolish boy at this period of Rome's history was necessarily a short one, and at the age of eighteen the soldiers killed him and let the Roman populace have the body to drag through the city streets. The worship of the Sun-god at once ceased, and no doubt, the stone also was thrown away.[10]

What is interesting about the accounts of the Black Stone – beyond it being conical – is its colour (black surfaces are a common feature of meteorites, caused by the scorching heat generated as they travel through the Earth's atmosphere), and the fact that its surface was said to be covered in "knobs", and "small projecting pieces and markings". Some researchers have suggested that this is another confirmation of the meteoritic nature of the 'Black Stone', as this description matches well with another feature of meteorites known as regmaglypts.[11]

Regmaglypts are concave impressions on the surface of larger meteorites that are likely formed by vortices of hot gas as the meteor passes through the Earth's atmosphere, giving them a knobby, eroded surface by the time they reach ground.

This suggestion might help explain another example of ancient iconography that has often baffled (or confused) anthropologists like James Frazer. For example, the original statue of Diana at the Temple at Ephesus (one of the ancient wonders of the world; it was known even to Greek historians of the 2nd century BCE[12] that the sanctuary of the Temple of Ephesus was extremely ancient, with

Meteorite with regmaglypts

claims that the Amazons themselves originally set up the worship of the goddess there) was also described by some as a stone fallen from heaven that was conical or pyramidal in shape, suggesting it was a meteorite. It is also mentioned in the Christian New Testament briefly (Acts of the Apostles 19:35), when the 'town clerk' of Ephesus notes that "the city of the Ephesians is the guardian of the temple of great Diana and of her statue that fell from heaven".

However, while modern excavations of the temple area have failed to recover the original statue, later copies of it (from the 1st and 2nd centuries CE) made of stone, metal and clay, and depictions on coins (dated to around 85 BCE), have been found elsewhere at Ephesus. These depictions show "a female, humanoid figure, standing erect with her arms bent and held forward, as if to hold loosely something staff-like vertically in each hand". But the distinguishing imagery of this depiction of Diana is that "her upper torso was draped with a series of ovoid objects, often in two or three horizontal rows. These have been interpreted as multiple breasts, eggs, fruits, bags of votive offerings, bull or human testicles."

These statuettes and images on coins vary in the different periods, but agree on the essentials. According to Frazer, they represent the goddess with a multitude of protruding breasts. The heads of animals of many kinds, both wild and tame, spring from the front of her body in a series of bands that extend from the breasts to the feets.[13]

Researchers have suggested that if this statue was in fact a meteorite, that – like the "small projecting pieces and markings" on the Black Stone discussed above – this "multitude of projecting breasts" might in fact have originally been regmaglypts[14] (compare the statue of Diana of Ephesus below to the image on the previous page).

Artemis of Ephesus with "multitude of projecting breasts" (Wouter Engler, CC by SA 4.0)

The Iron Bones of the Gods of Egypt

The conical or pyramidal shape ascribed to these ancient objects 'fallen from the sky' also brings to mind another sacred stone revered by the ancient Egyptians: the black, cone-shaped 'Ben-Ben' stone kept in the temple of Ra at Heliopolis. The influential Egyptologist E. A. Wallis-Budge made the connection in the 1920s, and others have made the comparison in subsequent decades (additionally, G.A. Wainwright has argued that the sacred object of Amun venerated at Thebes "gave many signs of a meteorite"). Given that the shape of the Ben-Ben stone is thought to have acted as the model for the capstones found on many of Egypt's famous pyramids and obelisks, could it be that the pyramids themselves were originally built to mimic meteorites, the 'gods fallen from the sky'?

The ancient Egyptians certainly knew about meteorites, and held them to be sacred. In 1922, when Howard Carter stunned the world with his discovery of the still-intact 'lost tomb' of the Egyptian King Tutankhamun (18th dynasty; 14th century BCE), two daggers were found within the wrapping of Tut's mummy: one with a blade of gold, the other with a blade made of iron from a meteorite.[15] And this wasn't just a case of the Egyptians coming across an iron meteorite 'rock' and using the exotic material without knowing the extraterrestrial source of the object, as their language specifically records that they were aware: the phrase *bja n pt* ("iron of the sky") was used to describe this material (given the dagger's age, it's sobering to remember that it was just 300 years ago that 'modern' scientists were debunking the idea that meteorites fell from the sky).

And around 2000 years before Tutankhamun was buried with his 'extraterrestrial dagger', at the very beginnings of ancient Egyptian civilization (ca. 3300 BCE) iron beads made from a meteorite were used in a burial.[16] According to Joyce Tyldesley, an Egyptologist at the University of Manchester who studied the trinkets, this is yet more evidence that "the sky was very important to the ancient

Daggers found buried with Pharaoh Tutankhamun

Egyptians", and as such "something that falls from the sky is going to be considered as a gift from the gods".[17] And the fact that these objects made of meteoritic iron have so far largely been found only in high-status graves suggests that this material was very strongly associated with royalty and power.

Furthermore, Campbell Price, a curator of Egypt and Sudan at the Manchester Museum has pointed out that during the time of the pharaohs, the gods were believed to have bones made of iron – and speculated that meteorites may have inspired this belief, with "the celestial rocks being interpreted as the physical remains of gods falling to Earth".[18]

Robert Bauval and Adrian Gilbert wrote about the veneration and use of iron meteorites by the ancient Egyptians in their 1994 book *The Orion Mystery* (Bauval had, in earlier papers, already made the argument that the conical/pyramid shape of the Ben-Ben stone may have been based on the similar shape of oriented meteorites), and note the many descriptions in the ancient Pyramid Texts of the bones of the king as *bja* (iron) and their connection to the stars. For instance, in PT1454 we find the passage "My bones are iron (*bja*) and my limbs are the imperishable stars."

> As these passages show, there was a belief that when the departed kings became stars, their bones became iron, the heavenly material (meteorites) of which the star gods were made. Such cosmic iron objects were the only material evidence of a tangible land in the sky populated by star souls, and it was easy to see why the stars were thought to be made from *bja*. Since the souls of departed kings were the stars, they too had bones made of iron.[19]

Interestingly, a little known fact about the ancient Egyptians is that they collected fossils of prehistoric animals – multiple tons of remains, consisting of thousands of black, sand-polished bones, have been excavated from shrines dedicated to the god Set. Some researchers have noted that these dark, heavy, fossilised bones share a strong visual similarity with desert-weathered iron meteorites, and as such have speculated that "they could be the source of inspiration for the Pyramid texts reference to the 'iron bones of gods'".[20]

Furthermore, given that many of the remains were bones of the hippopotamus, and were found at cult centres of the god Set – who was himself often depicted in artwork as a hippopotamus – perhaps we can see a possible connection here with the ceremonial adze used during the 'Opening of the Mouth' ritual during the funerals of pharaohs. According to Dr Bernd Scheel, an expert in ancient Egyptian metal-working and tools…

> Iron was [a] metal of mythical character…. According to legend, the skeleton (ie. the bones) of Seth … was of Iron, [and] was used in particular for the production of protective amulets and magic model tools which were needed for the ritual called the 'opening of the mouth', a ceremony which was necessary to prepare the mummy of the deceased for life after death.[21]

The 'Opening of the Mouth' of the pharaoh using the ceremonial adze

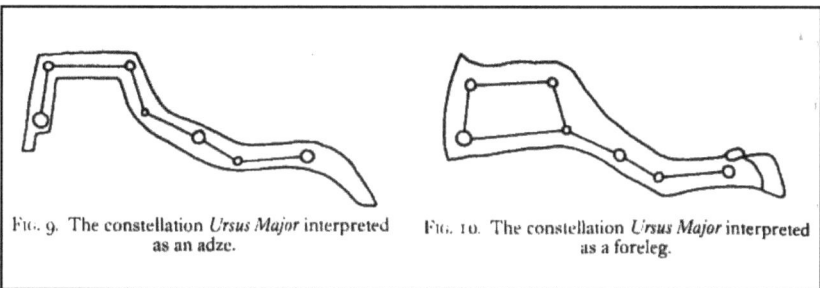

Fig. 9. The constellation *Ursus Major* interpreted as an adze.

Fig. 10. The constellation *Ursus Major* interpreted as a foreleg.

The constellation of Ursa Major representing both the adze and a foreleg (Image from Roth, Ann Macy, Fingers, Stars, and the "Opening of the Mouth": The Nature and Function of the Ntrwj-Blades.", *Journal of Egyptian Archaeology* 78)

So it is worth pointing out that Egyptologists G.A. Wainwright and Samuel Mercer both noticed that the adze used for opening the mouth was shaped in the form of the northern circumpolar constellation of Ursa Major – which the Egyptians called *mshtyw* ('the thigh'), and which in Egyptian sky imagery was actually held by Set-as-hippopotamus. Could this curious combination of tools made out of fallen stars, in the shape of animal legs visible as constellations in the heavens, be an indication that the ancient Egyptians (mistakenly) thought the blackened, polished animal fossils they collected were also fallen from the sky like the blackened iron meteorites they had found, and thus were the sacred 'iron bones' of the sky gods themselves?

Similarly, Robert Bauval has argued that the ancient Egyptians may also have confused – or at least, equated symbolically – black hard stones such as diorite, basalt and dark-grey granite with the "lustred, black appearance" of chunks of iron-meteorite, as "the resemblance can be uncanny". This could explain, he says, the use of these materials in the capstones of some pyramids:

> Not surprisingly, black basalt was called '*Bja-Kam*' meaning 'black iron', suggesting that basalt, and possibly similar black hard

stones viz. diorite and dark granite, were associated to meteoritic ironstone, and consequently to the 'bones' of star-gods. Most capstones of monumental pyramids were probably made of granite. The almost-black granite capstone of the pyramid of Amenemhet III in the Cairo museum is a fine example of this. It was discovered in 1902 by Maspero, who remarked that its surface had been 'mirror' polished ("poli a miroir"). Such a description is typical for the appearance of a freshly fallen iron-meteorite. Amenemhet III's capstone could well be the stylised man-made version of an oriented iron-meteorite symbolising his materialized star-soul.[22]

Rockin' All Over the World

While many of the examples given so far are from ancient locations around the Mediterranean, meteorite worship and use

Pyramidion capstones in the Cairo Museum (Ovedc, CC by SA 4.0)

of meteoritic iron for making tools and weapons appears to have been a worldwide phenomenon.

In the New World there have been multiple examples of apparent veneration of rocks fallen from the sky. For instance, a large (1500kg) meteorite was found in a ruined temple at Casas Grandes in Mexico, as well as a smaller iron meteorite that was wrapped and buried like a human mummy bundle, and said to be "similar to depictions and descriptions of the Aztec god Huitzilopochtli".[23] Other similar finds in the Americas suggest this might have been some sort of tradition: in 1915, a dig at a pueblo-style dwelling at Camp Verde, Arizona, found a meteorite wrapped in a blanket of feathers in what looked like a child's burial cist under the floor; further to the north, at Winona in Arizona, another meteorite was found in a similar stone cist beneath the floor of a dwelling.

According to one researcher, the Pawnee (who it must be noted were originally from Nebraska, quite a way from the Arizona finds) named meteorites "the children of Tirawhat" (their leading deity), and that one legend foretold that a marvellous being called Pahokatawa would one day come from the sky in the form of a turtle-shaped stone. Meteorite historian Alastair McBeath has noted that "the regmaglyptic markings often seen on larger meteorites...could certainly give a patternation reminiscent of that seen on a turtle's shell, while...a conical or lenticular form, something like a turtle, would not be unusual".[24] A similarly-shaped, 175kg meteorite was revered by the local tribes of Iron Creek in Alberta, Canada as a "medicine-stone", and was known by them to have fallen from the heavens.

The Cape York meteorite in Greenland, one of the largest iron meteorites in the world, was a site of pilgrimage for the Inuit of the region. The remains of a massive meteor that collided with the Earth nearly 10,000 years ago are split into multiple chunks, with Ahnighito (the Tent), weighing 31 metric tons; the Man, weighing about 20 metric tons; the Woman, weighing 3 tons; and the Dog, weighing 400 kilograms being among the largest found.[25] The Inuit would walk for 3 days to reach the meteorites, and used them as a source of iron for tools and harpoons for centuries – so much so that a 'rock wall' consisting of thousands of small stone boulders surrounded the meteorite named "Woman", having been left there after working the extraterrestrial iron.

(In the early 19th century stories about these massive meteorites sparked a number of expeditions by Westerners, and in 1894 Robert E. Peary eventually found and removed a number of them – selling the pieces for $40,000 to the American Museum of Natural History in New York City where they are still on display.)

There is some evidence that indigenous Australians also recorded meteor falls in their oral traditions, and regarded them as supernatural events. For example, the traditional name for the location of the Henbury crater field (created by an impact event <4,700 years BP) in the Northern Territory is *chindu china waru chingi yabu* (roughly translated, "sun walk fire devil rock").

Ahnighito meteorite

Indigenous astronomy researcher Duane Humacher notes that when a man named James M. Mitchell visited the site in 1921, his Aboriginal guide...

> ...refused to go near them, saying that it was a place where a fire "debil-debil" [devil] came out of the sky and killed everything in the vicinity. He visited the craters again in 1934 and took another Aboriginal guide with him. The guide said Aboriginal people would not camp within two miles of the craters or even venture within half a mile of them, describing them as a place where the fire-devil lived. He claimed they did not collect water that filled some of the craters, fearing the fire devil would fill them with a piece of iron.
>
> In March 1932, an unnamed resident of the area undertook independent research and spoke to local Aboriginal elders. According to the elders, all young Aboriginal people were forbidden from going near the craters. The elders described them as the place where "a fiery devil ran down from the sun and made his home in the Earth".
>
> ...The current evidence indicates that Aboriginal people witnessed the event, recorded the incident in oral traditions, and those traditions remained intact through the 1930s (and possibly later).[26]

In Japan, a meteorite was said to have been seen falling into the garden of a Shinto shrine on May 19, 861 in Nogata. This black-crusted meteorite has been kept at the shrine ever since in a small wooden box with the date of its fall engraved on it. And in Krasnojarsk, Siberia, a meteoritic mass of around 700kg was reported by a traveller in 1771 to have been long-regarded by the Tartars of the region as "a holy thing fallen from heaven".[27]

One of the world's major religions may even have a strand of meteorite veneration within it: many have claimed that the Islamic relic known as *al-Hajaru al-Aswad* (the 'Black Stone') – said to have been given to Abraham by an angel, and set into the eastern corner of the Kaaba at Mecca by him – is a fragment of a meteorite. Described as being a fragmented, metallic black stone with "a silver-grey, fine-grained interior in which tiny cubes of a bottle-green material were embedded", the Black Stone – according to other stories – was also said to have been originally worshipped by the Nabateans who visited the Kaaba as a site of pilgrimage in the pre-Islamic period.

However, given the sacred nature of the Black Stone, it has not been scientifically studied and so has never been confirmed to be meteoritic in origin. Additionally, as a part of the *tawaf* ritual during the *hajj* pilgrimage, as Muslims circle the Kaaba many try to touch and kiss the Black Stone – and so its blackened, shiny surface may be a consequence of human interaction (over centuries, involving millions of people) rather than scorching via atmospheric friction as it fell to earth.

Regardless of the still unknown origin of the Kaaba's Black Stone however, even in the last five centuries there are numerous accounts from around the world of meteorites being venerated or kept as sacred objects. In Ensisheim, Germany, a stone weighing nearly 150kg fell from the sky on November 16, 1492. The Emperor Maximilian is said to have had the stone brought to a nearby castle, "and a council of state was held to consider what message from heaven the stone fall had brought them". It eventually found its way to the local church, where it was hung with a strict command that it should remain there intact.[28]

In Durala, India, when a 10kg meteorite fell on February 18, 1815, the local people were said to have begun construction of a special temple over it due to its heavenly origin, until the East India Company took possession of it and sent it to the British Museum.

Woodcut illustrating the Ensisheim meteorite fall

And in Ogi, Hizen, Japan, two stones which fell in 1744 were used for more than 150 years in the temple to Shokujo on the festival of that goddess, as locals believed the stones had "fallen from the shores of the Heavenly River, or Milky Way, after they had been used by the goddess as weights to steady her loom" (one of these stones was also sent to the British Museum).[29]

And if you think that in the 21st century we're well past the 'primitive' idea that we would worship rocks fallen from the sky, it's worth pointing out that a 'Church of the Chelyabinsk Meteorite' was formed when the famous 2013 bolide made news across the world after exploding over Russia, injuring 1600 people.[30] The founder of the church, Andrey Breyvichko, has said that he believes the meteorite contains 'information' that "will help people live at a new stage of spiritual knowledge development". He (and his 50-or-so fellow believers) beseeched authorities to hand over any pieces of the recovered meteorite to them, as they wanted to house them in a (still-to-be-built) temple in Chelyabinsk. Breyvichko stated of the plan, "I think it won't hurt Chelyabinsk to become a truly holy city, home to a great temple that will be the object of pilgrimage for millions of people from across the world."

Given the similar accounts across the ancient world of temples housing sacred rocks fallen from heaven, it seems not that much has really changed.

Greg Taylor is the owner and editor of the online alternative news portal, *The Daily Grail* (www.dailygrail.com), and is also the editor of *Darklore*. He is widely read in topics that challenge the orthodox worldview, from alternative history to the mysteries of human consciousness. Greg currently resides in Brisbane, Australia. His most recent book *Stop Worrying! There Probably is an Afterlife* is an exploration of the evidence for the survival of consciousness after death.

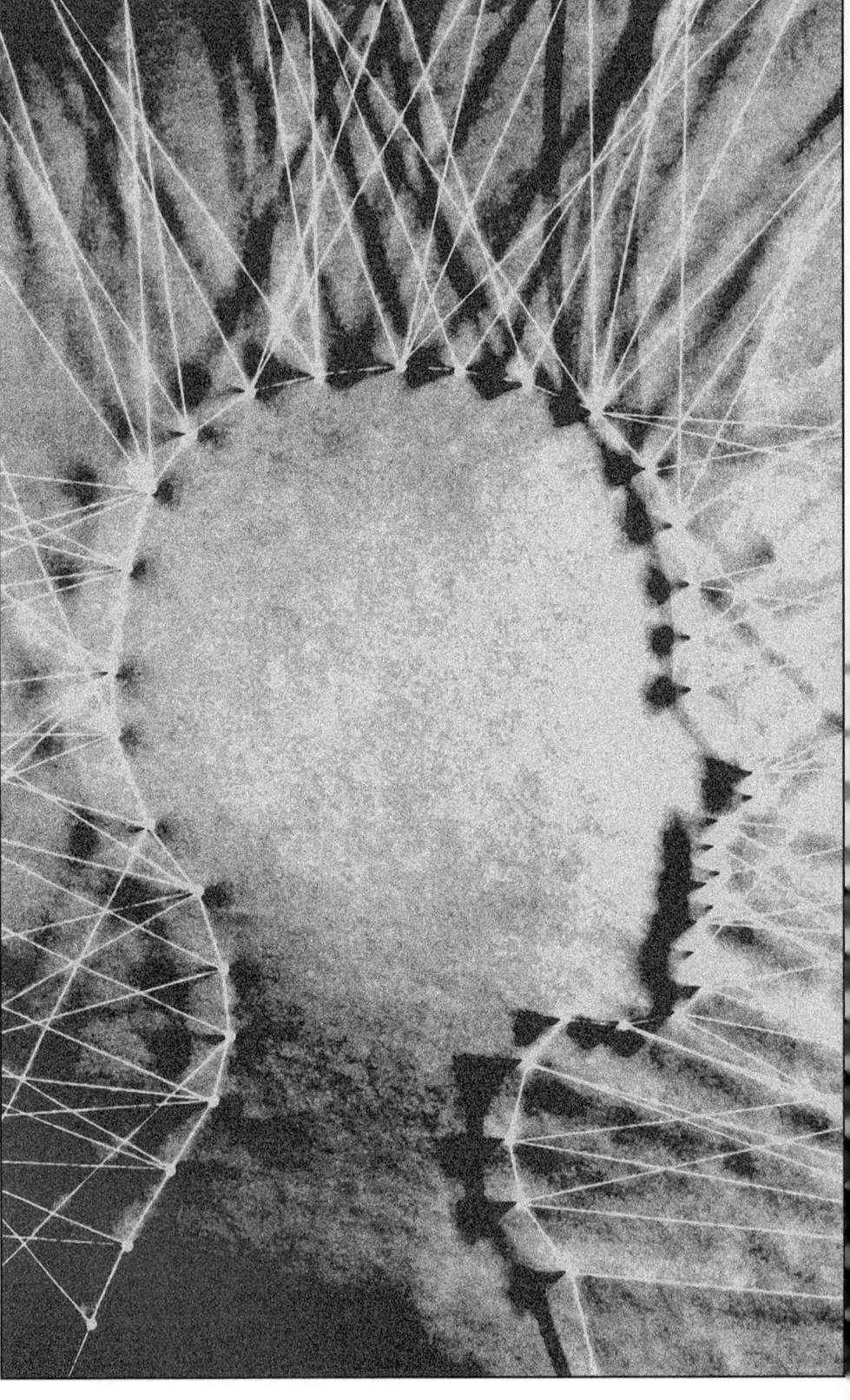

James Tilly Matthews and the Air Loom

The secret life and turbulent times of the first man to believe that his mind was being controlled by a machine

by *Mike Jay*

As the twenty-first century unfolds, the notion of the 'influencing machine' has entered the mainstream of our culture by stealth, from a thousand different sources. Covertly operated devices that use futuristic technology to send messages and control minds have become a staple of mass-entertainment science fiction and conspiracy narratives from *The X-Files* to *The Matrix* to *The Manchurian Candidate*. The Internet hums with rumours and first-person testimonies of mind control, electronic implants and subliminal influencing devices. The character who wears a tinfoil hat to deflect malign invisible rays has become a crude and parodic cliché of paranoia, and thus of madness itself. At the centre of this expanding web of fiction, technology, conspiracy and delusion, the influencing machine controls a new and disputed territory, accessible to all and none.

All this represents a striking transition from a century ago, when the influencing machine was just beginning to be glimpsed within psychiatric practice as a strange denizen from the far shores of insanity, recorded among the hallucinations of celebrated subjects such as Daniel Paul Schreber and August Strindberg, and yet to attract the attention of its first clinical interpreter, the gifted and tragic Victor Tausk. It is a challenge to the imagination, then, to comprehend just how uncanny it must have seemed a century earlier still when, in 1810, the prototype for all these spectral-cum-mechanical devices, James Tilly Matthews' Air Loom, was first presented to the public.

Nor was the Air Loom a distant ancestor, a rough sketch or fleeting glimpse that would need to be filled in with hindsight by succeeding generations. The influencing machine emerged fully formed. Where we might have expected to see confused jottings and frenzied scribbles, we have instead a precise and finely rendered technical drawing such as we might expect to find in a scientific journal of the time. Barrels, tubes, levers and cylinders are elegantly rendered and delicately shaded; figures are carefully dressed and artfully posed; components are finished with understated brass fittings and neatly keyed with copperplate lower-case initials. There is a coolness and conviction about the whole image, a sense that the artist has worked carefully to render complexity in its simplest form. Such coolness has a curiously unnerving effect. We wonder if we might have have been convinced of the reality of the machine, had it not been presented as the production of a long-term incurable inmate of Bethlem Hospital in London, the world's most famous asylum for lunatics.

But the reader of 1810 was not expected to admire the artistry of the Air Loom, or to contemplate the subtleties of the imaginative world that lay behind it. John Haslam, the resident apothecary at Bethlem – known popularly for centuries as Bedlam – included the image in his book *Illustrations of Madness*, at that time the longest psychiatric report ever written on a mad patient's delusions, with two clear purposes in mind. One was professional: as the title of his book

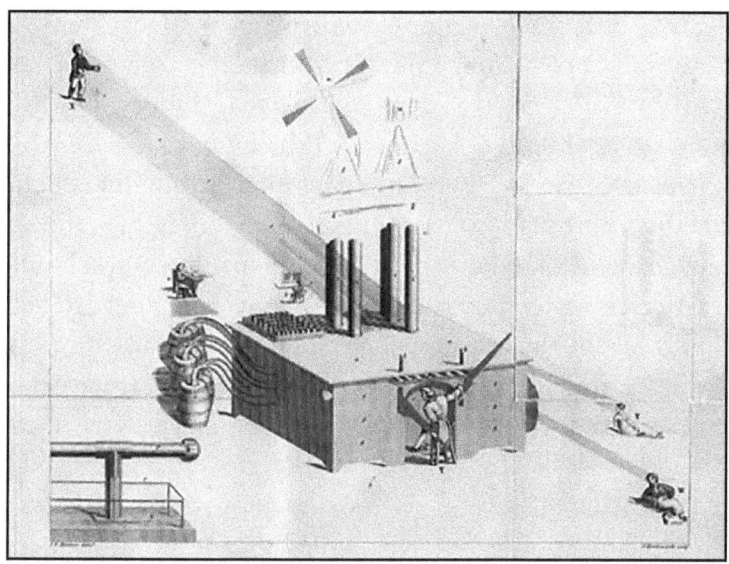

indicates, he wished to illustrate madness in its most florid form, and by the same token illustrate that he himself was the model for a new and specialist category of 'mad-doctor'. The other was personal: he was determined to prove, against contrary opinion from his family and others, that the artist, James Tilly Matthews, was indeed mad, and that those who had argued otherwise had proved themselves unfit to make such judgements.

The text that accompanied the illustration painstakingly reconstructed the world of the Air Loom, as conveyed to Haslam by his patient over many years. Matthews was convinced that outside the grounds of Bedlam, in a basement cellar by London Wall, a gang of villains were controlling and tormenting his mind with magnetic fluids and rays.

The machine they had developed for this purpose, the Air Loom, combined recent developments in gas chemistry with the strange force of animal magnetism, or mesmerism. It incorporated keys, levers, barrels, batteries, sails, brass retorts and magnetic fluid, and worked by directing and modulating magnetically charged airs and gases, rather as the stops of an organ modulate its tones. It ran on a mixture of foul substances including "spermatic-animal-seminal rays", "effluvia of dogs" and "putrid human breath", and the discharges of fluid extracted from these substances were focused to deliver thoughts, feelings and sensations directly into Matthews' brain. There were many of these modulations, or "event-workings", all vividly christened: "fluid locking", "stone making", "thigh talking", "lobster-cracking", "bomb-bursting", and the dreaded "brain-saying", whereby thoughts were forced into his brain against his will. To facilitate this process, the gang had implanted a magnet inside Matthews' head. As a result of the Air Loom, he was tormented constantly by delusions, physical agonies, fits of laughter and being forced to parrot whatever nonsense they chose to feed into his head. His confinement in Bedlam represented the success of their strategy in making him appear mad.

The Air Loom was being operated by a gang of undercover Jacobin revolutionaries, who had forced Britain into a disastrous war with Revolutionary France and were bent on maintaining hostilities between the two nations. These characters, too, Matthews could describe with eerie precision. They were led by their sadistic puppet-master and strategist, codenamed 'Bill the King'; all details were recorded by his sarcastic and punctilious second-in-command, 'Jack the Schoolmaster'. The French liaison was accomplished by a woman called Charlotte, who seemed to Matthews to be as much a prisoner as himself, and was often chained up near-naked. 'Sir Archy' was a woman who dressed as a rough, uncouth man and spoke in obscenities; the machine itself was operated by the sinister, pockmarked and nameless 'Glove Woman'. When Matthews slept, this gang materialised in his dreams, "forcing their phantoms and grotesque images on his languid intellect" and gathering the secret information they needed to plot his assailment for the following day.

But the gang's activity was not directed solely at Matthews; rather, he was the only witness to a conspiracy that had already engulfed

Europe. There were many Air Loom gangs all over London, influencing the minds of politicians and public figures, and with a particularly firm grasp of the Prime Minister, William Pitt, whom they could puppet like a child's toy whenever he addressed Parliament. In Paris, too, the French Directory was being manipulated by Air Looms, as were the crowned heads of Prussia and beyond. By poisoning the minds of politicians on both sides of the Channel with suspicious and belligerent "brain-sayings", the gangs were threatening national and international catastrophe. They were everywhere, lurking in streets, theatres and coffee-houses, where they tricked the unsuspecting into inhaling the magnetic fluid that would place them under the control of the Air Loom, and they carried magnetic batons that they could grasp to make themselves invisible if they were discovered.

John Haslam offered "the peculiar opinions of Mr. Matthews" not merely to titillate the reader with extravagant lunacy – though he clearly had the sensation-seeker in his sights – but, more urgently, to announce his theory of madness to his professional colleagues. "Madness being the opposite to reason and good sense", he patiently explained, "as light is to darkness, straight to crooked &c., it appears wonderful that two opposite opinions could be entertained on the subject". Let no doctor take refuge behind the idea that madness is in some sense in the eye of the beholder, an abstract or relative concept on which experts might agree to differ. "A person", Haslam insists, "cannot correctly be said to be in his senses and out of his senses at the same time". The only sure diagnosis of madness was by careful examination of the facts of the case, and this was the spirit in which the Air Loom was offered to the reader.

But the irony of *Illustrations of Madness* is that it is now virtually impossible to read it in the way the author intended. Too much of the revolutionary *zeitgeist* of the 1800s screams out at us from the page; too much of the subsequent progress of psychiatry sends beams backwards in time to illuminate this detail or that, and receives answering winks in reply. Most of all, the facts of James Tilly

Matthews' life before his admission to Bedlam make it clear that we are in a looking-glass version of a true story – a version not simply deranged but somehow artful, pointed, ironic, even playful. All this would be lost had Haslam not recorded it, but we must somehow bypass the author's intention to unlock its true meaning. It is a book that cannot simply be read: it demands to be hijacked.

The phrase that floats, like one of the Air Loom's brain-sayings, over Matthews' delusional world is "double agent". This is what the Air Loom made Matthews: a man operated at certain times by his own agency, at others by the gang who controlled the magnetic device. Modern psychiatric understanding of influencing machine delusions places them among the manifestions of 'passivity phenomena': the sense, associated with schizotypal disorders, that the subject is observing himself at one step removed, his own actions seemingly driven by forces over which he has no control. But Matthews was a literal double agent, too: a man whose confinement in Bedlam had been the last act in a drama of diplomacy and espionage that had already seen him incarcerated for several years in France as a counter-revolutionary spy.

James Tilly Matthews was a tea-broker, originally from Wales, who found himself, in London in the late 1780s and early 1790s, swept up in the movement for progressive political reform. He had accompanied his republican mentor David Williams on a visit to visit Paris in the winter of 1792. Williams, along with a handful of British republicans that included Tom Paine and Joseph Priestley, had been proclaimed a citizen of the new French republic, and had been invited by the revolutionary government to assist them in drafting a constitution. But the timing of their arrival was fraught: the trial of Louis XVI had begun, and France and Britain were edging towards war. Matthews, driven by a combination of ideological passion and political naivety, became a self-appointed peacemaker, undertaking secret diplomatic missions across the Channel to persuade both governments to abandon their sabre-rattling and forge an alliance.

Matthews may have been a novice at such cloak-and-dagger affairs, but he was persistent and ingenious. He drafted peace proposals and new constitutional arrangements, and presented them to the British Prime Minister William Pitt and the French Foreign Minister Jacques-Pierre Brissot. Even when the rush to war swept his initiatives aside, he refused to abandon his mission. He persisted with his peace proposals until he was arrested in Paris by the Committee of Public Safety in late 1793; he spent the next three years, throughout the height of the Terror, under house arrest and in prisons. Returning to Britain in 1796, he began a letter-writing campaign against the British government, attempting to hold them to account for abandoning him to the enemy and accusing them of increasingly far-fetched conspiracies. Receiving no reply, in December 1796 he interrupted a debate in the House of Commons to accuse the government minister Lord Liverpool of treason, as a result of which he was arrested and confined in Bedlam.

Here, perhaps, through the succession of traumas, arrests and confinements that came to swallow up Matthews' life, we can glimpse how the Air Loom might have made its entrance. The struggle between Matthews and the gang seems to have its origins in a struggle inside his own head. In his quest for peace on the brink of war, he found himself playing the role of British patriot and spy to Pitt and his government, and that of international republican – even, in his words, "true *sansculotte*" – to the French. As the two national agendas diverged into open hostility, so was the peacemaker torn in half. But the Air Loom offered an escape hatch for the double agent: a genuine double agency. Whichever persona he adopted, the troubling doppelganger who seemed to be fighting for the other side might be a puppet whose words and actions had been scripted and performed by covert magnetic workers. The Air Loom, whatever else it might have been, was perhaps a *deus ex machina*, a solution to the insoluble problem of the war that had consumed the world.

Indeed it seems from Haslam's account that, although Matthews located the Air Loom and its gang abroad in the wider world, their central locus was inside his head. It was here that they manipulated "puppets of uncouth shape, and of various descriptions" into obscene travesties of the waking world, simulating scenes and studying Matthews' reactions to them, enabling them to "glean his waking opinions on the mysteries which, during the night, have danced in his imagination". The gang, at their root here, were hobgoblins of the mind, night terrors, harbingers of the unconscious depths: they were frequently obscene, and Matthews believed they "lie together in promiscuous intercourse and filthy community" while their puppet-shows played on the screen of his unconscious mind. Those who have had similar experiences in the modern era have frequently described them by analogy with a private and internal cinema: movies flickering on the blank screen of their minds. In lucid states, they express amazement at the skill of the 'director', some part of their brain with which they have no conscious engagement that somehow sifts the lost archives and stitches what it finds into compelling narratives. The language of psychiatry echoes the same metaphor, describing the process as 'projection'.

Yet if the gang were ultimately malign munchkins in Matthews' head, they also reflected his real waking life and its adversities. They were, perhaps, all his tormentors conflated: the procession of secret police, political apparatchiks, magistrates, doctors, jailers, keepers and other functionaries of authority who kept him confined for what had by now become the majority of his adult life. The pretext for his confinement had shifted from political crimes to diagnoses of insanity, but the texture had remained constant: the gang became, for him, the über-tormentors, the puppet-masters behind the scenes of which the men in revolutionary uniforms or Bedlam's blue coats were merely the projected forms.

By the same token, the Air Loom itself reflects shards of the wider world, and Matthews' story offers hints about why the first influencing machine might have taken the shape that it did. The two technologies that combined to operate it, pneumatic chemistry and mesmerism, both carried a heavy freight of cultural and political meanings as symbols of the culture wars in which Matthews was deeply immersed.

Pneumatic chemistry – the chemistry of gases – was a new and potent field of science that was, in Britain, associated most prominently with one man: Joseph Priestley. Though remembered for his role in the discovery of soda water and oxygen, Priestley was a part time chemist better known in his day as a dissenting minister and political reformer. He saw no conflict between science and religion: both pointed in the same direction, towards political revolution. Nature was God's scripture; now that science was able to separate its elements and reconfigure them in new and powerful ways, the same process would revolutionise society. "The English hierarchy", he wrote in tones that would have resonated with Matthews, "has reason to tremble even at an air pump or an electrical machine".

As France and Britain headed towards war and the British establishment and public opinion lurched to the right, patriotic rhetoric flared into loyalist violence, and Priestley was an obvious target. On Bastille Day of 1791 he was forced to flee his laboratory as mobs under banners "For Church and King" set about destroying it, forcing him into exile in America. Across the Channel the other genius of pneumatic chemistry, Antoine Lavoisier, had suffered worse: he had been arrested in Paris in 1793, almost simultaneously with Matthews, and had been guillotined the same day.

Pneumatic chemistry embodied Matthews' hopes for the future, and the downfall of its heroes was linked with his own betrayal and persecution. Its appearance as the motive force of the Air Loom speaks of the war-torn world outside his Bedlam cell: one where the dream of its enlightened pioneers had been subverted by sinister forces bent on applying it not to progress but to destruction; where the pneumatic scientists' life-giving oxygen had been substituted with the foulest and most putrid substances imaginable; where the promised revolution had become a sightless, violent beast that had, in the famous phrase of the time, devoured its own children.

Matthews' personal connection to the other radical technology on which the Air Loom drew, animal magnetism or mesmerism, was closer still. This was the force that allowed the machine to torment and control the minds and bodies of its victims, and it had also had a turbulent journey through France's revolutionary adventure, with a trajectory that closely paralleled Matthews' own: from loyal ally to sacrificial victim.

Brought to Paris by Franz Anton Mesmer in 1778, its spectacles and miracle cures had rapidly made 'magnetism' a popular sensation. But when Mesmer's theories of magnetic fluids were rejected by the Academy in 1785 it had, like pneumatic chemistry, become a fellow-traveller with the revolutionary movement. Mesmer's protégé Nicholas Bergasse, an ardent revolutionist, had conflated his master's work with Jean-Jacques Rousseau's notion that primitive societies had been harmonious and self-regulating until modern institutions had disturbed their natural balance; thus, he maintained, despotic systems that ruled from above by the constant pressure of brute force always prevented a society from finding its true fluidic form. Only once such shackles were removed could society become whole once more, its equal but different components freed to maintain its natural, homeostatic harmony.

This theme was echoed by many of the early revolutionists, including Jean-Paul Marat, a bitter enemy of the Academy that had rejected his own scientific theories, and Matthews' future associate Jacques-Pierre Brissot, who was explicit about the rhetorical possibilities offered by the public fascination with magnetic fluids. "The time has now come for the revolution that France needs", Brissot argued, "but to attempt to produce one openly is to doom it to failure. To succeed it is necessary to wrap oneself in mystery; it is necessary to unite men under the pretext of experiments in physics but, in reality, for the overthrow of despotism". Mesmerism became a metaphor for invisible forces flowing

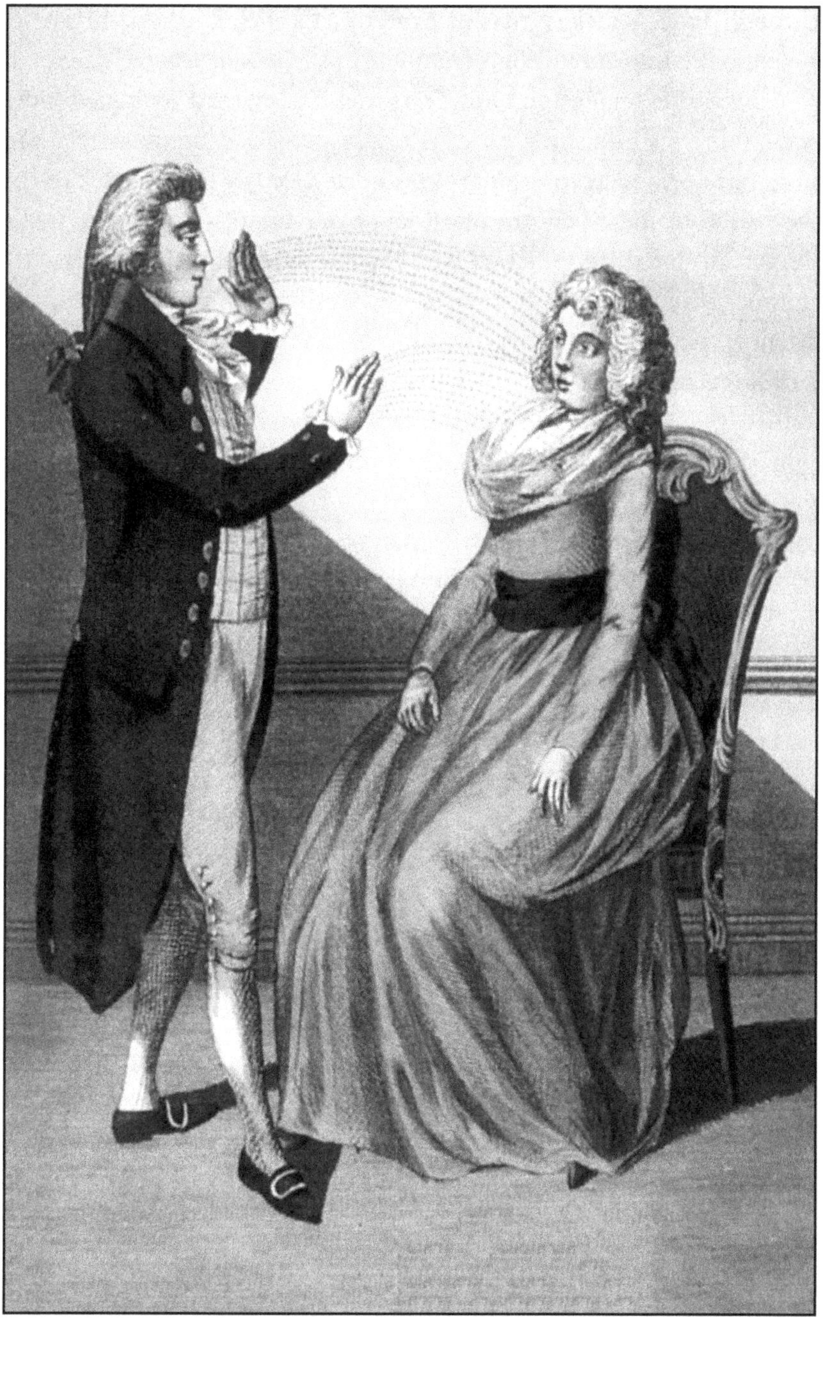

through French society that, if expertly channeled, could throw her body politic into convulsions from which she would emerge cured.

Come the revolution, however, mesmerism had switched sides once more. While some radicals had espoused it many others had not, and the new revolutionary orthodoxy swiftly coalesced into the view that, from its beginnings, it had been an aristocratic fad; as the Terror escalated, its practice had become punishable by death. Yet mesmerism remained a strange power, trailing behind it a mysterious science, transmitted covertly among an invisible underground. Although many leading mesmerists had become *emigrés*, there were skilled practitioners still in circulation who could demonstrate its powers under the cloak of occult drama that had so intoxicated the younger Brissot.

It was in this context that Matthews first encountered it personally, in circumstances transcribed by Haslam in *Illustrations of Madness*. In Pleissis prison outside Paris in 1795, a fellow inmate named Chavanay had asked him, "Mr. Matthews, are you acquainted with the art of talking with your brains?". When Matthews replied that he was not, Chavanay expanded mysteriously: "It is effected by means of the magnet". Matthews is silent as to whether Chavanay proceeded to mesmerise him, but it may be that the Air Loom was seeded by such an experience. For someone grappling with the confusing, overlaid identities within which Matthews was becoming lost, to find thoughts and feelings conjured up in his head by another, with no apparent input from his conscious mind, might have explained much. If it was possible for some people to control the minds of others, might that not account for the succession of disasters that had overtaken the world? Nobody had wanted war, and yet Europe was consumed by a war that seemed to have no end. The Revolution, so carefully conceived and courageously fought for, had been hijacked by a power that all seemed to fear but none could explain. Could the truth be that those apparently in power were, in fact, no longer the masters of their own will?

One of the most striking effects of being mesmerised is that the face that stares back at you from the mirror is no longer easily recognisable as your own. If Matthews was already becoming someone who could no longer easily recognise himself in the mirror, the experience might have given powerful external validation to this insight that the world had somehow become a strange shadowplay, its true face concealed from all but a few. By the time of his confinement in Bedlam, Matthews would have come to believe that his encounter with the mesmeric Chavanay was the point where he first became ensnared in the net of covert operators and magnetic spies who had become the puppetmasters of the world stage.

So we can locate the sources of the Air Loom both inside Matthews' head and in the convulsive events that had engulfed him, but there is a third and final place to look: within the walls of Bedlam itself. For here, too, there is a complex interplay between the delusional and the real, and one that suggests that the machine that was tormenting Matthews and the institution in which he was being confined were, when viewed from certain angles, one and the same. Before his confinement, his surviving writings are rich in bizarre plots and conspiracies, but the overarching frame of the Air Loom was yet to emerge: it was Bedlam that gave it shape. The London cellar from which he claimed that the gang operated was next to Bedlam; another gang, he added, plied their trade next to its rival asylum, St.Luke's. The Air Loom's subterranean, dungeon-like surroundings mirror Bedlam's damp and rotting basement, and the power-relations between the gang and their victim suggest a topsy-turvy version of the hospital and its staff: one where, as the gang frequently gloat in Matthews' dreams, Bedlam's true purpose is not to treat or cure him but to perpetuate his madness.

Among the looking-glass reflections that play between the Air Loom and Bedlam is the symmetry between mesmerism and psychiatry itself. Is the psychiatrist, in fact, so different from the magnetist? Both claim mysterious influence over their subjects on the basis of disputed scientific underpinnings; both generate stories of miracle cures and abuse of authority in roughly equal measure. This was a symmetry that had been observed since mesmerism first emerged, and one that had come to public attention during the madness of George III. In his famous treatment (and apparent cure) of the King, the Rev. Dr. Willis had made much of his use of 'the eye' in controlling the mad, claiming that there was not a lunatic alive whom he could not stare into submission by the peculiar force of his gaze. During a House of Commons committee hearing into his treatment of the King, the politician Edmund Burke had queried Willis' wisdom in allowing his Majesty to shave with a straight razor. What if "the Royal patient had become outrageous"?

"Place the candles between us, Mr Burke", Willis replied ominously, "and I'll give you an answer. There, sir by the EYE! I should have looked at him *thus*, sir – *thus*!"

Burke cowered before the doctor's "basiliskian authority", unable to hold his gaze, and the cross-examination was over. Here, mad-doctoring and mesmerism are virtually the same art: doctor and patient are barely distinguishable from the gang and their victim, the former exercising irresistable powers of coercion over the latter. Haslam himself was sceptical of 'the eye', but not of the need for patients to abandon their own will entirely to that of the doctor. The Air Loom's irresistable power, the senior functionary taking notes while his minions scurry around in the gloom, poking and prodding at their subject while cracking obscene jokes with one another, surely bear the imprint of Matthews' years under Haslam's care.

And if we were to follow this idea to its limits, might we not conclude that the Air Loom was ultimately not just Matthews' creation, but Haslam's too? Haslam was ambitious to become a specialist mad-doctor, and thus had a profound and personal – if unconscious – need to manifest appropriate specimens of madness. Matthews remained a peacemaker – the accounts of Bethlem staff stress that he was always striving to resolve conflicts – but Haslam, by insisting on imposing his will on his patients, made such resolutions impossible. The Air Loom, perhaps, was not merely the product of Matthews' unconscious mind, but of Haslam's too: forced into existence to satisfy the doctor's unacknowledged needs and desires. Matthews recorded that the gang frequently referred to him as their 'talisman', the key to their plan of world domination; but Matthews was equally Haslam's talisman, the doctor's secret weapon in his own grand schemes.

With or without such radical interpretations of authorship, *Illustrations of Madness* must nevertheless be regarded not simply as a doctor's psychiatric report on his patient but a genuine collaboration between the two men.

Matthews and Haslam were tireless antagonists throughout the years, each ready at any moment to denounce the other as raving lunatic or sadistic fraud. While Haslam was taking notes on his patient, Matthews was simultaneously taking notes on his doctor, and his lengthy accusations of ill-treatment would eventually see Haslam dismissed from his post and professionally disgraced. Yet Haslam commissioned the image of the Air Loom from Matthews, and Matthews was happy to oblige; Matthews read the finished manuscript, which included large sections in his own hand, and approved the final text. Haslam made a point of declaring that "these opinions have been collected from the patient…where inverted commas are used, the manuscript of Mr. Matthews has been faithfully copied; and that for thus introducing his philosophic opinions to the notice of a discerning public, he feels 'contented and grateful'." There is no reason to disbelieve Haslam on this – indeed, it was important to his claims of skilled observation that the patient should recognise the account that the doctor gave of him.

Rarely can a collaboration have taken place between two authors with such different intents. Haslam preserved the Air Loom for posterity to buttress his claims to psychiatric authority; Matthews contributed in order to warn the world of the dark forces that had already achieved the ultimate *coup d'état*, one that had taken control of the world in such a way that only one person had noticed. But two centuries later, the Air Loom has become something that neither of its authors could have guessed at: not the solipsistic ravings of a forgotten lunatic, but the first appearance of a myth of the modern age. The machine that controls the mind has emerged from its obscure corner of psychiatry to mesmerise the broader culture, its image now endlessly amplified and recycled through the mass media and the Hollywood dream machine. The Air Loom is a creature of the imagination that has become ever more recognisable as telephone, television and computer have colonised the texture of our reality, creating a world where rays, ethers, beams and particles assail us constantly, powering inscrutable machines that project shadow worlds into our minds from unseen basements and cellars, stimulating our senses and manipulating our thoughts.

In 1810, the Air Loom was real – but only to James Tilly Matthews. Now, perhaps, it is beginning to come into focus for the rest of us.

Mike Jay's book on James Tilly Matthews is *The Influencing Machine* (published in the US as *A Visionary Madness*). His latest book is *Mescaline: a global history of the first psychedelic.*

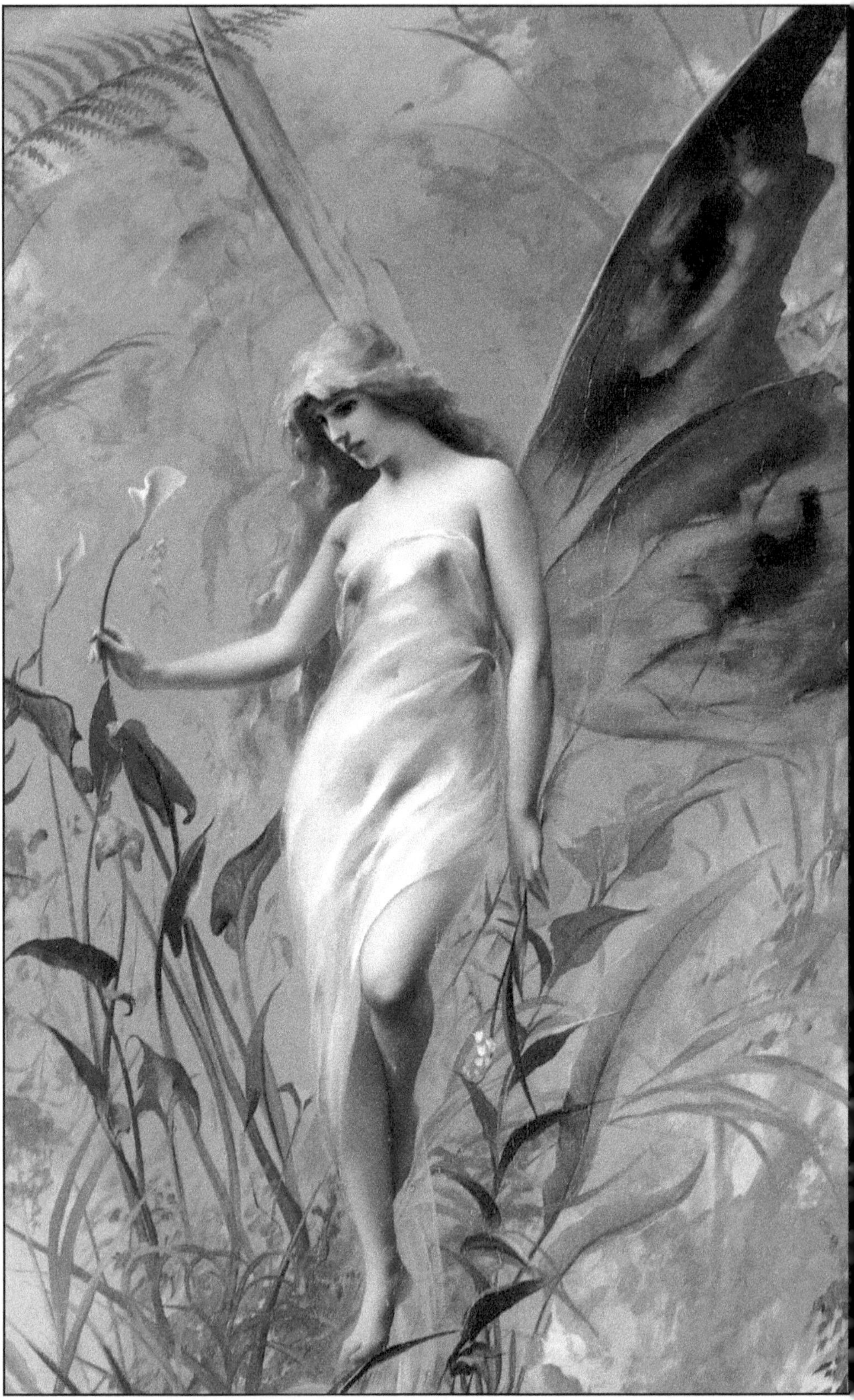

Some Faerie Metaphysics

An Ontological Investigation into Otherworldly Entities

by *Neil Rushton*

What are the faeries? Where do they come from and where do they go when they're not interacting with their human observers? Faeries have been an important part of the folkloric repertoire for hundreds (perhaps even thousands) of years, and while they are portrayed in the popular imagination through faerietales and have become Disneyfied through the 20th century, their main presence is in the myriad folktales and anecdotes from every part of the globe. They usually (though not always) take a humanoid form, and interact with human societies as ambivalent supernatural entities, appearing in our world to both co-operate with people and as general arbiters of mischief, while also living in their own Otherworld, sometimes accessible to humans either through accident or abduction. While the phenomenon is ancient, the belief in these metaphysical beings continues, and there are thousands of encounter reports from all over the world every year, as demonstrated by the recent survey by The Fairy Investigation Society, which includes around 500 testimonies.

But folklorists are usually ambivalent about the faeries; they are likely to keep their distance from them, so to speak. While happy to record and discuss the beliefs of people who tell stories and anecdotes about them, most folklorists speak the language (at least in official publications) of the reductionist, materialist worldview that has held sway in Western civilisation for the last few hundred years, and they'll often be reticent about assessing the potential actual reality of metaphysical beings. In the materialist's world, faeries simply cannot exist. They must be reduced into a categorised cultural belief system, and any discussion of them will usually be couched in the accepted language of scientific rationalism. This creates a problem for any folklorist (or anybody else) who wants to look behind the stories and investigate the possibility that the faeries can be incorporated into our consensus reality as a genuine phenomenon.

But the reductionist scientific orthodoxy has been challenged recently by a range of philosophical hypotheses such as Idealism, backed up by quantum mechanical theory and experiment, which reinstates consciousness (not matter) as the primary mover and creator of reality. When this is done, entities such as faeries are allowed back into the universe as an authentic phenomenon, and if we start to look in the right places, we begin to find that they are indeed everywhere…we just need to know where to look, or perhaps more accurately, how to look.

The Electromagnetic Spectrum, Dark Matter and Dark Energy

Our normal waking consciousness experiences less than 0.5% of the entire electromagnetic spectrum, with visible light being less than 0.1% of this. If we take into account the current

Some Faerie Metaphysics

(mainstream) scientific hypothesis that this electromagnetic spectrum itself composes less than 8% of the universe, with the mysterious Dark Matter and Dark Energy taking up the rest, then we are at a good starting point to understand that our version of reality is extremely compromised. We may have the technology to utilise the unseen wavelengths in the spectrum, but they are not accessible to our ordinary consciousness, whilst Dark Matter and Dark Energy are totally inaccessible to our technology, and remain for the moment, nothing more than theory based on the by-product of mathematical equations. We also have to take into account the recent theoretical mind-bender that the universe may actually be a virtual reality hologram, put in place by (depending on who you listen to) a supreme being, aliens or future versions of humans, the latter option coming from NASA scientist Dr Rich Terrile. With this level of uncertainty about the reality we inhabit, and in order to gain an understanding of the world in which we live (and the unseen entities that may exist alongside us), we might be advised to fall back on the only known certainty allowed us: consciousness.

The Origins of the Faeries in Altered States of Consciousness

Our earliest known artistic portrayals of the world, and how human consciousness interacted with it, come in the form of cave paintings from all parts of the globe, starting *c.*35,000 BCE. Many of these cave paintings include humanoids and therianthropes, otherworldly entities that have been recorded alongside geometric imagery, stylised animals and landscapes. They are in effect our earliest known folklore. But what state of mind were our Palaeolithic ancestors in when they were painting these strange entities in often difficult-to-access caves and shelters?

The anthropologist David Lewis-Williams has made the convincing argument that these cave and rock-shelter paintings were produced by shamanic cultures to represent reality as perceived in an altered state of consciousness. Twenty years ago this idea was anathema to anthropologists, but since the work of Lewis-Williams, and many others, the theory has tipped over to become an accepted orthodoxy. There are hundreds of motifs in the cave paintings that correlate with the visionary states of people in an altered state of consciousness, brought about most especially by the ingestion of a psychotropic substance. The basic premise is that the shamans of these Palaeolithic cultures transported themselves into altered states of consciousness and then painted the results of their experiences on the walls of caves and rock shelters – experiences that frequently included therianthropic beings and supernatural humanoids that correlate in many ways with later faerie types.

In his 2005 book *Supernatural*, Graham Hancock vividly utilises Lewis-Williams' work to discuss the continuity through time of entities experienced in altered states of consciousness, coming to the conclusion

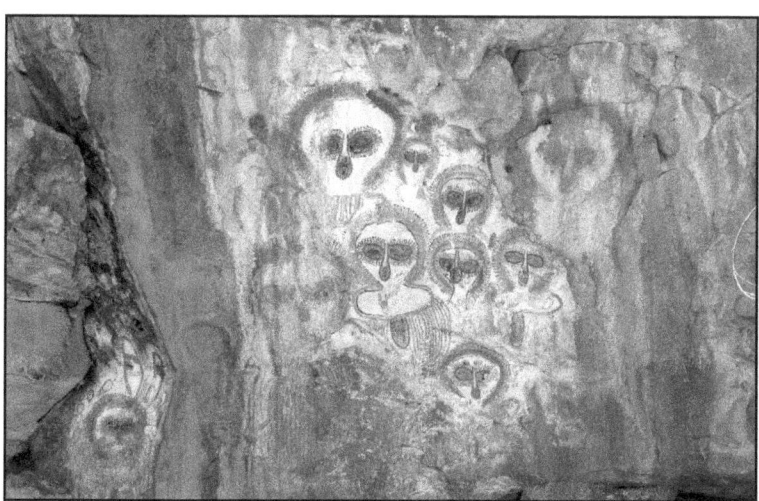

'Wandjina' rock art, Barnett River in Australia
(courtesy Graeme Churchard, Creative Commons licence)

that the faeries of our historic period are one and the same as those portrayed in prehistoric caves. And writers such as Carlo Ginzburg and Emma Wilby have argued that there is a direct link between prehistoric shamanic storytelling and the folklore embodied in classical, medieval and later periods that often incorporate entities such as nymphs and faeries; supernatural beings that interact with humanity when the conditions are right. Those conditions may well be reliant on the human participants undergoing an altered state of consciousness as a result of the ingestion of psychotropic compounds. There is certainly a preponderance of mushroom imagery associated with historic depictions of faeries, most especially the highly psychedelic red and white *Amanita muscaria* (fly agaric) mushroom, and the psilocybin mushroom, both prevalent in Europe and Asia. If these historic folkloric manifestations of interactions with supernatural entities can be linked to the cave art of prehistory and preliterate societies, then we have a continuation of relationship with an alternative reality, accessed through altered states of consciousness, over a very long period of time.

Many of the European faerie motifs repeated in stories and anecdotes through the centuries to the present day were already in place

during the medieval period. When folklorists began to collect these stories in earnest from the 19th century onwards, they found a belief in faeries amongst rural populations that was probably very close to the medieval belief and understanding of what faeries were and how they interacted with humanity. Many of the stories include situations where the protagonist interacts with the faeries in what seems an altered state of consciousness: Faerieland doesn't comply to Newtonian physics, it is consistently inhabited by strange humanoids and therianthropes (the faeries), and there are lots of recurring story motifs that are highly suggestive of an autonomous reality being described. But this is not consensus reality, this is the folklore recording stories from people operating outside consensus reality. The folktales about faeries have been overlain with much allegorical storytelling, but at their root the realities they describe are of people in altered states of consciousness, perhaps not too far from the realities experienced by the Palaeolithic cave painters and shamanic practitioners.

W. Y. Evans-Wentz, Rudolph Steiner and Metaphysical Nature Spirits

When the folklorist W. Y. Evans-Wentz travelled around the Celtic world at the beginning of the 20th century, collecting stories and anecdotal experiences about the faeries, it was clear that most of his interviewees rated clairvoyance as the best way of altering the conscious state to a position where it could interact with the faeries. Seership or second-sight was the method of entering – or at least viewing – an alternative reality inhabited by a relatively consistent cast of characters, usually recognised as the faeries. He met one such (un-named) Irish clairvoyant in Rosses Point, County Sligo. This seer talked about various types of faeries that inhabited the landscape of Sligo, "making them sound like a cross between nature spirits and mystical visions." But Evans-Wentz was just as interested in the mechanics of interacting with the faeries as he was with the stories themselves. How did the seer interface with them?

> I have always made a distinction between pictures seen in the memory of nature and visions of actual beings now existing in the inner world. We can make the same distinction in our world: I may close my eyes and see you as a vivid picture in memory, or I may look at you with my physical eyes and see your actual image. In seeing these beings of which I speak, the physical eyes may be open or closed: mystical beings in their own world and nature are never seen with the physical eyes."

The rural people interviewed by Evans-Wentz consistently affirmed that clairvoyant alteration of consciousness was the best sure-fire way to see the faeries. By the time Evans-Wentz visited these communities, there was a sense that the number of people gifted with second-sight was dwindling, cutting down on communication with the faeries. But at the same time as these rural communities were feeling the increasing pressures of modernism there was a reaction by organisations such as the Theosophical Society (first founded in 1875), which attempted to incorporate metaphysics into an understanding of reality. And their prime metaphysical technology was clairvoyance. The Austrian Theosophist Rudolf Steiner attempted to explain the mechanics of clairvoyance, when a person must transform their usually passive thought forms into something more dynamic. In normal consciousness, thoughts:

> …allow themselves to be connected and separated, to be formed and then dismissed. This life of thought must develop in the elemental world a step further. There a person is not in a position to deal with thoughts that are passive. If someone really succeeds in entering the world with his clairvoyant soul, it seems as though his thoughts were not things over which he has any command; they

are living beings… You thrust your consciousness into a place, it seems, where you do not find thoughts that are like those in the physical world, but where they are living beings. (Rudolf Steiner, *Perception of the Elemental World*, 1913).

Steiner described the specific elemental animating forces at work in the natural world, when perceived clairvoyantly, in what he calls the 'Supersensible World'. For Steiner the elementals in the Supersensible World existed as a range of beings, from devas, which are responsible for entire autonomous landscapes, through to the smaller nature spirits charged with the growth of vegetation. Steiner (basing his epistemology on that originally developed by the 15th-century alchemist Paracelsus) divides these entities into four main types corresponding to earth (Gnomic), water (Undines), air (Sylphs) and heat/light (Salamanders). This is the faerie realm, existing as a non-material autonomous reality that crosses over with ours, and which can be accessed via a clairvoyant altered state of consciousness. Steiner thought everyone has this innate ability, but they had to be taught how to use it…it had somehow become almost forgotten amongst humanity.

This idea finds common ground with the recent work of biochemist Rupert Sheldrake, who proposes that morphogenetic fields are the formative causation allowing life on earth. Sheldrake's description of this organising principle behind the natural world is issued in the language of biochemistry, but in effect, what he postulates is the same as Steiner's vision of nature spirits in action. There are invisible forces that are as essential in ordering life on earth as accepted non-material forces such as gravity. Sheldrake calls these morphogenetic fields "the memory of nature". In effect, Steiner saw nature spirits as anthropogenic representations of these morphogenetic fields, imposed upon them through the thought forms of the observer, who perceives them clairvoyantly.

The Faeries and DMT

But what allows this access to otherworldly realms and the entities that seem to exist there? What allows for clairvoyance, or second-sight? The answer may lie with the substance called N, N-Dimethyltryptamine – DMT. This molecule is one of the main active ingredients in the ayahuasca brew used by Amazonian shamans, but it is also produced endogenously in everyone's brain, potentially (but not definitely) in the pineal gland. It's usually safely dispersed around the brain and body for functional duties, but it seems that under certain circumstances, it can be released in higher quantities, causing an altered state of consciousness. This would require the DMT to be released in conjunction with Monoamine Oxidase Inhibitors (MAOI), which inhibit naturally occurring enzymes in the human body. This inhibition leads to increased levels of chemicals such as the neurotransmitters serotonin and dopamine. By slowing their metabolism, MAOIs can allow a surge of DMT production to have full effect and create radically transformed states of consciousness.

There is some evidence that this can happen during a frontal lobe epileptic seizure. This may be the root of the well-documented 17th-century Cornish story of Anne Jefferies' abduction by diminutive faeries when she suffered a 'convulsion fit' and was transported (at least in her mind) to a numinous world inhabited by the faeries. The author Eve LaPlante has used historic and contemporary examples to demonstrate that Temporal Lobe Epilepsy can provide access to an altered state of consciousness where the human mind participates in a reality several steps removed from the consensus material world. This often includes full immersion in alternative landscapes and contact with non-human intelligence.

The late and great Terence McKenna was an enthusiastic user of the synthesised form of DMT to access different realities, and coined the term 'self-transforming machine elves' for the creatures he regularly found there. As if to confirm Terence's assertions, a research study conducted between 1990 and 1995 in the General Clinical Research Center of the University of New Mexico Hospital by Dr Rick Strassman found that volunteers on the study injected with varying amounts of DMT underwent profound alterations of consciousness. This involved immediate cessation of normal consciousness, and transportation to a different realm of reality with divergent physical properties, inhabited by a range of creatures described as elves, faeries, lizards, reptiles, insects, aliens, clowns (yes, clowns) and various therianthropic entities. One woman even describes a pulsating entity that she called 'Tinkerbell-like'. The experiences, especially at higher doses, represented to the participants a parallel reality that was 'super real': not an hallucination, not a dream, but a substantial built reality with full sensory interaction + telepathy.

The experience reports from the study are irrational, absurd, frightening, illogical and surreal. There is no question of any of the volunteers physically leaving the hospital bed during their experiences, but for all of them (without exception) the DMT-world was every bit as real as the one their minds left behind. After the injections participants frequently talked about 'blasting through' or 'breaking through a barrier' after which they found themselves in a realm with its own laws of physical space and movement, and its own inhabitants.

There are dozens of recorded experiences from the study, and the participants all engaged in a non-physical reality directly with their consciousness, seemingly separated from their physical selves. Some of the experiences agree in type to certain aspects of the faerie phenomenon. But what the research demonstrates is that under the right conditions, human consciousness can operate within a distinct and separate universe inhabited by a range of apparently autonomous entities. These entities may be one and the same as the metaphysical beings recorded in prehistoric cave art and historic folklore, by people who were describing the beings encountered during various types of altered states of consciousness, brought on either actively or passively. The faeries may change superficially through time, adapting to the expectations of the culture they are part of, but if it is human consciousness they are interacting with, this is no surprise. Underneath the cultural masks, the faeries begin to reveal their true selves.

Materialism vs Consciousness

There are many reasons why folklore about the faeries exists, and it certainly seems that interacting with them during an altered state of consciousness is one of them. Are they real experiences? They are subjectively real, but what is the objective reality? A Theosophist clairvoyant would suggest that we need to override our five senses with a dynamic type of consciousness that commands prominence over the material world. They would probably agree with Aldous Huxley's description of a universal consciousness being 'Mind at Large' and that the brain is a 'reducing valve transceiver', that can be retuned by a variety of methods. Huxley did this with mescaline (and later LSD), describing the experiences in his 1954 book *The Doors of Perception*.

The brain certainly gives us a very limited view of what is actually going on around us. Altering the transmission to the brain seems to allow non-material consciousness more of a free rein. As in a dream, an altered consciousness is able to construct metaphysical realities. It is able to communicate with the entities it finds there, and bring back a report. The relative consistency of the inhabitants of this alternative reality may suggest that they live there all the time, non-physical, and are only able to interact with our physical world when conditions are right for an individual's consciousness. This is the crux: does consciousness create physical reality, or is consciousness an epiphenomenon of the brain? If the former, then the realities experienced in altered states of consciousness can be accepted as true, with their own autonomous existence. If the latter, then while entities such as the faeries may be subjectively real, they do not exist objectively within the electromagnetic spectrum. This is the materialist/physicalist view. Although even physicalism has to adhere to its own rules and allow for the hypothesis that over 90% of the universe consists of non-physical form: Dark Matter and Dark Energy. Maybe that's where the faeries are, waiting to be found.

Faeries and Aliens

But the ontological reality of faeries (in whatever form) has in recent decades become linked to other 'paranormal' activity types, primary of which is the intrusion into our consensus reality of entities usually known as aliens. The first person to suggest a definitive link between the the reports of faerie experiences and alien encounters was the astronomer and computer scientist Jacques Vallée. In his 1969 book

Passport to Magonia he put forward the theory that the faeries were one and the same as the alien beings who had been purportedly abducting people around the world for a couple of decades by that date. His hypothesis is that there is a commonality to the experiences reported in alien abduction scenarios, and the reports of interactions with faeries in folklore. He suggests the aliens and the faeries are essentially the same phenomenon, tuned through the cultural receptors of the time and then interpreted accordingly. He makes special reference to the regular motifs in faerie-tales of the abduction, by various means, of humans by faeries. There's a lot of data here – it's the most common motif in faerie folklore, and continues to be reported in anecdotal testimonies. For a variety of reasons humans are taken to an alternative faerie reality, either as midwives or nurses for faerie children, as servants to the faeries, for sex, as punishment or reward, or just because the faeries feel like it. These motifs, of course, coincide with many aspects of the consistently strange phenomenon of alien abductions, reports of which have grown at an exponential rate since the early 1950s. Vallée uses a range of evidence to tie-up faerie abductions from folklore and alien abductions from modern reports, and goes as far to state:

> … the modern, global belief in flying saucers and their occupants is identical to an earlier belief in the fairy-faith. The entities described as the pilots of the craft are indistinguishable from the elves, sylphs and lutins of the Middle Ages. Through the observations of unidentified flying objects, we are concerned with an agency our ancestors knew well and regarded with terror: we are prying into the affairs of The Secret Commonwealth.

The Secret Commonwealth was the term coined for the faeries by the Reverend Robert Kirk in a manuscript of 1691, which includes a detailed description of their appearance, habits and exploits, gleaned from both his own experiences and those Scottish Highlanders purporting to have second-sight, or clairvoyance. As Vallée points out, Kirk's descriptions of the faeries and their modus operandi bear more than a passing resemblance to the alien visitors of the 20th and 21st centuries.

Among their attributes was an ability to float through the air with insubstantial and fluid bodies, that they could make appear and disappear at will. This allowed them to 'swim' through the air and carry off mortals, usually to large circular abodes, that Kirk presumed were underground, and which were lit by a dim, unknown illumination. They even had 'ætheriall vehicles' to carry them around the sky. Kirk also asserted that the faeries had a nature intermediate between humans and angels. Their habit of abducting humans was usually for the purpose of wet-nursing faerie children or as midwives; a theme that fits in with the deluge of recent alien abduction reports (subsequent to Vallée's investigations in 1969) that would suggest one of the main reasons for abduction is to obtain both parents and wet-nurses for hybrid human-alien offspring. Vallée quotes the 19th-century folklorist Edwin Hartland's suggestion that such a programme of hybridisation was a primary reason for faerie abductions:

> The motive assigned to fairies in northern stories is that of preserving and improving their race, on the one hand by carrying off human children to be brought up among the elves and to become united with them, and on the other hand by obtaining the milk and fostering care of human mothers for their own offspring.

In 2005, Graham Hancock followed Vallee's lead and took the comparison of faerie and alien abduction much further in his book

Supernatural (after dealing with the elements of prehistoric shamanic cave-painting depictions of entities, discussed above). He compiled a range of faerie abduction reports from various time periods and geographical locations and set them against modern-day alien abduction events. He pays special attention to the faerie abduction of young women, such as Mrs Sheridan, an Irish woman, who seems to have spent much of the last decade of the 19th century being whisked off by the fairies for wet-nursing duties:

> Where they brought me I don't know, or how I got there, but I'd be in a very big house, and it was round, the walls far away that you'd hardly see them, and a great many faeries all about... but they wouldn't speak to me nor I to them.

These 'long-faced' faeries had a definite purpose for kidnapping her and weren't too concerned with her tearful appeals to release her – she had a job to do, and that was feeding their faerie babies. The correlation between these types of folkloric encounters and the alien abductions of women is striking. Hancock surveys the work of the late Harvard psychiatrist John Mack and the cultural historian David Jacobs, who have made extensive studies of people who claim to have been abducted by aliens, often using hypnotic techniques to extract memories from amnesic events. It's a minefield subject (mostly due to the vagaries of extracting memories from hypnosis), but John Mack in particular was a convincing advocate of the notion that whatever the experiences represent, they are genuinely real to the participant. The abductee, after being floated or beamed aboard the UFO is taken to a part of the ship where there seem to be drawers or tanks of hybrid alien-human babies, which they are expected to nurse. There is a consistency to these experiences (there are tens of thousands of them) that provides a dataset of testimony that Mack and Jacobs insist must be taken seriously as a phenomenon. For the abductees, the experience is often highly traumatic (Mack states that the best psychiatric diagnosis for many abductees is post-traumatic stress disorder), and no wonder, when they are confronted with alien hybrids often described as more like foetuses than babies. One abductee described to Mack their appearance, which is fairly typical:

> Their bodies were short for their heads. Their heads seemed oversized. They had very blue eyes. They had very thin, wispy hair… I would say they were probably three and a half feet tall, but they all looked the same age. 'You're our mother and we need you,' they said.

The evidence presented by Jacques Vallée and Graham Hancock makes a convincing argument for the tight relation between faerie abductions in folklore and alien abductions in the 20th/21st century. It is a relationship that has been skilfully investigated by Joshua Cutchin in his 2018 book *Thieves in the Night: A Brief History of Supernatural Child Abductions,* where he uses a wide range of folkloric, historic and modern testimony data to investigate child abductions by supernatural entities, coming to the conclusion that:

> The parallels between aliens and faeries are remarkable and extend deeply into the lore surrounding paranormal child abduction. The means and motivations behind both phenomena imply a shared ontological reality…

The experiences are culturally coded to time and place, but the correlations and similarities are intriguing, and suggest the possibility of a common source for the phenomena. But what is that source? Is it purely a metaphysical attribute interacting at the non-material level of consciousness, or is there a physical dimension? Perhaps more importantly, can we make the differentiation between consciousness and material reality?

Ontological Faeries

This brings us back to the ontology of faerie experiences; what are these entities that have been a part of human esperience for thousands of years, and where do they come from? They may be adapting to cultural codes, even evolving into new forms, but at what level of reality do they exist?

An answer may be to utilise David Luke's three-part interpretation for metaphysical entity contact. He used it to assess a study into the otherworldly beings (many of which had faerie-attributes) encountered by people who had altered their states of consciousness with DMT, but it is also a valid tool to evaluate what may be happening to anyone who reports a numinous experience that includes interaction with non-ordinary entities such as the faeries:

1. *They are hallucinations. The entities are subjective hallucinations.* Such a position is favoured by those taking a purely (materialist-reductionist) neuropsychological approach to the phenomena.
2. *They are psychological / transpersonal manifestations.* The communicating entities appear alien but are actually unfamiliar aspects of ourselves, be they our reptilian brain or our cells, molecules or sub-atomic particles.
3. *The entities exist in otherworlds and can interact with our physical reality.* A numinous experience provides access to a true alternate dimension inhabited by independently existing intelligent entities in a stand-alone reality, which exists co-laterally with ours, and may interact with our world when certain conditions are met. The identity of the entities remains speculative.

Of course, all three interpretations may be true at different times and under various circumstances. From a materialist-reductionist standpoint, all faerie experiences could be reduced to hallucinatory events. There is no physical residue as an after-effect of the interactions, and the reports are all limited to visual and audio experiences. While the specific adjuncts allowing for the hallucinations to take place cannot be properly analysed, seeing them all as aberrations of visual and audial fields remains one legitimate interpretation.

This explanatory model is reliant on the theory that consciousness is an epiphenomenon of the brain. The implication is that the brain, for whatever reason, is simply misconstruing sensory input from a physical world where things like faeries simply do not exist. This is the hard-and-fast materialist-reductionist standpoint, which is deeply embedded in Western culture. But, as discussed above, it is a standpoint that is now challenged at a fundamental level not only by religious and mystical traditions, but also by the recently reinvented philosophy of Kantian Idealism and by a growing number of quantum physicists, who (using a wide range of methodologies) suggest that the brain is a reducer of consciousness, not a creator of it. This model sees consciousness (not matter) as primary; it is everywhere and it is everything, and individual human (and animal) brains are merely conveying it within the remit of what then becomes physical reality. For the most part, this physical reality has a closely defined rule-set, but under certain conditions the usual laws break down and metaphysical events can occur. These supernatural occurrences are thus as legitimate as any natural occurrence. The philosopher Jeffrey Kripal describes this in relation to traumatic episodes that cause apparently non-ordinary experiences in his 2017 book written with Whitley Strieber, *The Super Natural: Why the Unexplained is Real*:

> The body-brain crafts consciousness into a human form through a vast network of highly evolved biology, neurology, culture, language, family, and social interactions until a more or less stable ego or 'I' emerges, rather like the way the software and hardware of your laptop can pick up a Wi-Fi signal and translate the Internet into the specificities of your screen and social media. The analogy is a rough

and imperfect one, but it gets the basic point across. Sometimes, however, the reducer is compromised or temporarily suppressed. The filtering or reduction of consciousness does not quite work, and other forms of mind or dimensions of consciousness, perhaps even other species or forms of life, that are normally shut out now 'pop in.' In extreme cases, it may seem that the cosmos itself has suddenly come alive and is all there. Perhaps it is.

While most faerie encounters are not the result of trauma, this helps us to perhaps understand preternatural faerie experiences as something metaphysical being allowed to 'pop in' from either a greater, transcendent form of consciousness, or from an alternative reality to which humans do not usually have access. This would fit with either of David Luke's second and third interpretations for supernatural entity contact. Simply put, a numinous zone has been entered and the participant is able to make contact with what usually resides external to their ordinary consciousness.

Experiences in numinous zones could be extended to a variety of preternatural encounters, from ghost apparitions through to Near Death Experiences and UFO abduction scenarios, but it would seem that the faeries, as an ontological taxonomic, remain a consistent, even persistent, form of entity that interact with our consensus reality. While reports of the faeries from history have often been turned into folkloric stories (frequently with a moral lesson inserted into the plot line), modern encounters usually take the form of anecdotal testimony. But the phenomenological types of faeries retain an adherence to their folkloric roots. They can receive an updated appearance, and cultural coding, but they remain recognisable as faeries. Graham Hancock has summed up what may be happening if we allow the faeries some type of metaphysical reality:

> If we are prepared to set aside the automatic scepticism and reductionism of our age, and if we spell out the problem in plain

language, then we find that we are contemplating the existence of highly intelligent discarnate entities belonging to an order of creation fundamentally different than our own…it really is almost as though the beings we are dealing with have been changing and developing alongside us for thousands of years, and that they therefore cannot simply be mass delusions, but must have a definite, independent reality outside the human brain.

Whatever their true nature, it seems that for the faeries to make contact with humanity they require our consciousness to become loosened from the usual restraints, and to enter a numinous zone. If the model of reality affirmed by Idealism is correct, then this zone may be allowing us to access a greater Over-Mind, where exist entities that represent either a stand-alone autonomous class of their own, or perhaps aspects of the human collective consciousness (as explicated by Carl Jung), which is usually filtered out through the reducing valve of the brain. Either way, it appears that the faeries are here to stay, functioning in some nebulous region where any interpretation of them is reliant on us finding a way to incorporate consciousness into physical reality. This is something that has eluded both philosophers and scientists for millennia, and so perhaps it is no surprise that the faeries – whether nature spirits, inter-dimensional beings, aliens, or products of our collective imagination – for the moment, remain an intangible part of our cultural zeitgeist.

Neil Rushton writes for a range of online sites and offline magazines, mostly on the subjects of folklore and archaeology. He had his first novel, *Set the Controls for the Heart of the Sun*, published in 2016. His website is https://deadbutdreaming.wordpress.com.

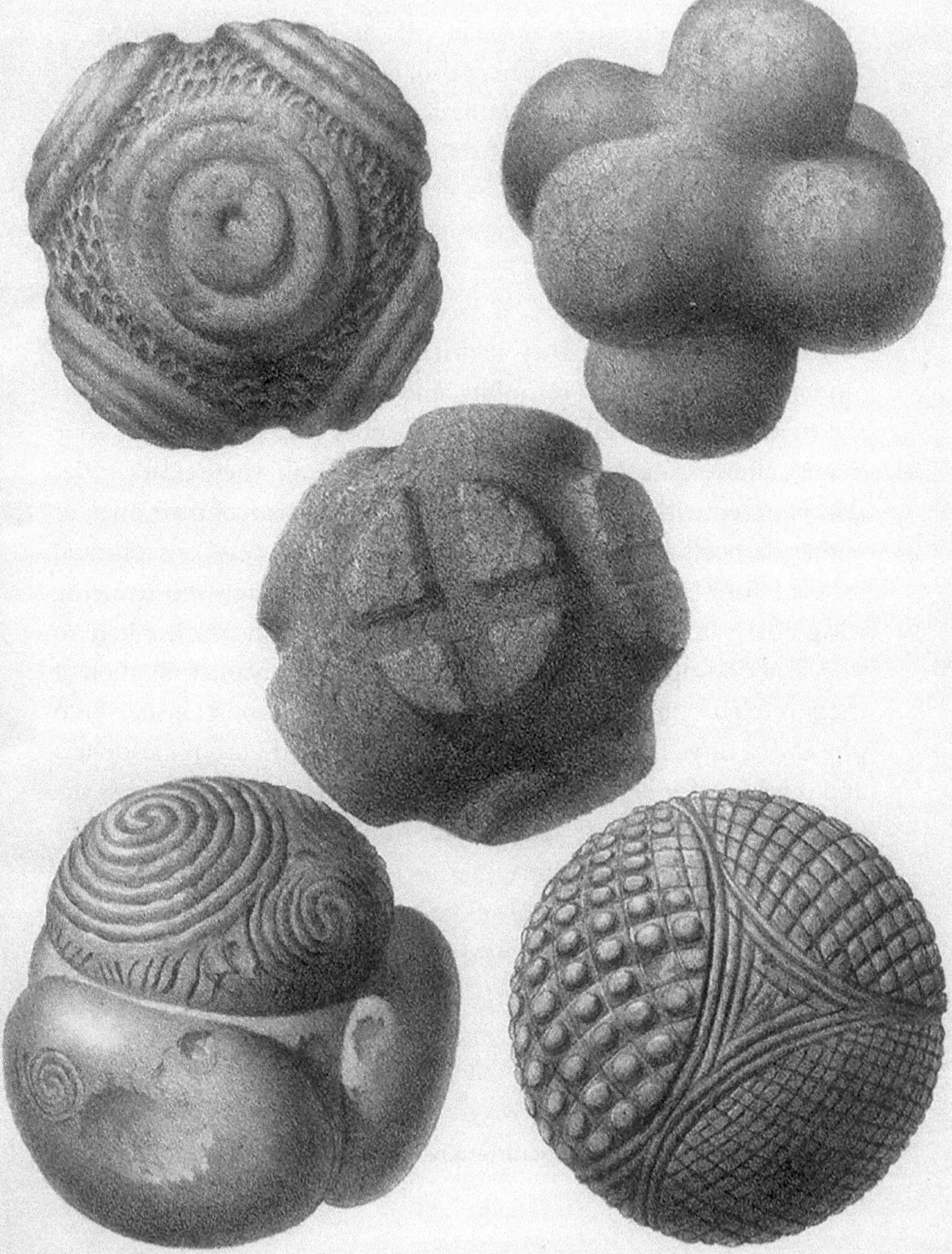

THE CARVED STONE BALLS OF SCOTLAND

WHO MADE THEM, AND WHY?

by *Jeff Nisbet*

Only about 400 of Scotland's 4,000-year-old carved stone balls have been found. They are of fairly uniform size, with the diameters of most measuring around 2.75 inches. Fitting nicely within the cupped hand, they are made from a variety of stone – from soft sandstones to hard granitics. The numbers of projections or knobs range from between three and 160, with six knobs being by far the most common. They display varying degrees of workmanship. A few, like the remarkable Towie Stone, display beautifully intricate carvings, while others are unadorned. All but five of the stones have been found in Scotland, with the majority discovered in the Aberdeenshire area.

Along with its vitrified forts and Loch Ness Monster, these carved stone balls take their place as one of Scotland's most enduring mysteries, and never fail to excite the inquisitive mind. Although many theories have been presented, no one is sure who made them or why.

In her exhaustive study of the balls, published in the 1976-77 *Proceedings of the Society of Antiquaries in Scotland,* Dorothy N. Marshall reports their distribution "is much the same as that of the Pictish symbol stones which led to the original idea that the balls were of Pictish origin," but goes on to say that the small collection found while excavating Skara Brae, a stone-built settlement in the Orkney Islands, place them firmly in the later Neolithic or New Stone Age period, which is too early for the Iron-Age Picts. Marshall also says, however, that the area where the majority of the balls were found "is also the area of good land which today, as well as in antiquity, can support the largest population," an observation we'll get back to later.

First, as listed in Marshall's paper, let's look at the various theories about how the balls were used.

- J. Alexander Smith, in an 1876 paper, believed the balls had been attached to sticks and used as weapons. But Marshall counters, "when one appreciates the skill and time which has been used in the fashioning of these balls, it does not seem possible that the owner would have risked their loss or damage in war or chase."
- Ludovic Mann also refuted Smith's belief in 1914, theorizing the balls were instead used as weights in primitive scales. While Marshall agrees that the balls' general uniformity of size and weight lends some credence to the theory, she cites the opinion of Major Colville, a farmer in Kenya, who said his farm workers "were suspicious of weighing, preferring to have their meal issued to them by measure," and felt that Neolithic people might feel the same.
- Marshall also relates the theory that the balls may have been used in competitive throwing games, but argues "if this had been the case surely more balls would have been chipped."
- A fourth theory is that the balls were used as oracles by rolling them on the ground and interpreting the future from both the

Illustration of Bayeux Tapestry showing maces, from J. Alexander Smith's 1876 article on the carved stone balls

way they rolled and their positions at rest. Marshall admits that this theory is a possibility, "although the diversity of shape in the balls would make interpretation of the signs different too."
- The last theory Marshall lists is that the balls may have been used as ceremonial speaking stones at important gatherings, with the right to speak given to the holder of the stone.

Unsatisfied with any of the theories made before the publication of her paper, Marshall concludes her presentation by quoting the opinion of archaeologists Stuart Piggott and Glyn Daniel that the usage of the balls is still "wholly unknown."

Left at such an unresolved juncture, it is not surprising that the mystery of the carved balls of Scotland continues to generate ever more theories.

One theory is that they were used as weights for fishing nets, which fails to mention why such time and care would be spent fashioning ornate objects for such a mundane task, and why not one of the balls, even if used to magically invoke a good catch, would have been discovered with the totem image of a fish carved on it. And why, too, have most of the balls been found inland?

Another theory, posted on the abovetopsecret.com forum by member MysterX, speculates that the carved balls were made to represent pollen, and posts microscopic images of pollen alongside photographs of the balls to make his case. While the comparison of the two is certainly visually intriguing, and might convince many less-than-scrupulous readers of his theory, MysterX wisely concludes his post with the following caveat: "The obvious question arises, if the stones are indeed representations of pollen, how could Neolithic people see microscopic pollen grains in order to carve them on the macro scale." The same argument could be leveled at the idea the balls are meant to represent the nuclei of atoms.

Yet another theory speculates that the Neolithic carvers were experimenting with solid geometry, and had knowingly or unknowingly discovered, and shown in the three-dimensional qualities of the balls, the five Greek Platonic Solids over one thousand years before Plato described them in his *Timeaus*, his dialogue on the nature of the physical world and its human inhabitants. Archaeologists and mathematicians have criticized this theory because not all of the Platonic Solids can be definitively found in the balls that have so far been discovered – some having far too many knobs to even remotely qualify, and some having no knobs at all. Dr. Alison Sheridan of the National Museums of Scotland is more than a little circumspect about the mathematical interpretation of the carved balls when she says that the interpretation "fails to take into account their archaeological background, and fails to explain why so many do not have the requisite number of knobs! It's a classic case of people sticking on an interpretation in a state of ignorance. A great shame when so much is known about Late Neolithic archaeology."

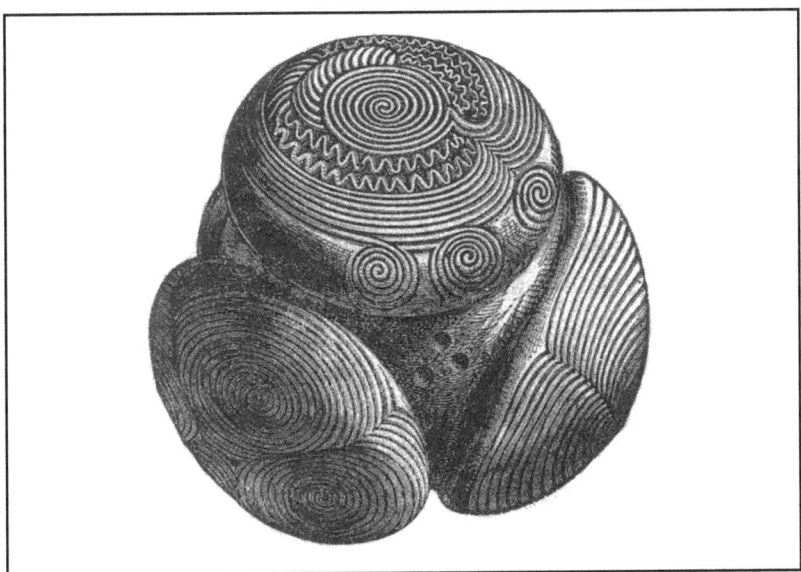

The Towie Stone

Finally, it has been speculated by Andrew Young, while an archaeology student at the University of Exeter, that the balls may have been used to move the huge stones found in Aberdeenshire's standing stone circles. While there is merit to the theory, it still does not explain why the balls were so elaborately carved, since smooth balls would have been more appropriate. The very act of carving the balls, in fact, would weaken their structural integrity, making them less fit for the task. And more damaged balls should certainly have been discovered.

As we can see, while there have been many theories put forth about Scotland's carved stone balls, the mystery still remains: who made them, and why?

I have a new theory.

Neolithic Résumés?

Hanging on the wall of my home office is the brass and iron fire poker my father gave me before he died. Regardless of its weight, it had been packed along with a very few other family keepsakes when we emigrated from Scotland to the USA in 1960, in spite of the fact that we would never again have to "poke up the fire" in a cold-water flat. It had clearly meant a lot to him, and it got me thinking …

He had made the poker, he said, as an "apprentice piece" – a requirement of his training as a British Railway "fitter." Railway fitters, especially during the Age of Steam, were often called upon to fashion parts for the huge locomotives out of raw metals, and his poker was a measure of his skill level at that time. The brass handle was made in the "thistle style," he added, and he had put a twist in the iron shaft for added strength.

I believe that as my father's poker verified, at its most basic level, my father's ability to work metals, so the carved stone balls of Scotland verified a mason's ability to work stone. As a 20th-century railway fitter, of course, my father didn't need his poker to find employment. He had a union card in his wallet that certified his proficiency in the trade, no matter where he looked for work. A Neolithic stonemason, on the other hand, would have needed some other type of certification, and an easily portable carved stone ball could have eminently suited that purpose.

Let's now return to Dorothy Marshall's conclusion that the small collection of balls found at Orkney's Skara Brae settlement place them firmly in the Neolithic Age (4000-2000 BC), which is too early for the Picts of the Iron Age (750 BC - 43 AD). While this rather mitigates the long-held theory that the balls are of Pictish origin, it does not necessarily preclude the possibility that the creation and usage of the balls could have spanned a much longer period of time – from the Neolithic or New Stone Age, through the Bronze Age, to the Iron Age and beyond. No matter what natural resources archaeologists have used to define these measures of historical time, stone has been worked in all of them, and still is.

While Marshall admits the distribution of the balls does seem to follow the distribution of the Iron Age Pictish symbol stones that dotted the landscape in Aberdeenshire, it is also true that more than 100 stone circle sites, dating as far back as 3000 BC, have been identified in the same area. This area where the majority of the balls were found, she says, "is also the area of good land which today, as well as in antiquity, can support the largest population."

It is as true today as it was then, I would add, that the larger the population of a region the more available work there is. Besides the symbol stones and stone circles, there would have been houses and walls to build, cist burial slabs to cut, and tools and weapons to make – all practical and marketable uses for the skilled stonemason's craft. Unlike the fishermen who sold their catch at the harbor, or the farmers who brought their livestock to the local market, stonemasons would have often been required to travel from job site to job site, and would have to prove they had the skills to handle the tasks at hand. Like the résumés and portfolios of today's workforce, the carved stone balls of the ancient stonemasons would be visible and tangible testimony of the work they were qualified to do.

In their 1992 book, *Scotland, Archaeology and Early History*, Graham and Anna Ritchie report that "very few balls have been found on archaeological sites, but those from Skara Brae clearly demonstrate their use in Neolithic times." Coincidentally, however, an undecorated six-knobbed ball was recently discovered within the Ness of Brodgar, an important Neolithic complex just 6 miles to the southeast of Skara Brae, causing a bit of excitement within the archaeological community.

The Ritchies also report "old records of balls having been found in burial cists suggest that their reverence if not their manufacture continued into Bronze Age times." While it is no doubt too late for these "old" discoveries, modern forensic study of the hand and forearm bones of those buried with the balls may, if future discoveries of that kind are made, be able to establish the professions of their owners.

Stones Lead to Rome

As my father's metal poker led me to the development of this theory, so the stonemason's carved balls serendipitously led me back to metalwork – specifically the cast-bronze objects known as Roman dodecahedrons.

Though younger in origin than Scotland's carved stone balls, but just as mysterious, the Roman dodecahedrons are so named because of their twelve pentagonal faces and because they have generally been found within the ancient boundaries of the Roman Empire. Dated from the 2nd or 3rd centuries AD, they are almost 3000 years younger in origin than the Skara Brae balls, are made of metal, not stone, and are hollow, not solid. Of the 100 or so that have been found, most have been found in France and Germany, and not one has been discovered in Scotland.

Like the stone balls, there are many theories about their usage, though none has been considered conclusive. Among the speculations are that they were made as candle holders, scepter decorations, dice, throwing toys, surveying instruments, flower holders, ring-size finger gauges, water pipe calibrators, rangefinders for siege machines, religious artifacts, bed warmers, and astronomical devices for determining optimal dates for planting and harvesting. Using a 3-D printed replica, one man even used it as a form on which to crochet a rather goofy looking pair of gloves. But because there is no mention

Two ancient Roman bronze dodecahedrons and an icosahedron (3rd c. AD) in the Rheinisches Landesmuseum in Bonn, Germany. The dodecahedrons were excavated in Bonn and Frechen-Bachem; the icosahedron in Arloff. (CCSA4 license, original author Kleon3)

of them in any known account of the day; their purpose is as big a mystery, now, as when the first one was discovered in 1793.

The dodecahedrons do, however, fit nicely in the cupped hand, just like Scotland's carved stone balls, and it is difficult for me to look at the two without feeling they were meant to perform the same simple function. Though separated by geography, time, and the materials of which they were made, I believe that each was meant to be nothing more than a portable example of an individual worker's skill level – the carved balls for stonemasons, and the dodecahedrons for metalsmiths – as well as a symbol of membership in the brotherhoods of their respective crafts. They functioned as résumés, portfolios, and union cards, all combined in small, eminently portable and entirely mundane objects.

If this is true, it would go a long way to explaining why a practical use for these objects has eluded discovery for so long: because, other

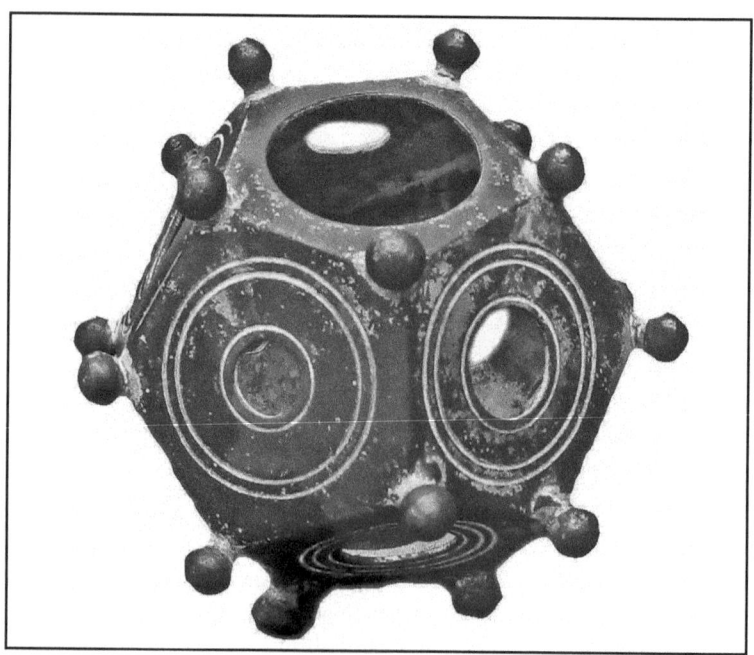

Roman dodecahedron (CCSA3 license, original author Lokilech)

than their skill-assessment and trade-recognition use, there was none. They would be valuable and necessary objects to the individual craftsmen, to be sure, but would be entirely useless to anyone else. Moreover, their intrinsic uselessness would have made them virtually theft-proof – no small consideration in those presumably wilder and woollier times.

But in these mundane objects we might still recognize, though separated by many centuries, the early roots of the medieval trade guilds, the arcane symbolism traditionally attached to those brotherhoods, and an ancient window through which to view our own work-a-day world.

Once cupped in ancient hands, these humble yet very personal objects can still give us a glimpse of who their makers were, bring us the curiously comforting knowledge that these craftsmen were not so very different from ourselves, and show us that even in our widely separated worlds our lives, indeed, may continue to play out on common ground.

Jeff Nisbet was born in Edinburgh, Scotland, and is a recently retired graphic designer living in the USA. The Art Director for *Billboard* magazine for 20 years of his career, it was a chance 1996 visit to 15th-century Rosslyn Chapel that sparked his abiding interest in arcane historical mysteries. His subsequent research has been published in numerous periodicals and anthologies, and has been reported on in the Scottish press. He can be reached at jeff@jnisbet.com.

John Anthony West and Robert Schoch at the Great Sphinx, 2016 (Courtesy of Robert Schoch & Catherine Ulissey)

THE ROGUE EGYPTOLOGIST

A celebration of the life of John Anthony West (1932-2018)

by *Robert M. Schoch, Ph.D.*

John Anthony West died on 6 February 2018. Not one for unnecessary sentimentality (he had a soft and kind soul housed in what could sometimes come across as a bitingly sarcastic façade), I know he would not want me to state it in any other way. Of course, if one knows anything about John Anthony West and his work, one realizes that I am referring to his physical death, not total annihilation of his consciousness, being, spirit, soul, or whatever term one may want to use. J. A. West fully believed that there was something more, much more, than this physicalist materialistic life on planet Earth.

On a personal note, the names we habitually used for each other, from the first day we met, were "West" and "Schoch". On occasion, when in the presence of other people, I might refer to him as, or call him, "John", but I do not remember him ever using any name other than "Schoch" for me. For the sake of convenience, however,

I will refer to him as "JAW" below, and indeed some people actually verbalized the word "Jaw" as a nickname for John Anthony West.

JAW was my friend and colleague for nearly three full decades. Despite being a generation apart (JAW was born a few months less than twenty-five years before I was), we were very close – not only as professional colleagues and collaborators in research, but as personal friends. I cannot express how deeply I miss him even now, and I do not believe it will become any easier in the future, but I do want to continue the research (as he always encouraged me to do) and thus perpetuate his memory and legacy. Here I will make a few brief comments relative to his life and work.

The End of the Physical Man

It seems it all happened very suddenly. In late December 2016 and January 2017, JAW was not feeling normal so he underwent a medical checkup and various tests. He was diagnosed with cancer that, originating in his left lung, had spread throughout his body, including into his brain. During the previous summer JAW and I had been in Egypt together once again, this time along with my wife Katie (Catherine Ulissey) and JAW's adult son Zeke, pursuing further research regarding our mutual interests, including the Great Sphinx. In late 2016, JAW led one of his famous tours to Egypt, but he began to show abnormal signs of fatigue, dizzy spells, and illness during the trip. Upon returning to the United States, he consulted a physician and as a result the cancer was discovered. JAW was scheduled to lead another two-week tour to Egypt in February–March 2017, but he found himself in the hospital instead (although still fully conscious and alert at that point). Out of friendship and at the request of the family, I rearranged my schedule and on a volunteer basis I led the tour in place of JAW. But the tour was still JAW's. I did my best to represent his points of view and analyses at the various sites we visited, from the Giza Plateau in Cairo to Abu Simbel in the far south. Additionally, I included my own observations and commentary as well.

The Beginning of a Friendship

I first met JAW in the late 1980s when he came to Boston University to present his work on Egypt at a college colloquium. And it was at the invitation of JAW that I first traveled to Egypt, in 1990, specifically so that I might apply my geological expertise to the problem of the dating of the Sphinx – a topic that has consumed much of my life ever since. As is generally well known (both JAW and I write about this in our various books and other publications), my analyses of the weathering, erosion, and seismic studies performed around the Great Sphinx determined that the core body of the statue (the head is a dynastic re-carving) originated thousands of years prior to the date of 2500 BCE which conventional Egyptologists assign to the statue. Our conclusions created an academic firestorm and I was vilified by various status quo university colleagues in archaeology, Egyptology, and history departments. Mind you, the vast majority of my geological colleagues have from the start been supportive of my work and conclusions – but then they have no personal vested interests in the age of the Sphinx.

JAW always relished the controversy surrounding our work together on the Great Sphinx. On the counter-attack, he was at his best. For my part, I have never enjoyed the punches back and forth. I would much rather have experienced immediate acceptance and praise for our findings, but that was not to be the case. Still I am grateful that now, decades later, our work on pushing back the age of the Great Sphinx – and with this work, the logical conclusion that there was an earlier cycle of civilization thousands of years prior to circa 3000 BCE – has found independent support elsewhere. In particular, the incredibly sophisticated site of Göbekli Tepe in southeastern Turkey, dating back to circa 10,000 BCE, confirms our premise that advanced societies inhabited our planet at a much earlier date than has been generally accepted by mainstream archaeologists.

Personal Thoughts and Reflections

There is much I could say about JAW, but here I will limit myself to a few thoughts as they come to me. The first thing that enters my mind as I reflect back are the wonderful times we had traveling and exploring together. There were many trips to Egypt over the decades (we traversed the country, although the primary focus was usually the Great Sphinx on the Giza Plateau). JAW and I also traveled together (along with my wife, Katie) to Milan for a conference at which we were both invited to speak; there was a trip to Norway (at the kind invitation of, and arranged by, David McCall) where we not only spoke, but were able to study ancient petroglyphs; and of prime importance for our on-going collaborative research, we traveled to Turkey together in 2010 to study Göbekli Tepe. Besides the overseas trips, another thing that comes immediately to mind are the wonderful visits to, and long discussions at, "Westhenge" (JAW's studio-home) in Saugerties, New York.

JAW realized that he would be best remembered for our work on re-dating the Great Sphinx. It was the Sphinx research that brought him (indeed, both of us) to the attention of the world with the first airing of the Emmy-winning documentary *The Mystery of the Sphinx* on NBC-TV in 1993. It has been re-aired many times since, including after having been translated into and voiced over in various languages; JAW once estimated that it has been seen by hundreds of millions of people around the world.

John Anthony West and Robert Schoch at the rear of the Great Sphinx, 2016
(Courtesy of Robert Schoch and Catherine Ulissey)

The re-dating of the Sphinx is not just a matter of pushing back the age of what is arguably the greatest and most famous statue on the face of the planet (a senior professor once said to me that I, and by implication JAW as well, would always be associated with the Great Sphinx, and thus always remembered as long as the Sphinx is remembered). The implications of an older Sphinx are profound. There existed a cycle of civilization, as I like to refer to it, before civilization is said (according to the standard story) to have originated, and we can now date the end of this earlier cycle of civilization to the end of the last ice age, circa 9700 BCE. This, as JAW pointed out in his 1979 book, *Serpent in the Sky*, raises the issue of "Atlantis" – that is, advanced civilization before civilization is supposed to have existed (JAW was never one to be seeking a specific geographic location for Atlantis). JAW was in agreement with my work demonstrating that the demise of this early civilization was due to a major eruption from our Sun which occurred nearly 12,000 years ago and snapped us out of the last ice age (see my 2012 book, *Forgotten Civilization: The Role of Solar Outbursts in Our Past and*

Future). In fact, JAW was fascinated by, and found quite compelling, the petroglyph evidence for this that we examined together during our trip to Norway (which ties in with a much larger body of evidence, discussed in *Forgotten Civilization*).

Given his work in, and love for, Egypt, JAW sometimes referred to himself as a "rogue Egyptologist" (although he had no formal training in Egyptology). He espoused the Symbolist interpretation of Ancient Egypt developed by R. A. Schwaller de Lubicz (1887–1961) – see my comments below on JAW's book *Serpent in the Sky*. He was an autodidact in the field, but he had learned well, devoting an immense amount of time to his meticulous studies; it is a shame that he died before a university formally recognized his achievements and granted him an honorary Ph.D., something that he was hoping for.

JAW had a love-hate (admittedly mostly hate, or rather disgust) relationship with academia. He despised most academics as rather petty narrow-minded upholders of the current societal dogmas and standard paradigm. In general, he referred to academics as "quackademics", and felt that the educational system was primarily a system of propaganda in support of the status quo. Despite his quarrels with established academia, JAW was a true scholar and agreed with me that we must follow the evidence wherever it may lead. To give a straightforward example, we traveled together to Yonaguni (Japan) and studied the submerged formations off the coast of the island, hoping to find definitive evidence of advanced civilization at the end of the last ice age (which would complement our Sphinx work). However, after diving the site, we both agreed that the "Yonaguni structures" are primarily natural.

Surprisingly to some, given various conferences where he spoke and his popularity among certain groups, JAW had little tolerance for unsubstantiated claims promulgated by members of what has been termed the "New Age" movement. He was known to use the term "unicorns" as a descriptor for certain New Agers, fake psychics, uncritical believers, and the like. He did not hesitate to express his opinions about anyone at almost any time, whether or not it was civil or politically expedient. As he often told the story, by the age of twelve or thirteen he had come to the conclusion that there are major problems with our modern society and its norms. The way he liked to describe it is that we are living in a lunatic asylum. As JAW viewed himself, his purpose and goal in life was to expose the nonsense and hypocrisy, the shortcomings and lies. Early in his life, JAW realized that he had been born into the lunatic asylum known as "modern civilization". He compared himself to the story of the little boy who was the only one willing to say "The emperor has no clothes". In terms of the Hindu Yuga Cycle, JAW and I agreed that we are in the depths of the Kali Yuga, and it will most likely get worse, much worse, before things improve.

JAW was an adherent of "The Work" of George Ivanovich Gurdjieff. JAW and I passed many happy hours discussing the teachings, philosophy, and practices of Gurdjieff (as well as P. D. Ouspensky, Rodney Collin, and others). West was convinced that The Work descended from ancient traditions and knowledge going back to an earlier cycle of civilization, a concept that I find quite credible. From Gurdjieff's teachings, JAW learned to live in the lunatic asylum (rather than retreat to a monastery, for instance), even as he opposed societal norms and conventional wisdom. And he learned from Gurdjieff that he should "use everything" – even experiences and circumstances that seemed, on the surface, to be negative or setbacks. All experiences, good and bad, are useful to a writer, JAW often told me. And he learned the lesson not to allow others to "push your buttons", for anyone who can emotionally rattle you can control you. JAW sometimes liked to paraphrase Gurdjieff regarding education: "Either do something that no one has ever done before – or just stay in school and do nothing."

JAW also liked to paraphrase past great writers. Two of his favorites paraphrases were that "a gentleman fights for lost causes" (Jorge Luis Borges) and "there is nothing stronger than an idea whose time has come" (Victor Hugo). Regarding the latter, JAW was quick to point out that the "idea whose time has come" need not be a good idea.

JAW had an abiding interest in many other diverse subjects (too many to mention here), from classic cars to fine art and music. One of the subjects that fascinated him was parapsychology (the scientific study of psychic phenomena), and he was delighted that I take a serious interest in it too. Another was alchemy, an interest which we shared as well. As JAW was quick to point out, Schwaller was an alchemist. Here is JAW's view of alchemy, which I would contend he applied to his own life:

> The true alchemist was not a deluded proto-scientist out to turn lead into gold for gain. His rituals with lead, mercury, and sulfur served as mnemonic aids in the quest for spiritual self-perfection. As the carnal became the spiritual on the inner plane, so – according to the medieval theory of hierarchy and correspondences – the gross

John Anthony West and Robert Schoch, Göbekli Tepe, Turkey, 2010
(Courtesy of Robert Schoch and Catherine Ulissey.)

would become fine on the physical plane. Though the method may not wash as science, it is singularly apt when applied to art. All art is alchemical in the sense that it distills the raw stuff of experience into something rarer and finer. Understood metaphorically, every real artist is an alchemist. (JAW, 1991, foreword to a reprint of *The Death Ship* by B. Traven [a pseudonym; there is still not 100% agreement as to the true identity of the author]. Brooklyn, New York: Lawrence Hill Books, p. vi)

In a more mundane sense, one might classify cooking as a type of alchemy, an alchemy in which JAW excelled. He was not only a great cook, but had a refined palate and appreciated good food. And all who knew him well knew of JAW's love of good vodka. I sometimes joked with him (actually, it was not a joke at all) that if I attempted to drink a fraction of the vodka he could consume in a day, it would no doubt kill me.

A Very Brief Timeline of the Life of John Anthony West

In answer to questions that many readers may have regarding when he was born, where he lived, and so on, I have put together a brief timeline of JAW's life. This is based on my own knowledge and recollections, supplemented by comments from others that I have picked up over the years.

JAW was born in New York City, 9 July 1932. His family owned a clothing store on Fifth Avenue.

He attended Lehigh University (Bethlehem, Pennsylvania, USA), College of Business and Economics, 1949-1953, graduating with a B.S. in Economics. He never spoke much to me about his Lehigh years; he generally despised the formal educational system in America. I do know that one of his professors at Lehigh was Dr.

Ray L. Armstrong, Professor of English. JAW thought enough of him that he presented Dr. Armstrong with an inscribed copy of the American edition of his first book, *Call Out the Malicia* (see below for a list of JAW's published books).

JAW served in the U.S. Army in Europe for two years in the 1950s. He had a German girlfriend at the time and a white Porsche that he used to tour Europe during his free time. After his army tour was over, he returned to the United States and fell madly in love with a woman "who would not have him" (as he put it). He also found a good job on Madison Avenue, New York City, writing advertisement copy and other such work, but his true aspiration was to be a genuine writer. His first short story, "Journey to Moonhowler's Isle" (a fictional story, which I suspect was partially autobiographical, as so much of his fiction was, about a young man at summer camp), was accepted for publication on 15 October 1957, a date that he said was more important to him than his actual birthday, for it was his birth as a true writer. JAW decided that America was not big enough for both him and the woman who would not have him, and he had long wanted to escape the lunatic asylum of America and the evils of modern society, so around early 1958 he moved to the then remote hideaway of Ibiza, a small island off the east coast of Spain. (His story first came out in the paperback volume *New World Writing #13*, published in June 1958 by the New American Library; I believe this was after he had already moved to Ibiza.)

On Ibiza, JAW joined the Bohemian community of writers, artists, and intellectuals who had settled there. Although I never heard him use the term, he was essentially a part of the late "Beat Generation" – he was a "beatnik" according to societal norms of the time, although "beatnik" carries somewhat derogatory connotations and I certainly never mentioned the term around him. His home on Ibiza, "Rum Place", was famous for the parties held there and the gatherings of intellectuals.

Early during his time on Ibiza, JAW fell madly in love with the Finnish painter Anita Snellman (1924-2006). It was, by his account, a short but wildly passionate affair. Snellman became the model for the character Janine Lindemann in JAW's 1966 novel *Osborne's Army* (discussed further below).

JAW loved the Ibizan hounds, and he acquired two on the island, Frontis (or Frontes) and Leo. Interestingly, the Ibizan hounds were descended from the hunting dogs, the Greyhounds of Horus, of Ancient Egypt. JAW did not yet have any particular interest in Egypt; the dogs seemed to presage things to come. He raised a number of Ibizan hounds over the years, right up until the time of his illness. JAW was also always fond of cars. On Ibiza he was the proud co-owner of a 1926 Morris Cowley which he and his friend Gordon Gardner drove from London through Spain and had transported to the island. During his Ibiza years, JAW's first book was published, *Call Out the Malicia* (first edition, 1961; discussed below).

While on Ibiza, JAW met the Welsh actress Catherine (Cate) Dolan (she was from Port Talbot, Wales). They married in 1966, and JAW thereby became the stepfather of her son Geraint Hughes (who would go on to make a name for himself as a musician – a "musical genius", as JAW described him to me; JAW always expressed an incredible fondness and admiration for his stepson). JAW and Catherine Dolan moved to Ealing, London. *The Case for Astrology*, which JAW co-authored with Jan Gerhard Toonder (whom he knew while living on Ibiza), was first published in 1970 during the London years. It was through research for this book that JAW became familiar with the work of R. A. Schwaller de Lubicz. Cate Dolan and JAW lived in London from around 1966 to 1972/1973. JAW became involved with Gurdjieff circles during his London years, and remained a Gurdjieffian for the remainder of his life. In 1972/1973 they moved to an old farmhouse at Garreg Fawr, Carmarthenshire, South Wales, where they lived until 1976/77. I recollect JAW telling me about living in the old, rather leaky and cold, farmhouse in Wales

John Anthony West and his Ibizan hounds, from the back cover of his book *Osborne's Army* (1967, photo by Martin Reichenthal)

where he worked on the manuscript of his book, *Serpent in the Sky*. I believe he wrote much of the text prior to his first trip to Egypt.

JAW and Catherine Dolan parted ways in 1977. She died of breast cancer in 1991. JAW returned to New York, and ultimately settled in upstate New York in the general Woodstock area. For most of the years I knew him he lived in either Saugerties or Athens, New York. JAW married Celesta Kramer; together they had two children (now adults), Zeke and Zoë. From his base in upstate New York, JAW spent his time researching, writing, and pursuing various endeavors (such as working at times with Gerald Celente of the Trends Research Institute). He also led tours to Egypt on a regular basis, working in particular with our mutual close friend Mohamed Nazmy (died mid-August 2018), president of Quest Travel.

During 2017, seeking treatment for his cancer, JAW's family took him to the Burzynski Clinic in Houston, Texas. He returned to upstate New York toward the end of 2017, and ultimately passed away in a hospital in Albany, New York, at 9:42 p.m. local time on 6 February 2018.

In the last years of his life, JAW was one of the behind-the-scenes supporters of the not-for-profit Organization for the Research of Ancient Cultures (ORACUL) that I helped to co-found for the purpose of pursuing the type of research that JAW had initiated. (For more information regarding ORACUL, see the description and link on my website, www.robertschoch.com).

John Anthony West and Egypt

JAW loved Egypt, there can be no doubt, but his interest in Egypt was not what many people may assume. He was not simply another Egyptophile.

There is one idea that John Anthony West always held above all others. He believed in and presupposed…

...a universe in which consciousness, meaning and order are written into the fabric of its creation – as all traditional religions and societies have always insisted. And in this universe, on this particular planet, humanity has been placed for a reason; with unique privileges and unique responsibilities. (JAW, *The Case for Astrology*, Viking Arkana, 1991, p. 500)

According to JAW:

If we believe that the universe is a conscious creation and that humanity is on earth for a purpose, then whatever serves that purpose is practical (whatever does not serve that purpose is at best a waste of time, at worst, evil...). Knowledge of that purpose is science; Sacred Science. There cannot be the slightest doubt that this science of order, purpose, meaning and the transformation of the carnal or material to the spiritual was what once prevailed on Earth. For a civilization to be worthy of the name, it must be based upon a sacred science. Through the efforts of a number of brilliant scholars over the past couple of centuries, key elements of the lost sacred science have been rediscovered or reformulated. (p. 499)

This 'sacred science', JAW believed...

...provided those who understood its laws with the guidelines for carrying out their pre-ordained responsibilities, that inner transformation of the carnal, material and merely rational beings they were by birth into the spiritual beings we all are by birthright. (p. 500)

In Ancient Egypt, JAW found a civilization that understood these principles. This was the basis for JAW's profound interest in, and relationship with, Egypt.

Of Horsemen and Cowboys

Due to overlapping interests, and on occasion we would all appear at the same conference, some people have referred to John Anthony West, Graham Hancock, Robert Bauval, and me (Robert Schoch) as "The Four Horsemen". The basic concept, as I understand it, is that the four of us, each in our own way, are somewhat like the Four Horsemen of the Apocalypse (*The Book of Revelation*, attributed to St. John) in terms of spreading death and destruction among the old guard academics, archaeologists, and historians when it comes to the timeline and interpretation of ancient civilization. Now one of the horsemen has departed. The basic names or attributes often associated with the four horses and horsemen are Conquest, War, Famine, and Death. I am not sure which appealed to JAW the most, or which horseman he envisioned himself as. For better or worse, when the Four Horsemen in the context of the four of us have been mentioned or illustrated at conferences or elsewhere, I (Schoch) tend to be the one on the white horse.

> And I saw, and behold a white horse: and he that sat on him had a bow; and a crown was given unto him: and he went forth conquering, and to conquer. (Revelation 6:2, King James Version of the Bible)

JAW wanted me to continue the fight, to go out and conquer, even after he had passed on. This he told me.

Also playing on the concept of the Four Horsemen, in the last decade or so of his life, JAW – ever the satirist – liked to speak about his concept of the Five Cowboys of the Apocalypse 2.0, which he also referred to as the Posse of the Church of Progress, out to capture and destroy any subversive elements who might dare to question modern technological Western society. The Five Cowboys are: Capitalism, Patriotism, Democracy, Technology, and Entertainment. To paraphrase JAW ever so briefly regarding these Five Cowboys:

Capitalism is the concept of "all for me and none for you".

Patriotism is the concept of "all for us and none for them".

Democracy is, for example, when the dishwashers of a restaurant elect one of their own as the chef. This is not a restaurant where JAW would care to eat. The new chef may be a good chef after all, but it is unlikely and not worth taking the risk.

Technology is a mixed bag. It has some benefits, but it also has the ability to deprive people of their livelihood and basic worth. Technology can cripple creativity, enhance and promote anti-social behavior, and can turn individuals into effectively mindless zombies who simply serve the powers to be and are subservient to the technology. Technology, I would add, if applied improperly, can be incredibly destructive of nature. In upstate New York, JAW loved that he was surrounded by nature and relished his walks in the woods with Sabu, his Ibizan hound. (He owned more than one Ibizan hound over the years named Sabu.)

Entertainment, as JAW liked to say, is "what one does to kill time before time kills you".

And, I would add, JAW often pointed out that education, or should we say indoctrination and propaganda, is a powerful tool utilized by the Five Cowboys to keep everyone in line.

To the end, JAW was the little boy who did his best to point out the nakedness and emptiness of the emperor, of modern society and the power structure that props it up.

Books (and More) by John Anthony West

Here I list and briefly comment on JAW's published books. JAW did not publish a plethora of books, but those he did publish are deep and profound, and his non-fiction works are scholarly and well-researched, yet accessible to the educated reader. I have no doubt that his books will stand the test of time; as long as there are readers to read, JAW's books will endure.

Because of their importance to him personally, I also include below his play, *Jarry*, and the NBC television documentary *The Mystery of the Sphinx*. In addition to his published books, JAW wrote many articles, plays, forewords for diverse books (fiction and nonfiction; books for children and for adults); he helped edit and even ghostwrite various articles and books; he was interviewed many times for print and other media; and he was involved in numerous radio, television, film, video, and other projects throughout his career (some of which, I always felt, distracted him and took too much of his time – precious time he could have spent working on books, including books he and I planned to write together, or other more serious scholarly and literary pursuits – but then he did not anticipate dying so soon). JAW always stressed to me that he was, above all else, a writer – and a very good writer indeed, if he did say so himself.

1) John Anthony West, *Call Out the Malicia*. London: William Heinemann, 1961. New York: E. P. Dutton, 1963.

JAW's first published book – a collection of ten short stories, some of which had been published previously. (There are some differences between the 1961 and 1963 editions.) These short fictional pieces have sometimes been classified as a combination of fantasy and horror; they are mostly a bit on the bizarre side, and indeed several fit the definition of macabre. The Spanish "malicia" of the title can be translated as malice, wickedness, or mischief, and this is an appropriately mischievous book. The back of the dust jacket of the 1963 American edition reproduces a portrait of JAW by his friend, the artist Alan Schmer (died 2013). I do not know the context or date, but JAW presented a copy of *Call Out the Malicia* (1963 edition) to the well-known Armenian-American writer David Kherdian and his wife Nonny Hogrogian with the following

inscription, which gives insight into how JAW viewed himself and his writing career at the time:

> For David & Nonny,
> Hope you'll enjoy
> these first baby steps –
> in steel-toed boots.
> Love
> John Anthony West

In the various characters who populate the stories of *Call Out the Malicia*, I can recognize different aspects of the JAW I knew. There is the misunderstood artist Alain Marsh, with an interest in telepathy, clairvoyance, and the nature of time, who only gained the recognition he deserved after his death ("What, Exactly, Do You Mean by 'Cheese'?"). And there is the struggling and hard-drinking writer Henry Scherfzon who shares an apartment with a painter of "vibrant" canvases and has a Dutch friend who drops by when in town ("Roses, Roses Riotously" – in real life, JAW had a Dutch friend in Ibiza, Jan Gerhard Toonder, who was the coauthor with JAW of the 1970s version of *The Case for Astrology*).

One of the stories in *Call Out the Malicia* is "George" (1963 American edition, pp. 136-156), and I have the impression that this may have been in some ways JAW's favorite tale of the lot; at any rate, he spoke to me about it numerous times and he also turned it into a play. At the end of the story, George dies. Marjorie, his wife, demands, "What do you feel? I've got to know, George." The words JAW put in George's mouth could be considered prophetic, or at least hopeful:

> "It's not so bad," he said, speaking slowly, his voice thickening with each syllable. "Not bad at all. I... I..." And he had to summon every reserve of strength for his last words: "I... I sort of like it," he said.

2) John Anthony West, *Osborne's Army*. London: Eyre & Spottiswoode, 1966. New York: William Morrow, 1967. Harmondsworth, Middlesex, England: Penguin, 1969.

The novel is set on the imaginary island of Escondite ("Hidden" or "Hideaway" in Spanish) in the Caribbean; however, there can be little doubt that it reflects many aspects of Ibiza, where JAW was living and writing at the time. The book was initially inspired by a trip JAW took to Puerto Rico; the idea germinated (as JAW described it) for three years and he took another six years to write the novel. Some of the characters from *Call Out the Malicia* reappear in *Osborne's Army*. The story climaxes with grockles (tourists) and other intruders invading the island and ultimately despoiling it. Amos Osborne leads the fight, even taking grockles hostage, to free the island and restore it to its pristine condition – but unfortunately Osborne's army is ultimately defeated.

As noted above, in *Osborne's Army* JAW utilized and popularized one of the terms that became closely associated with him – "grockle". According to the unabridged *Oxford English Dictionary*, the term "grockle" may have originated in the early 1960s in the seaside resort town of Torquay (Devon, England) and was first popularized in the 1964 British film *The System* (which was shown under the title *The Girl-Getters* in America). JAW adopted "grockle" wholeheartedly in *Osborne's Army*; years later, taking groups to Egypt, he never failed to use the term liberally and with his trademark satirical humor, often defining a "grockle" as "any tourist other than us" (you never wanted JAW to refer to you as grockle). Cheap souvenirs offered by local venders are "grockle-bait" intended to draw in and trap the unwitting grockles, while hotels are "grockle coops". Decades after the publication of *Osborne's Army*, JAW found himself in the position of a "grockle-herder".

Those who knew JAW well will remember that he often liked to inveigh against the technological "advances" of modern society, such as striped toothpaste and hydrogen bombs (two of his favorite examples), a theme that can be found in *Osborne's Army*, in which he wrote regarding the possibilities for technological advances that actually might be worthwhile,

> ... centuries of mindless gadgetry was bound to produce something less silly than striped toothpaste, and something less sinister than hydrogen bombs, if only through the law of averages... (1966, p. 117)

JAW once told me that *Osborne's Army* was almost made into a movie. He bemoaned that, like many things in his life, it was almost made, but never actually came to be.

3) John Anthony West, *The Case for Astrology*. London: Viking Arkana, 1991. (This is a rewrite and update of an earlier book: John Anthony West and Jan Gerhard Toonder, *The Case for Astrology*. London: Macdonald, 1970. New York: Coward-McCann, 1970. Harmondsworth, Middlesex, England: Penguin, 1973.)

This is not your typical frivolous or superficial astrology book (there is nothing at all frivolous about it), and it certainly is not a manual of astrology. Rather, ultimately, it is a critique of modern scientism (particularly the arch Skeptics and Debunkers, purposefully capitalized) and the "Church of Progress", as JAW referred to the dogma that humanity only progresses from dumb old "them" to intelligent and technologically sophisticated "us". Yes, it does consider astrology specifically and the evidence that there are correlations between Earth and the Heavens, such as the work of Michel Gauquelin (1928-1991). JAW and I often discussed the hermetic concept that is so aptly summarized in the phrase "As above, so below". Importantly, for the development of JAW's future path, it was through researching material for *The Case for Astrology* that JAW developed an interest in Schwaller and Egypt.

4) John Anthony West, *Serpent in the Sky: The High Wisdom of Ancient Egypt*. New York: Harper and Row, 1979. Updated edition: Wheaton, Illinois: Quest Books, 1993.

This is JAW's famous, and magisterial, study of the work of R. A. Schwaller de Lubiz and the "Symbolist School" of interpretation when it comes to Ancient Egypt. In a nutshell, Schwaller argued that the surviving monuments of Ancient Egypt, such as the Temple of Luxor (the "Temple of Man", as Schwaller referred to it), are not only masterpieces of harmony and proportion, but that they incorporate into their designs meaning and symbolism reflecting the ancient wisdom, along with advanced knowledge, which unifies the disparate fields we now think of as science, medicine, religion, theology, philosophy, art, and so forth. As JAW would often point out, reading Schwaller directly, even in English translation (and when JAW originally wrote *Serpent*, there were no English translations of Schwaller readily available), is virtually impenetrable for most people. *Serpent* made Schwaller and Symbolist Egypt accessible. But *Serpent* is much more than simply an explanation and analysis of Schwaller's work and the "sacred science" of Ancient Egypt. *Serpent* contains many insights original to JAW, and also discusses such topics as classical numerology, sacred geometry (so popular in certain circles nowadays, even if the advocates and practitioners do not always understand the fundamentals of the field), and the issue of "Atlantis" and a forgotten civilization that preceded dynastic Egypt, as evidenced by the Great Sphinx – for it was Schwaller who noted that the Great Sphinx was weathered and eroded by water, not sand and wind, and therefore the statue must have its origins long before the rise of Dynastic Egypt around 5,000 years ago. Many people, among whom I am included, consider *Serpent* to be JAW's masterpiece. He was very proud of the book, and rightfully so.

5) John Anthony West, 1980. *Jarry: A Spectacle*. A play written by JAW that was performed under the direction of Beuva Rosten in April 1980 at the Perry Street Theater, New York.

I consider this to be JAW's most important and influential play, based on the life and work of the novelist, essayist, and playwright

Alfred Jarry (1873-1907) whom JAW greatly admired. Jarry rejected many of the conventions and much of the received wisdom of his time (themes close to JAW's heart and head). Jarry is often viewed as a forerunner of Dadaism, Surrealism, and Futurism, and his 1896 play *Ubu Roi* set the stage for (some say founded) the Theatre of the Absurd. JAW explores and extends these themes in his play about Alfred Jarry.

6) John Anthony West, *The Traveler's Key to Ancient Egypt: A Guide to the Sacred Places of Ancient Egypt*. New York: Alfred A. Knopf, 1985. Updated edition: Wheaton, Illinois: Quest Books, 1995.

Without doubt, this is the best "on the ground" introduction to Symbolist Egypt and the thinking of both Schwaller and JAW (and I am pleased to note that JAW included mention of me in the 1995 edition of *Traveler's Key* as well as in the 1993 edition of *Serpent*). *The Traveler's Key to Ancient Egypt* is a true travel guide, even physically designed to be slipped easily into a pack, pouch, or large pocket (the printed book is about four and a quarter inches [10.8 cm] wide by eight and a half inches [21.6 cm] tall by one and one-eighth inches [2.9 cm] thick), with travel tips regarding, and in-depth analyses of, all the major ancient sites of Egypt. But it is much more than simply a travel guide, and can be read to advantage as an introduction to, and armchair tour of, Ancient Egypt (in this day and age, perhaps supplemented by photos found on the Internet). When I took over JAW's final Egypt trip, the one he could not lead because of his severe condition, I carried a copy of *The Traveler's Key* everywhere. I did not personally need it; JAW taught me well and for the guests I did my best to impart JAW's wisdom (as well as my own thoughts and insights) throughout the two weeks and at all of the sites, but it was a comfort having it with me. Of course, my mind was always on JAW and his battle with cancer.

For a number of years JAW told me that he was working on an update and revision of *The Traveler's Key to Ancient Egypt*. The problem always was, as JAW readily admitted, that he tended to be a bit disorganized and, at least in his later years, incredibly inefficient at getting things done, plus new endeavors were always coming up that would distract him. In this respect, he reminded me of Leonardo da Vinci, a brilliant genius who began more projects than he was able to ever complete. And JAW always told me that he was going to live to be 120; I am not sure he actually believed that, but he certainly expected to live at least well into his 90s and hopefully surpass the century mark.

7) NBC (National Broadcasting Company), *The Mystery of the Sphinx* (television documentary). Hosted by Charlton Heston; featuring John Anthony West and Robert M. Schoch; directed by Bill Cote; executive producer, Boris Said; produced by Robert Watts. First aired in the United States, 10 November 1993, 9–10 p.m. Eastern Standard Time.

The version of the show that is currently generally available on DVD, YouTube, and other outlets, is not the original show; it was re-edited and expanded with supplementary and extraneous material. I had no control or input over this re-editing and I object to some of the material included in the expanded version; honestly, this was a serious point of friction between us. Nevertheless, *The Mystery of the Sphinx* helped introduce our work to the world at large.

8) David Solomon with John Anthony West, *The Dead Saints Chronicles: A Zen Journey through the Christian Afterlife*. Dead Saints Media, 2016.

David Solomon was a longtime friend of JAW. Solomon died in April 2016, just after *The Dead Saints Chronicles* was published. Solomon had been working on materials for this book when he was diagnosed with brain cancer (glioblastoma multiforme). JAW spent two years (beginning in April 2014) editing and seeing to completion *The Dead Saints Chronicles*, to the detriment of his own research and literary output (I write this without malice; it is simply an observation). Reading the book, I see much more of

Solomon than of JAW in the text, particularly in terms of the spiritual, religious, and philosophical aspects of the book. Given that it was the last major literary project that JAW was involved with that saw publication prior to his death (I do hope that some of his other projects can be completed and brought to press posthumously), I mention it here. I note, with great appreciation, that David Solomon took an active interest in, and was very supportive of, our work on the Great Sphinx and the confirmatory evidence of Göbekli Tepe.

As I bring these brief notes to a close, a sentence that JAW wrote, in his Afterword to *The Dead Saints Chronicles* (p. 375) comes to mind, and consoles me:

> The Afterlife is real, and every one of us would do well to start preparing for it.

John Anthony West, Mena House Hotel, Cairo, Egypt, 2016
(Courtesy of Robert Schoch and Catherine Ulissey.)

John Anthony West spent a lifetime preparing. No doubt he is on his way to becoming a star, as the Ancient Egyptians believed. I wish him well on his glorious new journey.

Robert M. Schoch, Director of the Institute for the Study of the Origins of Civilization at Boston University, a full-time faculty member at B.U.'s College of General Studies, and an Honorary Professor at the Nikola Vaptsarov Naval Academy, earned his Ph.D. in geology and geophysics at Yale University. Best known for re-dating the Great Sphinx, he is the author of *Forgotten Civilization: The Role of Solar Outbursts in Our Past and Future*, and many other books. Website: www.robertschoch.com

Endnotes

Maria J. Pérez Cuervo - The Lost Children of Hamlin (p. 9)

Acknowledgements:

First published in *Fortean Times* no. 264

Notes:

1. As quoted in Elisa Gutch's "The Pied Piper of Hamelin", *Folklore*, vol. 3, no. 2, Jun 1892.
2. See Justus Friedrich Carl Hecker's *From The epidemics of the middle ages.* Accessed through Google Books.
3. See Dado of Rouen: "Life of St. Eligius of Noyon", *Medieval Hagiography: An Anthology,* ed. Thomas Head. Accessed through Google Books.
4. Gutch, op. cit.

Ray Grasse - Uncovering the Lost Tomb of Osiris (p. 23)

Notes:

1. Gordon White, *STAR.SHIPS: A Prehistory of the Spirits,* Scarlett Imprint, 2016, p. 174.
2. Robert Temple, *Egyptian Dawn: Exposing the Real Truth Behind Ancient Egypt*, Arrow Books, 2011, pgs. 43-80.
3. Ibid, p. 79.
4. https://web.archive.org/web/20090813082309/http://heritage-key.com/egypt/exclusive-interview-dr-zahi-hawass-indianapolis

5. In early January of 2015, archaeologists announced the discovery of another purported "Tomb of Osiris," this one supposedly built during the 25th Dynasty between 760 and 525 BCE, and located on the west bank of the River Nile near Luxor, Egypt. The fact that there may be more than one Tomb of Osiris should come as no surprise, since any one of them is only a symbolic replica of the original site described in mythology (although some would argue that the the Giza site takes on special significance due to its location on the Plateau). To use a simple analogy, every Christian church that sports a empty crucifix near its altar is commemorating the crucifixion and resurrection of Jesus, without claiming to be the actual location of the original story itself.

Kelvin F. Long - The Apkallu Initiative (p. 57)

Acknowledgements:

The author dedicates this article to the efforts of Graham Hancock and Randall Carlson, whose significant research inspired this initiative. It was written to garner scrutiny of the idea, before deciding whether to proceed or not. Feedback is invited.

John Reppion - Diabolus in Musica (p. 81)

Notes:

1. In the earliest printing of the *Il trillo del diavolo,* at that point in the third movement where the "Devil's trill" begins, an annotation reading "the Devil at the foot of the bed" can be seen. The idea of The Arch Fiend at the foot of Tartini's bed, playing the violin with speed and accuracy so impossible it might drive a musician to give up his calling altogether, was the inspiration for French artist Louis-Léopold Boilly's 1824 work "Tartini's Dream". That image of the horned Devil with a violin in his hand has proved an incredibly powerful one; visually cementing that connection between the demonic and the musical for a new age. A version of the image currently serves as part of the logo for Goblin - an Italian progressive rock band internationally renowned for their horror soundtrack work.
2. The Black Sabbath riff was undoubtedly inspired by "Mars – the Bringer of War" from Gustav Holst's *The Planets* suite (written between 1914-16), whose satanic sound also comes from the tritone AKA The Devil's Interval (*diabolus*

in musica). The tritone interval is created by three adjacent whole tones played together, producing a dissonance which seems ominous and "unnatural" to the listener. It was long believed that the use of the tritone was once banned by the church because of its demonic associations, but this has proved to be untrue. It was merely the fact that it sounded so unpleasant which led to its exclusion from (most) Christian music for a long time. The tritone has become a cornerstone of Metal music thanks to its use in Black Sabbath, used in songs such as Metallica's "Enter Sandman", Iron Maiden's "Hallowed Be Thy Name", and pretty much everything by Slayer.

References:

http://www.catholic.org/saints/saint.php?saint_id=2271
https://en.wikipedia.org/wiki/Theophilus_of_Adan
http://www.thefreedictionary.com/Faustian
Voyage d'un François en Italie, fait dans les années 1765 & 1766 by J.J. Le Français de Lalande (https://archive.org/details/voyagedunfranoi00lalagoog)
https://www.britannica.com/biography/Giuseppe-Tartini
https://aviolinslife.org/tartinilipinski/
https://en.wikipedia.org/wiki/Niccol%C3%B2_Paganini
http://www.vam.ac.uk/blog/tales-archives/henry-cole-and-the-devils-violinist
http://www.musicradar.com/news/guitars/history-of-the-acoustic-blues-567109
http://robertjohnsonbluesfoundation.org/biography
https://en.wikipedia.org/wiki/Witchcraft_Destroys_Minds_%26_Reaps_Souls
https://www.npr.org/2017/10/25/559501959/shocking-omissions-coven-switchcraft-destroy-minds-reaps-souls
http://www.blacksabbath.com/history.html
http://www.complex.com/pop-culture/2015/02/what-is-the-illuminati-conspiracyand-who-are-its-members/are-they-real

Eric Wargo - The Great Work of Immortality (p. 101)

References:

Blackmore, Susan J. (1992). *Beyond the Body*. Chicago: Academy Chicago Publishers.

Bruce, Robert. (2009). *Astral Dynamics*. Charlottesville, VA: Hampton Roads.
De Jong, H. M. E. (2002). *Michael Maier's Atalanta Fugiens*. York Beach, Maine: Nicolas-Hays, Inc.
Eli Luminosus Aequalis. (2013). *MUTUS LIBER Loquitur*. Charleston, SC: Sacer Equestris Aureus Ordo Inc.
Fox, Oliver. (1980). *Astral Projection*. Secaucus, NJ: The Citadel Press.
Freud, Sigmund. (1965). *The Interpretation of Dreams*. New York: Avon Books.
Fulcanelli. (2000). *Le Mystere des Cathedrales*. Las Vegas, NV: Brotherhood of Life.
Graziano, Michael S. A. (2013). *Consciousness and the Social Brain*. Oxford, UK: Oxford University Press.
Hillman, James. (1979). "Peaks and Vales." In J. Hillman, ed., *Puer Papers*. Dallas, TX: Spring Publications.
Jung, Carl. (1993). *Psychology and Alchemy*. Princeton, NJ: Bollingen.
Kingsley, Peter. (2003). *Reality*. Point Reyes, CA: The Golden Sufi Center.
Lecouteux, Claude. (2003). *Witches, Werewolves, and Fairies*. Rochester, VT: Inner Traditions.
May, Edwin C.; Rubel, Victor; Auerbach, Lloyd. (2014). *ESP Wars East and West*. Palo Alto, CA: Laboratories for Fundamental Research.
McLean, Adam. (1991). *A Commentary on the Mutus Liber*. Grand Rapids, MI: The Phanes Press.
Monroe, Robert A. (2001). *Journeys Out of the Body*. New York: Broadway Books.
Muldoon, Sylvan J.; Carrington, Hereward. (1952). *The Projection of the Astral Body*. New York: Rider & Company.
Naydler, Jeremy. (2005). *Shamanic Wisdom in the Pyramid Texts*. Rochester, VT: Inner Traditions.
Powell, Arthur E. (1969). *The Etheric Double*. Wheaton, IL: The Theosophical Publishing House.
Strassman, Rick. (2001). *DMT: The Spirit Molecule*. Rochester, VT: Park Street Press.
Thompson, Evan. (2015). *Waking, Dreaming, Being*. New York: Columbia University Press.
Tilton, Hereward. (2013). "Of Ether, Entheogens, and Colloidal Gold: Heinrich Khunrath and the Making of the Philosophers' Stone." In A. Cheak, ed., *Alchemical Traditions*. Melbourne, Australia: Numen Books.
Uždavinys, Algis. (2008). *Philosophy as a Rite of Rebirth*. Westbury, UK: Prometheus Trust.

Waite, A. E. (1999). *The Hermetic Museum*. York Beach, Maine: Samuel Weiser, Inc.
Wallace, B. Alan. (2012). *Dreaming Yourself Awake*. Boston: Shambhala.
Wangyal, Tenzin. (1998). *Tibetan Yogas of Dream and Sleep*. Ithaca, NY: Snow Lion.
Wargo, Eric. (2016). "Psi's Big Guns: Sleep Paralysis and Astral Time Travel." *The Nightshirt*. http://thenightshirt.com/?p=3773
Wargo, Eric. (2018). *Time Loops*. Charlottesville, VA: Anomalist Books.
Wilhelm, John L. (1976). *The Search for Superman*. New York: Pocket Books.

Notes:

1. An earlier version of this article appeared on the author's blog, *The Nightshirt*.
2. In this article, I use the term OOBE to reflect this phenomenology—feeling like you are out of body—without necessarily assuming this is what is "really" happening.
3. Muldoon & Carrington, 1952.
4. Monroe, 2001.
5. Bruce, 2009.
6. See, e.g., Graziano, 2013.
7. Blackmore, 1992.
8. Thompson, 2015.
9. Kingsley, 2003.
10. Naydler, 2005.
11. Uždavinys, 2008.
12. See Wilhelm, 1976.
13. May et al., 2014.
14. Jung, 1993.
15. Lecouteux, 2003.
16. Powell, 1969.
17. Waite, 1999, 280.
18. Bruce, 2009.
19. Waite, 298.
20. De Jong, 2002.
21. Fulcanelli, 2000.
22. McLean, 1991.
23. Aries is a ram, of course. Sheep, whose guardians (shepherds) notoriously

are given to slumber, are another ancient symbol for dreams. You would be rewarded rereading many parts of the Old and New Testaments with this in mind.

24. Ibid.

25. Eli Luminosus Aequalis, 2013.

26. Freud, 1965.

27. See Wallace, 2012.

28. Lecouteux, 2003.

29. Waite, 276.

30. Ibid.

31. Rick Strassman's (2001) argument that dimethyltryptamine (DMT) is a "spirit molecule," associated with the pineal gland and somehow facilitating the departure of consciousness from the body, is an echo of Descartes.

32. Hillman, 1979.

33. Waite, 304.

34. Tilton, 2013.

35. Fox, 1980.

36. Wallace, 2012; see also Wangyal, 1998.

37. Information about lucid-dream-conducive over-the-counter supplements and vitamins is readily available on the Web.

38. The "greats" of remote viewing, Joe McMoneagle, Ingo Swann, and Pat Price, all traveled out of body both deliberately and, in McMoneagle's case, during near-death experiences. John L. Wilhelm's 1976 book *The Search for Superman* (Wilhelm, 1976) is a great resource on Price and Swann. Pat Price reported to Wilhelm that it was in an OOBE during early Scientology training that his formidable psychic abilities, dormant the first fifty years of his life, awakened: "I was asked to sit down and look at some other guy for period of time and do nothing. After about three minutes I found myself outside of my body, looking at him looking at me" (p. 228).

39. See Wargo, 2016. My own adult, recorded OOBEs have all proven to be vivid, essentially video-quality precognitive phenomena corresponding to later waking experiences in my body (but not in bed). On this basis I suggest sleep paralysis may be the same thing, but instead precognizing lying awake in bed a few minutes into the future. (Regular sleep paralysis experiencers may note that their eyes are not in fact really open during these experiences.) The possible precognitive dimension of phenomena that feel discarnate because of this confusing temporal displacement (and the impossibility of "source monitoring") is a ripe area for future research (for more on this, see Wargo, 2018).

Blair MacKenzie Blake - Making the Unbelievable Believable (p. 127)

Acknowledgements:

The books pictured throughout the article are from the personal collection of Blair MacKenzie Blake.

Notes:

1. "In his last years, according to those who knew him, Barker grew deeply unhappy as he battled financial problems and wrestled with personal demons." (*The Emergence of a Phenomenon: UFOs from the Beginning through 1959* {i.e. *The UFO Encyclopedia, Volume 2*} by Jerome Clark). According to James Moseley writing in 1998, Barker died after "the more or less simultaneous failure of various organs due most probably to AIDS (though it was not diagnosed as such in those days.") This according to John C. Sherwood's article in *Skeptical Inquirer* Volume 26.3, May/June 2002.

Greg Taylor - God is My Rock (p. 149)

Notes:

1. https://onlinelibrary.wiley.com/doi/full/10.1111/j.1945-5100.2012.01409.x
2. http://blogs.nature.com/news/2012/09/buddhist-iron-man-found-by-nazis-is-from-space.html
3. https://onlinelibrary.wiley.com/doi/full/10.1111/j.1945-5100.2012.01409.x
4. https://descrier.co.uk/science/is-the-space-buddha-a-counterfeit/
5. King, Edward, *Remarks concerning stones said to have fallen from the clouds, both in these days and in antient times,* 1796
6. Ibid.
7. Bauval, Robert, "Investigations on the Origins of the BenBen Stone: Was it an Iron Meteorite?", *Discussions in Egyptology,* vol 14, 1989
8. Wylie, C.C. and Naiden, J.R. "The Image which Fell Down from Jupiter", 1936
9. Book V of Herodian's *History*
10. Newton, H.A. "The Worship of Meteorites"
11. McBeath, A. and Gheorghe, A.D. "Meteor Beliefs Project: Meteorite worship

in the ancient Greek and Roman worlds", *WGN, Journal of the International Meteor Organization*, vol. 33, no. 5.

12. Pausanias' *Description of Greece*

13. Wylie, C.C. and Naiden, J.R. "The Image which Fell Down from Jupiter", 1936

14. McBeath, A. and Gheorghe, A.D. "Meteor Beliefs Project: Meteorite worship in the ancient Greek and Roman worlds", *WGN, Journal of the International Meteor Organization*, vol. 33, no. 5.

15. https://www.dailygrail.com/2016/06/king-tut-was-buried-with-a-dagger-of-extraterrestrial-origin/

16. https://www.dailygrail.com/2013/05/ancient-egyptians-mined-iron-from-space/

17. https://www.nature.com/news/iron-in-egyptian-relics-came-from-space-1.13091

18. Ibid.

19. Bauval, Robert and Gilbert, Adrian, *The Orion Mystery*

20. https://www.dailygrail.com/2016/10/the-ancient-egyptians-collected-fossils/

21. Bauval, Robert and Gilbert, Adrian, *The Orion Mystery*

22. Bauval, Robert, "Investigations on the Origins of the BenBen Stone: Was it an Iron Meteorite?", *Discussions in Egyptology*, vol 14, 1989

23. McBeath, A. "Meteor Beliefs Project: Meteorite Veneration in the New World", *WGN, Journal of the International Meteor Organization*, vol. 38, no. 6.

24. Ibid.

25. https://en.wikipedia.org/wiki/Cape_York_meteorite

26. Hamacher, Duane W. "Recorded Accounts of Meteoritic Events in the Oral Traditions of Indigenous Australians", *Archaeoastronomy* vol. 25

27. Farrington, Oliver. "The Worship and Folklore of Meteorites", *The Journal of American Folklore*, 1900.

28. Ibid.

29. Ibid.

30. https://www.rt.com/news/meteorite-church-established-russia-971/

Mike Jay - James Tilly Matthews and the Air Loom (p. 173)

Acknowledgements:

A version of this article first appeared (in English and German) in the catalogue of the Prinzhorn Collection's exhibition *The Air Loom and Other Dangerous*

Influencing Machines (2006). It was reproduced (English only) in the catalogue of *Ghosts in the Machine* (New Museum, New York 2012).

In 2002, the artist Rod Dickinson built the Air Loom from James Tilly Matthews' plans. It has been exhibited at the Laing Gallery in Newcastle (2002-3), the Prinzhorn Collection in Heidelberg (2006-7), and the Bethlem Museum of the Mind (2016-17). Images are archived at www.theairloom.org.

Jeff Nisbet - *The Carved Stone Balls of Scotland* (p. 213)

Acknowledgements:

This article is dedicated to my father, for reasons that will become obvious, and to Robert Brydon, FSA Scot, who passed along his own torch of inquiry on May 21, 2014.

I am grateful to the Society of Antiquaries of Scotland for permission to reproduce images of the stone balls. They originally appeared in J. Alexander Smith's "Notes on small ornamented stone balls found in different parts of Scotland, &c., with remarks on their supposed age and use", *Proceedings of Antiquaries of Scotland Vol. XI (1874-76)* pp. 29-62. The Roman Dodecahedron shown on page 3 is a Wikimedia Commons image, uploaded by user LoKiLeCh.

Lightning Source UK Ltd.
Milton Keynes UK
UKHW042326210219
337760UK00001B/156/P